Language and Decoloniality in Higher Education

Multilingualisms and Diversities in Education series
Editors: Kathleen Heugh, Christopher Stroud and Piet Van Avermaet

Multilingualism and diversity are fast becoming defining characteristics of global education. This is because human mobility has increased exponentially over the past two decades, bringing about an increase in socioeconomic, cultural and faith-based diversity with consequences for citizenship, identity, education, and practices of language and literacy (among others).

The **Multilingualisms and Diversities in Education** series takes a global perspective of the 21st-century societal diversities. It looks at the languages through which these diversities are conveyed, and how they are changing the theoretical foundations and practice of formal and non-formal education. Multilingualisms and diversities in this series are understood as dynamic and variable phenomena, processes and realities. They are viewed alongside: classroom practices (including curriculum, assessment, methodologies); teacher development (pre- and in-service; and in non-formal education); theory-building; research and evaluation; and policy considerations.

Volumes in the series articulate the opportunities and challenges afforded by contemporary diversities and multilingualisms across global settings at local, national and international levels. A distinctive aim of the series is to provide a platform for reciprocal exchanges of expertise among stakeholders located in different southern and northern contexts.

Forthcoming in the series:

Functional Multilingual Learning for Inclusive Education, Sven Sierens, Stef Slembrouck and Piet Van Avermaet
Shifting Linguistic Identities and Multilingual Pedagogies, edited by Belinda Mendelowitz, Ana Ferreira and Kerryn Dixon

Front cover. Bronze sculpture by David Hlongwane, 1995, University of the Western Cape. This statue of a mother (represented as a domestic worker) and her graduating son reflects the hopes of millions of black South Africans for education, opportunity and a better life in post-Apartheid South Africa.

Language and Decoloniality in Higher Education

Reclaiming Voices from the South

Edited by Zannie Bock and Christopher Stroud

BLOOMSBURY ACADEMIC
LONDON • NEW YORK • OXFORD • NEW DELHI • SYDNEY

BLOOMSBURY ACADEMIC
Bloomsbury Publishing Plc
50 Bedford Square, London, WC1B 3DP, UK
1385 Broadway, New York, NY 10018, USA
29 Earlsfort Terrace, Dublin 2, Ireland

BLOOMSBURY, BLOOMSBURY ACADEMIC and the Diana logo are trademarks of
Bloomsbury Publishing Plc

First published in Great Britain 2021
This paperback edition published 2023

Copyright © Zannie Bock, Christopher Stroud and Contributors, 2021

Zannie Bock, Christopher Stroud and Contributors have asserted their right under the
Copyright, Designs and Patents Act, 1988, to be identified as Authors of this work.

Cover design: Anna Berzovan
Cover image © Zannie Bock

All rights reserved. No part of this publication may be reproduced or
transmitted in any form or by any means, electronic or mechanical, including
photocopying, recording, or any information storage or retrieval system,
without prior permission in writing from the publishers.

Bloomsbury Publishing Plc does not have any control over, or responsibility for,
any third-party websites referred to or in this book. All internet addresses given
in this book were correct at the time of going to press. The author and publisher
regret any inconvenience caused if addresses have changed or sites have
ceased to exist, but can accept no responsibility for any such changes.

A catalogue record for this book is available from the British Library.

Library of Congress Cataloging-in-Publication Data
Names: Bock, Zannie, editor. | Stroud, Christopher, editor.
Title: Language and decoloniality in higher education : reclaiming voices
from the South / edited by Zannie Bock and Christopher Stroud.
Description: London ; New York : Bloomsbury Academic, 2021. |
Series: Multilingualisms and diversities in education|
Includes bibliographical references and index. |
Identifiers: LCCN 2020055558 (print) | LCCN 2020055559 (ebook) |
ISBN 9781350049086 (hardback) | ISBN 9781350049093 (ebook)|
ISBN 9781350049116 (epub)
Subjects: LCSH: Education, Higher–Developing countries. |
Language and education–Developing countries. |
Multilingualism–Developing countries.
Classification: LCC LC2610 .L36 2021 (print) | LCC LC2610 (ebook) |
DDC 378.009172/4–dc23
LC record available at https://lccn.loc.gov/2020055558
LC ebook record available at https://lccn.loc.gov/2020055559

ISBN:	HB:	978-1-3500-4908-6
	PB:	978-1-3502-3845-9
	ePDF:	978-1-3500-4909-3
	eBook:	978-1-3500-4911-6

Series: Multilingualisms and Diversities in Education

Typeset by Integra Software Services Pvt. Ltd.

To find out more about our authors and books visit www.bloomsbury.com
and sign up for our newsletters.

Contents

List of Figures	vi
Notes on Contributors	vii
Series Editors' Foreword	x
Foreword: A Decolonial Project	
Lynn Mario T. Menezes de Souza	xiii

1. Loving and Languaging in Higher Education: A Decolonial Horizon, *Christopher Stroud and Zannie Bock* — 1
2. Decolonizing Higher Education: Multilingualism, Linguistic Citizenship and Epistemic Justice, *Christopher Stroud and Caroline Kerfoot* — 19
3. Indigenous Texts, Rich Points and Pluriversal Sources of Knowledge: *Siswana-sibomvana*, *Antjie Krog* — 47
4. Affect, Performance and Language: Implications for an Embodied and Interventionist Pedagogy, *Miki Flockemann* — 67
5. Linguistic Citizenship as Decoloniality: Teaching Hip Hop Culture at an Historically Black University, *Quentin Williams* — 85
6. Teaching Modern South African History in the Aftermath of the Marikana Massacre: A Multimodal Pedagogy for Critical Citizenship, *Marijke du Toit* — 111
7. Delinking from Colonial Language Ideologies: Creating Third Spaces in Teacher Education, *Soraya Abdulatief, Xolisa Guzula and Carolyn McKinney* — 135
8. When Linguists Become Artists: An Exercise in Boundaries, Borders and Vulnerabilities, *Marcelyn Oostendorp, Lulu Duke, Simangele Mashazi and Charné Pretorius* — 159
9. Decolonizing Linguistics: A Southern African Textbook Project, *Zannie Bock* — 181
10. Afterthoughts: Multilingual Citizenship, Humans, Environments and Histories, *Duncan Brown* — 201

Index — 216

Figures

5.1	Poster for Hip Hop lecture series, AHHI	93
5.2	Emile YX? performing his lecture	95
5.3	B-boys Malis and Muis performing a Khoi San dance	96
5.4	Graffiti artist Sergio (seated on the floor) starts to draw	101
5.5	Mak1One (standing) narrates over drawing	102
5.6	Finished Graffiti drawing by artist Sergio and Mak1One	102
6.1	Marijke at three years old. Personal property	119
6.2	My great grandparents, *c* 1930s. Personal property	120
6.3	Photograph by Miss Buyske, *Die Huisgenoot*, 1917	121
6.4	Lecture slide with quote from letter to *Ilanga lase Natal* in isiZulu and English translation. Courtesy *Ilanga lase Natal*	128
6.5	Example of annotated text from assignment on language and power	129
7.1	Nicky (second from right) uses body percussion to make the sound of rain by clapping her hands on her thighs	141
7.2	Multilingual and multimodal newsprint poster created by Group 2	142
7.3	Lisa (second from right) performing and the lecturer (far right) joining in here	144
7.4	Tracey (second from left) reading the Afrikaans poem off the left-hand bottom corner of the poster	144
7.5	Creating a multilingual word wall of scientific terms	154
8.1	Multimodal assessment task	162
8.2	Exhibited multimodal pieces	163
8.3	Little Europe task	168
8.4	Little Europe display	172

Contributors

Soraya Abdulatief is completing her PhD in Education at the University of Cape Town on the academic literacy practices of multilingual Postgraduate Certificate in Education (PGCE) students learning to be science teachers. Other research interests include decolonial and multimodal theory, technology in education, and debates around race and gender. She co-authored a book chapter with Xolisa Guzula titled 'Emerging Academics: Using WhatsApp to Share Novice and Expert Resources in a Postgraduate Writing Group'.

Zannie Bock is Associate Professor in Linguistics at the University of the Western Cape, South Africa. Her current publications are in narrative and discourse analysis with a focus on racializing discourses of university students and decolonial pedagogies. She has a long-standing interest in literacy and adult education and is the project coordinator and co-editor of the southern African textbook, *Language, Society and Communication: An Introduction*.

Duncan Brown is Professor of English in the Centre for Multilingualism and Diversities Research at the University of the Western Cape. He has published widely in the field of South African literary and cultural studies. His research interests include orality and performance, religion and spirituality, identity and belonging, environmental issues, and creative non-fiction. He is currently Principal Investigator (PI) of an A.W. Mellon–funded project on 'Rethinking South African Literature(s)' and PI of the South African section of the 'Global Trout Project' funded by the University of Oslo.

Lulu Duke is currently completing a master's degree in linguistics at Stellenbosch University. Her interests include academic writing, decolonial pedagogies and arts-based methodologies. Her current research focuses on citation and discursive construction in academic writing.

Marijke Du Toit is a teaching and learning specialist in the Faculty of Arts and Humanities at the University of the Western Cape. Before that, she was a lecturer in history at the University of KwaZulu-Natal. Her early research includes gender, nationalism and state social welfare in early twentieth-century South Africa. She has had several photographic exhibitions on urban histories of segregation and Apartheid and has also co-authored the book, *Breathing Spaces: Environmental Portraits of South Durban* (2016). Her current research includes African print cultures and the materialities of paper archives.

Miki Flockemann is Extraordinary Professor in the Department of English at the University of the Western Cape. Her primary research interest is the aesthetics of transformation. Her publications include comparative studies of diasporic writings from South Africa, the Americas and the Caribbean with an emphasis on migrant experiences. She has also published extensively on contemporary South African theatre trends with a recent emphasis on the transformative potentiality of affective performance aesthetics.

Xolisa Guzula is a lecturer in multilingual and multiliteracies education at the University of Cape Town. She is interested in language and literacy as social practice, biliteracy development, emergent literacy, critical literacies, multimodality, third spaces and bilingual children's literature. Her doctoral research is on third spaces as a way of disrupting monoglossia and monomodal education. She has run and researched children's literacy clubs.

Caroline Kerfoot is Professor in Bilingualism at the Centre for Research on Bilingualism, Stockholm University. Her current research focuses on entanglements of language, race and social inequalities in schools. She has extensive experience of education policy work with trade unions and community-based organizations in South Africa. Her book *Postracial Potentials: Language, Identity, and Epistemic Justice in Multilingual Schools* will appear in the Bloomsbury Multilingualisms and Diversities in Education Series.

Antjie Krog is a poet, writer and professor at the University of the Western Cape. She has published twelve volumes of poetry, three non-fiction books, and co-authored an academic book, *There Was This Goat* (2009), with two colleagues Kopano Ratele and Nosisi Mpolweni. A volume of her academic essays was published as *Conditional Tense – Memory and Vocabulary after the South African Truth and Reconciliation Commission* as part of Seagull Books' African List in 2013.

Carolyn McKinney is Associate Professor in Language Education at the University of Cape Town. Carolyn's research focuses on language ideologies, multilingualism as a resource for learning, critical literacy and relationships between language, identity/subjectivity and learning. She is a member of the bua-lit language and literacy collective: www.bua-lit.org.za. She recently published *Language and Power in Post-Colonial Schooling: Ideologies in Practice*.

Simangele Mashazi obtained her MA at Stellenbosch University. Her research was on the linguistic repertoires and embodied experiences of under-represented language groups at Stellenbosch University: inclusion, exclusion and resilience. She is currently a junior lecturer at the Department of General Linguistics at Stellenbosch University.

Marcelyn Oostendorp is a senior lecturer in the Department of General Linguistics at Stellenbosch University. Her current publications are in multimodal discourse analysis and multilingualism with a focus on educational settings. She is also interested in alternative methodologies such as arts-based research methods and humour as a methodological tool.

Charné Pretorius has recently completed her master's degree in General Linguistics at Stellenbosch University with a focus on linguistic and semiotic landscapes. Her research has specifically focused on residence hall spaces at Stellenbosch University. Charné has presented her research at the 2018 *Decolonizing Knowledge, Teaching and Learning in Higher Education Conference*. She has also presented at two international conferences: *Inscape's 2019 (Linguistic Landscapes Symposium)* and *Unsettling Paradigms: The Decolonial Turn in the Humanities Curriculum*.

Christopher Stroud is Emeritus Professor of Linguistics and former Director of the Centre for Multilingualism and Diversities Research (CMDR) at the University of the Western Cape. He is also Professor of Transnational Bilingualism at Stockholm University. He has worked on multilingualism and literacy in a variety of contexts, including Mozambique, Papua New Guinea, Sweden and Singapore. His current research focuses on practices and ideologies of multilingualism in southern Africa, specifically *Linguistic Citizenship*, as a way of rethinking the role of language in brokering diversity in a decolonial framework.

Quentin Williams is Associate Professor of Linguistics at the University of the Western Cape. He is also the new Director of the Centre for Multilingualism and Diversities Research (CMDR, UWC), co-editor of the journal *Multilingual Margins*, and co-editor of *Neva Again: Hip Hop, Art and Activism in Post-Apartheid South Africa* (HSRC Press, 2019).

Series Editors' Foreword

It is little more than five years since students in South African universities ignited what seems to have become a compelling clarion call from university campuses around the world to 'decolonize the curriculum'. This began a challenge that has captured the imaginations of academics and students in many different contexts, particularly those who experienced or were in some way connected with European colonization between the sixteenth and twentieth centuries. Although this discussion has only just begun in many northern institutions and is still to reach others, it is perhaps not too much of an exaggeration to suggest that this is probably the most significant challenge yet to rock the very foundations of western and northern conceptualizations of higher education. For reasons set out below, the editors and authors of this volume are well-placed to articulate decolonial responses that have been circulating in institutions in South America, Africa and South Asia for the last seven decades or more. This volume brings those that have been germinating in universities in South Africa, especially the University of the Western Cape, an institution that has provided much of the recent leadership in these developments and where many of the contributors are based.

Student-initiated resistance to colonial or northern-centric influences, while not something unique or surprising to university campuses, took a dramatic turn in 2015 with a well-documented and vigorous campaign to dislodge a large statue of the British colonial entrepreneur and mining magnate, Cecil John Rhodes, on land owned by the University of Cape Town on the Devil's Peak side of Table Mountain. What came to be known as the #RhodesMustFall movement reverberated almost immediately at Oxford University, the institution from which many hundreds of international recipients of prestigious Rhodes Scholarships have, since 1903, completed post-graduate studies and from which they have moved on to illustrious careers. In South Africa, meanwhile, #RhodesMustFall mutated to #FeesMustFall, spearheaded predominantly by black students agitating for lower fees that would increase access to university studies. This, in turn, was swiftly followed by a broader cry to rally support for #decolonisethecurriculum. This had to do with the kind of curriculum, pedagogies and assessments that students faced once enrolled in undergraduate and post-graduate programmes. As a result of high rates of attrition and resistance to what students perceived as hegemonic northern-centric epistemologies in southern, post-colonial institutions, students demanded an end to what they perceived to be discriminatory, racist and ultimately neo-colonial curriculum and practices. In the context of a multilingual country like South Africa, language has always been a locus of political contestation and discontent. Vexatious issues relating to languages, medium of instruction, and who are included or excluded in courses provided in English, Afrikaans or an African language, have been bitterly debated since the end of the South African (also known as the Anglo-Boer) War in 1902.

This volume responds precisely to the most recent, explosive, challenge from students to decolonize the curriculum in 2015. The editors, Zannie Bock and Christopher Stroud, and a wide cross-section of authors (new and well-established scholars) offer historical and contemporary insights on decolonizing practices and processes in higher education, particularly in relation to multilingualisms in democratic, inclusive, socially just and transformative higher education. The University of the Western Cape has a proud history of anti-Apartheid and decolonial resistance from the moment of its establishment in 1960 to serve students designated 'coloured' by the Apartheid government. After sixty years of developing theoretical and pedagogical practices in higher education to resist discrimination, exclusion and racism, this university has much to offer institutions of higher education elsewhere that are in search of substantive responses to decolonial pedagogies and curriculum development. Notably, the Linguistics Department at the University of the Western Cape has attracted the largest cohort of students enrolled in linguistics courses anywhere in the world. In large part, this has much to do with the approaches developed by teaching academics in conversation with students to decolonize the study of linguistics with a focus that brings alive the exuberance and possibilities of multilingualisms in education not only in higher education but also across education systems. Together these have contemporary and ethical relevance for students' social and working lives beyond the university with a vision for care and love of humanity at a time of both domestic and global disruption and turbulence.

Several of the authors have played a significant role in activities of the 'Southern Multilingualisms and Diversities Consortium' which emerged from conversations between the Centre for Multilingualism and Diversity at the University of the Western Cape and the Research Centre for Languages and Cultures at the University of South Australia in 2012. These conversations have led to a series of collaborative publications and research projects that include researchers and research centres in many parts of the world that explore the dynamics, ethics and features of southern and decolonial linguistics, and which have ignited, reanimated and joined related conversations of Indigenous Knowledge Systems and decoloniality through Africa, the Américas and the Asia-Pacific. These conversations now infuse applied, educational and sociolinguistic studies in both southern and northern contexts. In a global world confronting a host of social issues, such as racism, patriarchy, poverty and pandemics – not to mention environmental sustainability – we are becoming increasingly aware of the potential for multilingualisms to craft a humanity as *Homo Sapiens Amans*, a genre of the human that lives with love, in mutual care and through hope. It is this vision of humanity that may well prepare higher education students and academic teacher-researchers, wherever they are located, to engage with and prepare the way for ethical and sustainable futures.

Finally, as Series Editors of Bloomsbury's *Multilingualisms and Diversities in Education*, we wish to encourage new and established authors who have developed, discovered or initiated approaches to bilingualism and multilingualism that strengthen diversity and inclusivity anywhere in the world, whether these are in formal, informal or non-formal education, to submit book proposals to this series.

Kathleen Heugh, Piet van Avermaet and Christopher Stroud
January 2021

Foreword: A Decolonial Project

Lynn Mario T. Menezes de Souza

In relatively recent developments of sociolinguistics, applied linguistics, literacy and pedagogy, there seems to have been a counter-hegemonic move away from previously dominant *norms* that privileged the abstract, the universal and the homogeneous to *practices* that focus on the situated, the local and the heterogeneous.

Thus, Blommaert and Rampton (2011: 4) in their appraisal of sociolinguistic 'superdiversity' in Europe declare that 'rather than working with homogeneity, stability and boundedness as the starting assumptions, *mobility, mixing, political dynamics and historical embedding* [my emphasis] are now central concerns'. In her discussion of *translanguaging* pedagogy, Garcia (2009) speaks of 'acts performed' by bilingual students, involving 'communication' and not 'language itself'. Seidlhofer (2005: 340), in turn, defends a sociolinguistic-pedagogical notion of English as a lingua franca and postulates that 'linguistic descriptions alone cannot, of course, determine what needs to be taught and learnt for *particular purposes and in particular settings*' (my emphasis) based on the consideration that they may 'not provide sufficient guidance for what will always be pedagogical decisions'. In relation to literacy, Cope and Kalantzis (2008: 196) describe the recent change in focus as being now on the 'big picture, [on] the changing word and [on] the new demands being placed upon *people as makers of meaning* – in changing workplaces, as *citizens in changing public spaces* and in changing dimensions' (my emphasis).

What may be seen in these developments, in their move away from abstraction, universality and homogeneity towards a focus on 'acts or practices', is a growing awareness of the role of historical and social context in issues related to language and pedagogy and the need to focus on the subjects involved: language users, learners, meaning-makers.

What is implicit and what has mostly not been the focus of explicit consideration in these theoretical developments are the political and ideological issues involved. In other words, what is the ideological and political import of bringing subjects into discussions of language, pedagogy and meaning-making?

Why were they not there to begin with? What are the implications of not identifying or associating subjects with meanings and theories?

Marking the Unmarked

The recent theorizations of 'decoloniality' (Castro-Gomez and Grosfoguel, 2007; Dussel, 1993, 1995; Grosfoguel, 2011; Menezes de Souza, 2019; Mignolo, 2013; Walsh and Mignolo, 2018; Quijano, 2000) and 'epistemologies of the South' (Santos, 2018) question the apparent universality of knowledge and meaning-making undertaken for centuries in the West and associate it with the history of colonization which since the sixteenth century established the hegemony of Europe over the rest of the world as the sole source of valid scientific knowledge.

According to these theories, though it may have been recognized that knowledge production did occur elsewhere, this latter production was seen as having limited worth. Thus, whereas Eurocentric knowledge was *unmarked* and seen as universally valid, the knowledges produced elsewhere were local and *marked*. The origin of this process of 'unmarking Europe' is seen to lie in the process of colonization and the ensuing development and propagation of capitalism. Mignolo (2013) and Grosfoguel (2012) describe the 'geo-politics' that characterized colonization and that established Europe on a world scale as the centre of economics, industry, science, knowledge-production and power; Mignolo and Grosfoguel connect this with what they both call a 'body-politics of knowledge and being'.

Dussel (1993) refers to this process as 'coloniality' and describes it as a particular pattern of a hegemony of races, knowledges, languages and beings put in place at the moment of colonization by the European colonizers. Dussel sees the origin of coloniality in a process of racialization through which, at the moment of colonization, the European colonizer saw himself as superior to the indigenous native of the land. The superiority of the self-image of the colonizer depended constitutively on establishing the native as inferior. The most visible sign of the native – the colour of his skin – was then used as a signifier for the inferiority of all that pertained to the native – knowledge, language etc., thus initiating the process of racialization in the colonial relation. Curiously, though this process originated in the factor that most marked the visibility of the colonized native, the resulting pattern of coloniality that then became hegemonic made 'invisible' the same colonized native and all that pertained to him.

Dussel goes on to explain that, though 'colonization' as a political and economic fact may have terminated, 'coloniality' persisted as a hegemonic relation that racialized and established the inferiority of the native and all things pertaining to him. Santos (2007) enhances the concept of coloniality with the concept of the 'abyssal line'; the line as a concept was established during colonization and manichaeistically produced, on one side, the visibility and purported sole existence of all things pertaining to the colonizer – race, knowledge, language etc. The line then 'produced as invisible', on its other side, the race, knowledges and languages of the colonized. Both concepts, coloniality and the abyssal line, have their origins in the thinking of Frantz Fanon (1967) and his description of colonial thinking and spatial organization. For Fanon, the European colonizer established a conceptual line that separated a 'zone of being' from a 'zone of non-being'. Like the abyssal line, everything pertaining to the colonizer was granted ontological existence and existed in the 'zone of being'; in contrast, the ontological existence of all that pertained to the colonized native was negated and relegated to the 'zone of non-being'.

Coloniality, the abyssal line and the zones of being and non-being interconnect with Mignolo's and Grosfoguel's concept of the 'body-politics of knowledge and being'. Grosfoguel describes the process whereby the European philosophies of Descartes and Kant disconnected knowledge from the subjects that produced it, emphasizing what was said and enunciated as 'knowledge', but concealed the subjects that produced it. Where the subject, producer of knowledge, was taken into account, the historical and geographical particularity of its locus of enunciation was taken as universally applicable. The two related moves in the body politics of knowledge were therefore (i) to 'hide the body' and thus the situatedness of the European producer of knowledge and/or (ii) to treat the situatedness of the body of the European producer of knowledge as not just local, but also 'universal'.

This body politics of knowledge acquired more than epistemological validity. Interconnected with coloniality and the abyssal line, by 'negating visibility and existence' to knowledge produced by the colonized non-European, it also acquired ontological value. Through this process, as an effect of coloniality, European knowledges, produced by powerful concealed bodies, were taken to be universal and therefore 'unmarked', and the knowledges of the colonized, produced by negated, value-less bodies, were seen as 'marked' and as having only limited and local validity.

Given that the efficacy of coloniality and the abyssal line lies in their power to 'negate' the existence and knowledge-producing capacity of subjects from formerly colonized regions, the critical strategy proposed by decolonial theories and the theories of the epistemologies of the South is three-pronged: it involves *identifying* coloniality, *interrogating* coloniality and *interrupting* coloniality.

For Dussel (1977, 2012), given that coloniality negates the existence and capacity of the subjects it has excluded, and given that to interrupt coloniality involves 'negating the negation' inherent in it, then ethically the critical strategy to interrupt coloniality demands initiation from a counter-hegemonic or non-hegemonic location (i.e. one already negated by coloniality). The reason is that one cannot effectively be located as a beneficiary of coloniality and cannot also seek to interrupt it. Though Grosfoguel (2011) makes clear that being situated in a Southern or peripheral, or non-hegemonic location, is no guarantee that 'epistemologically' one speaks *as* or *from* the South, Dussel insists that coloniality can only be challenged from such a non-hegemonic location. Dussel of course is here referring to the necessity of an *epistemological and ethical* perspective (that from the margins or periphery – a perspective from the South) and not merely a physical or geographical one.

The importance of the issue of location in the initiation of a decolonial critique emphasizes the significance and insufficiency of the connected concepts of 'situated knowledge' and 'locus of enunciation'. In the context of Dussel's and Grosfoguel's reservations above, in a decolonial critique it is necessary, but not sufficient, to declare oneself as speaking from a non-hegemonic locus of enunciation. Also important is the need to identify and interrogate if and how coloniality traverses one's locus of enunciation, in terms of the knowledges/languages that one takes for granted, the knowledges/languages that one deems insignificant, and the interlocutors one sees as existent or not (and therefore as worthy or not worthy interlocutors). According to Dussel, if coloniality is identified as traversing one's locus of enunciation, after being interrogated it has to be interrupted.

The strategy of negating the negated, that is, of identifying, interrogating and interrupting coloniality and the abyssal line in oneself and in what one is working with, seeks as its objective not just an emancipation from coloniality but also an unleashing of a plurality and diversity of previously subjugated knowledges deemed invisible and non-existent.

Dussel refers to this critical strategy as moving beyond a mere negation of previous negation and being proactively positive and enabling in transforming the negation into something positive; this makes emancipation not just an event or a fact but a process of transformation and production. Dussel (2012: 49) is furthermore emphatic that a critical strategy must be preceded by a project and traces the outlines of a possible and productive critical project. Firstly, he says, one has to affirm

> the self-valorization of one's own negated or devalued cultural moments … Secondly, those traditional values ignored by [hegemonic coloniality] should be a point of departure for an internal critique, from within the culture's own hermeneutical possibilities. Thirdly, the critics should be those who, living in the bi-culturality of the "borders", can create critical thought. Fourthly, this means a long period of resistance, of maturation, and of the accumulation of forces.

Dussel portrays this final phase as consisting of the 'creative and accelerated cultivation and development of one's own cultural tradition'.

Dussel speaks of the need for 'dialogue' in this critical strategy and, like Veronelli (2015) and Lugones (2006), warns that due to the persisting effects of coloniality, a dialogue between the participants involved, some of whose very existence may have been more negated by coloniality than others, may be inhibited. Adding to this complexity of dialogue, Alcoff (2007) describes what she calls 'instituted ignorance'. As any social group undergoes a process not dissimilar to coloniality, hierarchically and epistemically organizing what is known in such a way that any member of the group knows only what has been established by the convention of that group and what has circulated within that group, a member of a particular group may not know what is known by members of another group. This 'instituted ignorance', like coloniality, may inhibit dialogue and communication between groups.

Freire and the Unmarking of the Marked

Though he worked and produced his theories decades before decolonial theories and the theories of the epistemologies of the South, parallels may be drawn between these theories and the work of the Brazilian educator, Paulo Freire. His pioneering pedagogical work in the 1960s was also based on a strategy of critique and interruption of a hegemonic relation of inequality which marginalized large sectors of the Brazilian population in poor and underprivileged urban peripheries and rural communities.

On a par with the concepts of coloniality and the abyssal line which negated the very existence and the knowledge-producing capacity of members of these invisibilized and marginalized communities, Freire (1963, 2003) saw the need to emancipate them by educating them to be *autonomous* subjects. Given the authoritarian and undemocratic social and political structure of Brazilian society at the time (its parallels with coloniality), many citizens had no access to schools, to literacy and therefore to citizenship in the sense of having a voice and capacity to defend their own interests. The problem facing Freire was how to produce such autonomous subjects in a non-authoritarian manner in a situation in which autonomy did not exist.

Freire's strategy of critique, similar to that of Dussel, began with the notion that before critique one needs a project. How should one negate the negated existence and knowledge-producing capacity of a community silenced and therefore invisibilized by not being literate in a hegemonically literate nation? Like Dussel, Freire would have to move beyond a mere negation of a previous negation (the silencing and exclusion of the community) and develop something 'proactively positive' which could 'transform the negation into something positive', something which would bring the members of such a community into subjecthood and make them agents of their own actions. As mentioned above, for Freire also, emancipation could not be just an event or a fact; it had to be made into a 'process of transformation and production'. His final objective was to make the members of such marginalized communities into autonomous subjects.

The dilemma that faced Freire was not dissimilar to the dilemma that faced Dussel, when Dussel identified the ethical need to work 'from the margins' of coloniality and not from 'the midst' of coloniality in order to interrogate and interrupt coloniality.

For Freire this involved beginning the process of emancipation from the bottom-up or beginning from the local and the marginal to attain the 'universal' or hegemonic. Promoting the development of autonomous subjects meant producing subjects capable of going beyond the limits of their 'local, marked' knowledges in order to have access to and interact with those hegemonic knowledges deemed 'unmarked or universal'. However, Freire did not want to do this in a hegemonic, directive, authoritarian, top-down manner. This could run the risk of maintaining the marginalized subject in a position of subordination as a lesser being incapable of knowledge production, and this could jeopardize the possibility of his learners attaining autonomy.

The pedagogic project on which Freire's counter-coloniality strategy was based began with developing an awareness among the prospective educators of their instituted ignorance. This involved leading the educators to unmark the local knowledge of the community, previously seen as not having value, and marking their own hegemonic knowledge as 'local' as that of the community – 'local' in the sense of also having originated in a particular socio-historic context.

This process of unmarking was done through encounters with the prospective students of the local community in what Freire called 'Circles of Culture' (Freire, 2003; Lyra, 1996). In these encounters, Freire and the prospective educators would promote a dialogue with the prospective learners enquiring about words which denoted significant aspects of life in their community. For example, a fishing community identified words such as 'fish', 'boat' and 'net'. An urban peripheral community identified words such as 'brick' and 'building'. This stock of 'generative' words would then be used as the basis of literacy teaching, whereby each word was broken down into syllables and recombined to form other words.

In the process of identifying with the learners words which were significant to them, the instituted ignorance of the educators from the hegemonic culture became apparent. The latter did not have the knowledge that the community of the learners considered to be of significance.

To go beyond the local, marked knowledges of the community, Freire's approach was to discuss with the students the chosen words of significance to them and denaturalize them. In a well-known example, Freire used the word 'brick' as the basis for a discussion of how their labour as builders was exploited, how the value of land for building was subject to market interests and how exploitation resulting from the ignorance of the market value of both their labour and their land could make them vulnerable. This dialogue between educators and learners, in which each of the parties involved was ignorant of something and knowledgeable of something, sought, in Freire's words, to rehumanize these learners as capable of learning something they did not know. It also sought to make the learners aware of how they were historically 'produced' as 'marked', 'local' and 'ignorant' and how their purported ignorance made them vulnerable to exploitation by those who had access to hegemonic knowledge.

This process of dialogue, questioning, denaturalizing or 'un-marking the marked' sought to make these subjects conscious, critical and autonomous subjects capable of producing knowledge. Freire's purpose was not to give them access to knowledge in a cumulative manner; this would only confirm the quantitative idea of knowledge that they had been exposed to (in which they 'knew less' and had to be dependent on those that 'knew more'). Instead, Freire sought to give them 'transformative' knowledge – knowledge that would 're-humanize' them and enable them to transform the negative conditions in their places of residence without convincing them that they should aim at becoming upwardly mobile and move out of their places of residence into a better 'somewhere else'. The objective of making these learners autonomous subjects and knowledge producers was that they could transform their own locality into something else, extending the process of unmarking the marked. They would themselves become producers of culture. For Freire (2003: 51), it is in this manner that '[m]an takes control over his reality. He humanizes his reality. He adds to it things which he himself has made. He gradually becomes aware of how the process of history affects geographic space. He makes culture'.

In this manner, similar to the four phases mentioned above that Dussel envisaged as parts of a decolonial strategy, Freire's strategy of unmarking the marked also foresaw firstly the self-valorization of the previously negated subject, followed by the need for internal critique, through which the subject perceived how he was produced as incapable by the hegemonic discourse and how his naturalization and introjection of this discourse convinced him this was indeed the case. Following this came the need for the subject to understand that now having access to both his own local knowledge and the hegemonic knowledge, he is in a better position to critique both. Finally came the perception that transformation may not be immediate as it may involve a long process of maturity, but in order to occur, the process needs to be initiated.

For the educator, Freire's proposals taught that in order to be effective, autonomy and the capacity to transform cannot result from an authoritarian directiveness which sees some – the educators, as the knowledge-producers and others – the learners, as knowledge consumers. A dialogue has to occur in which both parties involved in the dialogue see themselves as capable of producing certain knowledges and also as ignorant of other knowledges. Both parties have to mark what they had previously considered to be naturalized and universal and unmark what they had considered to be local. This process brings back the body (its spatial and historical/ideological location) into the process of knowledge production and interrupts the body politics of knowledge and being which had negated the very existence of so many communities.

Finally, we need to come back to the recent developments in sociolinguistics, applied linguistics, literacy and pedagogy, mentioned at the outset, and the accompanying move from a concern with abstract norms to a concern with situated practices. The reason that many theories of diversity, translingualism, English as a lingua franca, literacy and pedagogy stop short of constituting decolonial strategies may be firstly because they do not identify, interrogate and interrupt the coloniality present in them: many still seem to speak in universal terms, unaware of how their locus of enunciation, located epistemically within the hegemonic North, may impact positively or negatively on the knowledge they produce and the knowledges of those of whose existence they are unaware.

Secondly, and perhaps just as important, many of those who see themselves as critiquing established theories, which are deemed as having ignored certain phenomena, may in fact be using established theories to enable their critiques. In other words, though they seem to desire the 'local' and the 'particular', they are still bound to an unspoken and unchallenged valorization of the universal and the abstract. Though they focus on practices of apparently situated subjects, little consideration is given to the political and ideological aspects of their theoretical proposals. In the guise of an example, consider the fact that in the move from a focus on *abstract norms* as bounded and systematic (reflecting an established hegemonic and positivist concept of science as dealing with the palpable and measurable) to a focus on *practices,* many theories still seem tied to notions of boundedness and systematicity, be it in diversity, translingualism, English as a lingua franca, literacy or pedagogy. Furthermore, how do these theories relate to processes of exclusion and inequality of the subjects involved?

On the other hand, in the critical strategy of the theories of coloniality and the theories of the epistemologies of the South, and in the political-pedagogical proposals of Freire, much more than strategies of opposition to established norms, what is involved is a strategy of 're-existence', a strategy of bringing *visibility and humanity* to what had previously been denied even mere existence.

It is in this spirit of decolonial critique and of making visible the knowledges of the South that this volume embodies not only a critical strategy but also an enabling project.

References

Alcoff, L. M. (2007), 'Epistemologies of Ignorance: Three Types', in S. S. N. Tuana (ed.), *Race and Epistemologies of Ignorance*, 39–50. Albany: SUNY Press.

Blommaert, J. and B. Rampton (2011), 'Language and Superdiversity: A Position Paper'; *Working Papers in Urban Languages and Literacies: Paper 70.* Ghent: University of Ghent.

Castro-Gomez, S. and R. Grosfoguel, eds (2007), *El giro decolonial: Reflexiones para una diversidad epistémica más allá del capitalismo global.* Bogotá: Siglo del Hombre Editores.

Cope, B. and M. Kalantzis (2008), 'Language Education and Multiliteracies', in Hornberger, N. H. (Org.). *Encyclopedia of language and education*, v.1, 195–211. New York: Springer.

Dussel, E. (1993) *Europa, modernidad y eurocentrismo.* México: Editorial Trotta.

Dussel, E. (1995), *The Invention of the Americas: Eclipse of 'the Other' and the Myth of Modernity*, trans. M. D. Barber, New York: Continuum.

Dussel, E. (2012), 'Transmodernity and Interculturality: An Interpretation from the Perspective of the Philosophy of Liberation', *TRANSMODERNITY: Journal of Peripheral Cultural Production of the Luso-Hispanic World*, 1 (3): Available online: https://escholarship.org/uc/item/6591j76r (accessed 12 December 2019).

Dussel, E. D. (1977), *Filosofia na América Latina: filosofia da libertação*. São Paulo: Loyola.

Fanon, F. (1967), *Black Skin, White Masks*. New York: Grove Press.

Freire P. (1963), *Discurso do Professor Paulo Freire, em Angicos, ao encerramento do curso de alfabetização de adultos*. Instituto Paulo Freire. Série Obras de Paulo Freire. Subgrupo Angicos (RN) 1963. Disponível em: Available online: http://acervo.paulofreire.org/xmlui/handle/7891/1707.

Freire P. (2003), *Educação e atualidade brasileira*. São Paulo: Cortez Instituto Paulo Freire.

García, O. (2009), 'Education, Multilingualism and Translanguaging in the 21st Century', in A. Mohanty, M. Panda, R. Phillipson and T. Skutnabb-Kangas (eds), *Multilingual Education for Social Justice: Globalising the Local*, 128–45. New Delhi: Orient Blackswan.

Grosfoguel, R. (2002), 'Colonial Difference, Geopolitics of Knowledge and Global Coloniality in the Modern/Colonial Capitalist World-System', *Review*, 25 (3): 203–24.

Grosfoguel, R. (2011), 'Decolonizing Post-Colonial Studies and Paradigms of Political Economy: Transmodernity, Decolonial Thinking, and Global Coloniality', *TRANSMODERNITY: Journal of Peripheral Cultural Production of the Luso-Hispanic World*, Available online: http://escholarship.org/uc/item/21k6t3fq (accessed 12 December 2019).

Grosfoguel, R. (2012), 'Descolonizar as esquerdas ocidentalizadas: para além das esquerdas eurocêntricas rumo a uma esquerda transmoderna descolonial', *Contemporânea*, 2 (2): 337–62. ISSN: 2236-532X.

Lugones, M. (2006), 'On Complex Communication', *Hypatia: A Journal of Feminist Philosophy*, 21 (3): 75–85, Available online: DOI: 10.1111/j.1527-2001.2006.tb01114.x (accessed 12 December 2019).

Lyra, C. (1996), *As quarenta horas de Angicos: uma experiência pioneira de educação*. São Paulo: Cortez.

Menezes de Souza, L. M. (2019), 'Glocal Languages, Coloniality and Globalization from Below', in M. Guilherme and L. M. Menezes de Souza (eds), *Glocal Languages and Critical Intercultural Awareness: The South Answers Back*, 17–41. New York: Routledge.

Mignolo, W. (2013), *Historias Locales/diseños Globales: colonialidad, conocimientos subalternos y pensamiento fronteirizo*. Madrid: Akal.

Mignolo, W. and C. Walsh (2018), *On Decoloniality Concepts, Analytics, Praxis*. Durham: Duke University Press.

Quijano, A. (2000), 'Coloniality of Power, Ethnocentrism, and Latin America', *NEPANTLA*, 1 (3): 533–80.

Santos, B. de S. (2007), 'Beyond Abyssal Thinking: From Global Lines to Ecologies of Knowledges'. Review (Fernand Braudel Center), 30 (1): 45–89.

Santos, B. de S. (2018), *The End of the Cognitive Empire: The Coming of Age of Epistemologies of the South*. Durham: Duke University Press.

Seidlhofer, B. (2005), 'English as a Lingua Franca'. *ELT Journal*, 59: 339–41. http://dx.doi.org/10.1093/elt/cci064.

Veronelli, G. (2015), 'Sobre la colonialidad del linguaje'. Available online: https://revistas.javeriana.edu.co/index.php/univhumanistica/article/view/11432/11947 doi:10.11144/Javeriana.uh81.scdl (accessed 12 December 2019).

1

Loving and Languaging in Higher Education: A Decolonial Horizon

Christopher Stroud and Zannie Bock

Introduction

This volume brings together a collection of diverse chapters, all centring on language, decoloniality and higher education. It brings together a set of different voices that reflect the authors' cumulative years of experience as educators in higher education in different southern contexts. Using case studies of praxis and explorations of different epistemic perspectives, the authors use a range of decolonial lenses to reflect on questions of knowledge, language and learning in higher education and to build a reflexive praxis of decoloniality through multilingualism. While some of these lenses would be familiar to readers (e.g. the writings of Walter Mignolo, Lynn Mario T. Menezes de Souza, Boaventura de Sousa Santos and Catherine Walsh), this volume also explores an emerging conceptual framework, Linguistic Citizenship, developed, over the past two decades, by scholars in southern Africa (see below and extended discussions in Chapters 2, 5 and 9). In this collection, we use Linguistic Citizenship as a lens to 'think beyond' the inherited colonial matrices of language which have shaped this region (and many other southern contexts) for centuries and to 're-imagine' multilingualism – and semiotics, more broadly – as a transformative resource in the broader project of social justice.

This volume was written in conjunction with a Mellon Foundation grant awarded to the editors, Zannie Bock and Christopher Stroud, at the University of the Western Cape and Marcelyn Oostendorp at Stellenbosch University within the programme *Unsettling Paradigms: The Decolonial Turn in the Humanities Curriculum at Universities in South Africa*. We would like to thank Kathleen Heugh most sincerely for her insights and inputs on this chapter and the pre-final book manuscript. We would also like to thank Elaine Ridge for her meticulous, insightful and invaluable editorial work on this volume.

In this sense, then, the case studies in this volume offer insights for educators working in a globally transforming world, which, in recent years, has begun to confront a host of social issues, including inequality, racism, migration, poverty, pandemics and environmental sustainability. Given that South Africa has been grappling with these issues for decades (and particularly since the first democratic elections in 1994), the chapters in this volume would have relevance to other contexts undergoing similar socio-economic transformations. All chapters explore the issue of 'voice', and the conditions under which students and educators make themselves heard and visible. Some reflect directly on teaching praxis, others consider local and marginalized sources of knowledge and the validation of different world views and ways of relating, while others focus on the histories of 'language making' and 'the literacies of place' that shape these contexts. What may be of particular interest to global scholars are authors' recounts of how they have grappled with leveraging the country's multilingual resources in the project of promoting academic access and success in the face of historical hierarchies of language and social power.

The authors in this volume speak from a particular geographic 'locus' as educators in South African universities, in particular, from the Western Cape region. All authors (with the exception of Lynn Mario Menezes de Souza) are (or were) based at one of three regional universities: the University of the Western Cape (UWC), Stellenbosch University (SU) and the University of Cape Town (UCT). All three institutions have very different histories: the first, UWC, was established in 1960 by the Apartheid state for people designated 'coloured', as part of the grand scheme of 'separate education for separate races'.[1] Since then, UWC has emerged as a leading 'historically disadvantaged' institution, both in terms of the number of black students that it graduates each year and in terms of its research rankings. Both SU and UCT are leading 'historically advantaged' universities established over a century ago for people considered 'white' under both the former colonial structures and the more recent Apartheid regime (1948–94). SU has historically catered for Afrikaans-speaking white students, and UCT for English-speaking white students. Thus, the South African higher education landscape reflects more than a century of stratification based on racial and linguistic privilege, and all institutions have had to grapple with how to transform their historical identities and positions and become more inclusive in the face of rising pressures for socio-economic justice and student calls for decolonization. This history, then, provides the backdrop to the case studies in this volume which chart the different authors' journeys towards 'decolonial horizons' (Walsh (2014)).

Loving and languaging in higher education

A prerequisite for an education which is capable of driving a new benevolent human relationality is an adequate understanding of the role of language and, in particular, multilingualism in human relations. In this chapter, we wish to explore the thinking of several (lesser known) Chilean neurobiologists, Maturana and Cabezon (2001) and Maturana and Varela (1980), and their work on language and the biological basis of human relations. We refer to their work as it offers a theory of language emerging as a species-specific, structured system of coordination between humans. At the same time, they link language to the biological basis of communication among all species. These close, cooperative engagements, they argue, are the prerequisites for the survival of the species. Among humans, they argue, language emerged in this context of 'loving' and social engagement. We find this a useful overarching frame for the chapters in this volume as it foregrounds the importance of language in social relationalities. This is the hallmark of Linguistic Citizenship, which we see as a tool to pursue educational goals, which would hopefully lead to the creation of new voices, new knowledges and stronger, more cohesive societies.

Maturana and Cabezon (2001) characterize the human condition as caught between the forces of *Homo Sapiens Amans* and those of *Homo Sapiens Arrogans* or, in their terms, as lives lived between a culture founded in love and one of patriarchy. 'Patriarchy' is the culture 'founded in the negation of the other, that emphasized relationships of appropriation, competitiveness, struggle, success and control' (Maturana and Cabezon, 2001: 244). On the other hand, 'love', in Maturana and Cabezon's (2001) usage, refers neither to the physical relationship between intimates, nor to any religious significance. It is rather 'the biological dynamic system that constitutes trust and mutual acceptance in body and spiritual relations of nearness and intimacy' (Maturana and Cabezon, 2001: 242) – 'the biological basis of social phenomena' (Maturana and Varela, 1980: 268–9). We might hazard the guess that patriarchy is recognizable as what many other authors would call coloniality-modernity, the dark global forces of human and environmental destruction, which manifested (historically) as slavery and colonization and today as (neo)capitalism and environmental destruction.

Such a stance informs a particular interpretation of 'decoloniality', which would then comprise a 'delinking' of our humanity (Mignolo, 2007) from patriarchy (the inheritance of coloniality) in order to reinstate a 'culture of love' and relink with the memories, praxes of living and thinking that were disavowed by coloniality-modernity. Recapturing a life in love would mean an approach to social and personal transformation that is significantly about recalibrating relationships among selves and others and vanquishing or banishing the arrogance and spite that conserves oppressive orders and their institutions. In the particular South African context, a decoloniality of this cut would acknowledge the historical entanglements of life and thought among diverse people and would seek to dismantle categories that divide, such as race, ethnicity and sexuality. Taking account of Fanon's (1967) observation that black and white subjectivities are constructed in spaces of non-relationality, the decolonial project would involve re-crafting the human to create liveable worlds constituted by cooperation, mutual recognition and non-racialism. It would, quite simply, imply recovering entanglements that bind us together, which in turn would open spaces of relationality. If we are who we are because of our entanglements with others, it is our relationships to others that must be foremost. This would mean engaging critically with ideas and practices that deny, obscure or obfuscate those historical entanglements. The question must be: how can this happen? Through what means can we relearn how to love?

While there is no obvious blueprint for establishing a decoloniality based in 'loving relationships', it is clear what does *not* constitute a way forward. This cannot be a decoloniality of repatriation and restitution of essentialized identities and distinct knowledges, but a search for historical entanglements across imaginary social and epistemological divides. It cannot be a decoloniality that focuses its energies solely on the 'capture' of institutions and structures such as universities and schools. For example, the point cannot be to merely replace existing curricula and content with other knowledges or introduce new languages that themselves have long histories of colonial engineering in the hope that they will act as catalysts for change. Although change in curricula and languages must and should happen, experience shows these strategies do not *in themselves* guarantee a decolonial outcome. Throughout history, countless social movements and innumerable initiatives of individuals and groups have demonstrated time and again that change does not come about easily through protest, political transformation or institutional engagement alone. Racism, sexism and climatism remain scourges of our time (depressingly so, even within the very movements that advocate decolonial delinking). This has prompted Papadopoulos (2018: 3) to ask

> what if we approach social movement action not as targeting existing political power but as experimenting with worlds? What if we see social movement action not as addressing existing institutions for redistributing justice but as the creation of alternative forms of existence that reclaim material justice from below?

To the extent that existing institutions are in the hands of our worst selves, *Homo Sapiens Arrogans*, our decolonial futures lie beyond the structured and institutional present. This does not mean, however, that institutional change should not also be a priority. Rescaling the decolonial project to the human – or better still the relational – does not mean denying the importance of structural and institutional transformation. It does mean, however, vigilance as to how established structures work to accommodate and defuse the potentiality for radical structural transformation in, what Papadopoulos calls, 'a politics of irregularity'. This is where divergence and difference in thinking and being find affirmation, are co-opted and accommodated, in extant workings of system without fundamental change to these systems (cf. Papadopoulos, 2018: 58). It is to recognize that there are many ways of engaging thinking and knowing, and many modes of thought in the 'mundane ontologies of everyday life' (Papadopoulos, 2018: 58, 213) that are 'invisible' to the workings of formal structures.

In fact, there is an excess of ways of knowing and relating – what the German philosopher Ernst Bloch would call 'utopian', that is, a better way of living that is 'foreshadowed' in the present (as in the past) but as yet 'unrealized' (cf. Anderson, 2008). Utopian foreshadowings do not fit well with regulated, formal procedures, but inhabit rhizomatically the cracks, fissures and joins that permeate all such structures. It is these utopian seams that must be 'mined' for radical, transformational potential and that will ultimately change the structures and institutions in ways not possible to imagine in the current order of doing and thinking.

Decoloniality in this sense comprises the imaginations, creativities and practical crafting of the everyday and its relationships – the getting by, getting along – for which there can be no formal prescription or one size that fits all. The radical utopian possibilities come out of 'the making of invisible alternative spaces' – what Bayat (2010) calls 'social non-movements', the grassroots socialities that allow people to relate variously, that craft new actors, agencies and forms of awareness out of which alternative ways of relating are made possible when building a world with its own emerging logic and dynamics. It is this that subsequently, and often imperceptibly, supersedes conventional ways of doing things and forces a redesign of existing structures. (On the link between everyday life and social transformation, cf. also Savransky, 2017.)

Acknowledging others (and oneself) through love should lie at the very core of an education which should provide a space for 'experimentation'. Education is 'the process by means of which adequate relational behaviors (i.e.

cognitive, affective and psychomotor behaviors) are triggered through which another (or oneself) arises as a legitimate other in coexistence with oneself' (Maturana and Cabezon, 2001: 245). For Maturana and Cabezon, life and cognition are inseparably linked and to 'learn is to live together' (2001: 244). They go on to note with respect to intelligence that it is about coordination and acknowledgement rather than (as we tend to assume) about solving (difficult) problems with facility. It is 'the capacity to participate in a new or old consensual domain that a person, or in general any living being, may exhibit in the course of its interactions' (2001: 240). Once again, Maturana and Cabezon point to the centrality of love as paramount: 'Only love expands intelligence, because love as the domain of those behaviors through which the other arises as a legitimate other in co-existence with oneself, opens a human being to see and enter in collaboration' (2001: 243).

Such a stance on education, love and the human also informs Maturana and Cabezon's understanding of 'language'. Although there is an increasing emphasis on the centrality of language in decoloniality, few have interrogated in depth what the idea and practice of decolonial 'languaging' require. Not surprisingly, for Maturana and Cabezon, there is an essential link between language and love in the sense of the consensual coordinations of relationality between self and others. Humans are essentially 'loving, languaging animals' and the evolutionary history of humans is 'a history of social life centered on consensuality and cooperation, not on competition or aggressive strife' (2001: 243). At the same time, human beings exist in language – every facet of our lives is permeated by languaging. Thus, language as a 'manner of loving must have arisen in the history that gave origins to humans some three million years ago' (Maturana and Cabezon, 2001: 242).

Thus, if decoloniality is 'about recovering and conserving what makes us human', then language has an absolutely key role to play – a much larger part than we are accustomed to accord it. Language as 'love' rather than 'label' (i.e. language as 'human relationality' rather than 'named entities') is the means, modality and medium, where energies and relationalities are mobilized in ways that 'generate *alternative and autonomous* spaces of existence' (Papadopoulos, 2018: 3, our emphasis). Together with others, Papadopolous refers to these 'spaces of otherwise' as 'new ontologies' or, in Crain Soudien's words, 'ontological refashionings' (Soudien, 2014). Maturana and Varela (1980) also inform us that the understanding of language as a domain where relationality with self and others is coordinated in emotions of love requires a theory of language beyond 'language as a tool of communication' or symbolization. It also involves recognizing that the idea we have of language and the way we politicize and practise it is still determined by coloniality and its beneficiary lineage, the *Homo Sapiens Arrogans*.

Linguistic Citizenship

A view of language and multilingualism that is commensurate with relationality is that of Linguistic Citizenship (Stroud, 2001, 2018). Linguistic Citizenship was originally coined out of research into multilingual educational contexts in the geopolitical South (Mozambique and South Africa) (Stroud, 2001, 2009; Stroud and Heugh, 2004; Kerfoot, 2011; Williams and Stroud, 2015) and further developed elsewhere (Lim et al., 2018; Milani and Jonsson, 2018; Rampton et al., 2018). It attempts to capture precisely the essential relationality of language, in particular multilingualism, thereby addressing Maturana and Varela's (1980) point that humans live in the relational space of language. Its point of departure is the critique of a politics of language (e.g. one defined by a notion of Linguistic Human Rights) that is *institutionally* driven and which understands language as a particular sort of 'object' delimited by 'rights discourses'. Studying acts of Linguistic Citizenship is thus an attempt to reach an understanding of what language *is* – what comprises its particular form of relationality.

Acts of Linguistic Citizenship are the semiotic means whereby speakers create transient or more permanent interpersonal engagements, feelings of conviviality and belonging, and a sense of mutual care. They craft new subjectivities that do not necessarily need to be immediately recognized or represented as such in formally regulated Habermasian public spaces. Rather, through exercising – or creating a Linguistic Citizenship – speakers use language to create new sensibilities and open up possibilities for imagining themselves differently – as actors and agents in the process of becoming. Acts of Linguistic Citizenship are at root processes of 'ontological refashioning', where speakers approach and 'redefine' both the nature of themselves and their circumstances alternatively. They involve the expansion or 'retooling' of available linguistic resources and implicate language both as a 'target' of change and as a 'medium' for social, ontological and epistemic transformation. This is why Linguistic Citizenship, where language is both medium and message, is key to understanding language in the context of education. Thus, approaching education through Linguistic Citizenship means understanding how new subjectivities and agencies are co-developed in synchrony with new registers and styles of speech, including multilingual and multimodal repertoires.

With respect to theories of decolonial change, Papadopoulos's idea of decoloniality as 'rescaling' and Maturana's emphasis on 'relationality' and 'love' merge in a notion of Linguistic Citizenship that essentially addresses 'the remaking of everyday existence below the radar of control in mundane and yet unexpected ways' (Papadopoulos, 2018: 4). It does so by attending to the 'small, everyday spaces' and local relationalities where alternative ways of being and seeing are crafted.

In this volume, the authors explore the role of Linguistic Citizenship in crafting the potentialities for education to afford spaces for experimentation, for the creation of alternatives which are radically different from the realities in which we find ourselves. Our focus on higher education in this volume is especially important given that this is a space where students have a unique opportunity to *disengage* with 'discipline' and structures and to live creatively and with imagination and empathy for the worlds of others. We suggest that education built around Linguistic Citizenship can offer an alternative institutional context for working out the necessary reconnect with the *Homo Sapiens Amans* that we are and assist in the design of alternative futures.

Linguistic Citizenship and Higher Education (in South Africa)

Acts of Linguistic Citizenship as fundamentally acts of humanity are illustrated in a number of ways in this volume. In Stroud and Kerfoot's chapter, acts of Linguistic Citizenship are seen as an essential strategic component of local struggles for agency, self-identification and voice. The authors illustrate this with speakers of an emerging variety of Afrikaaps (a local 'stigmatised' linguistic variety, related to the more powerful standardized 'white' variety, Afrikaans) who, through acts of Linguistic Citizenship, 'enregister' new forms of language and create alternative 'indexical orderings' (cf. also Williams, 2019, and Williams, this volume). These practices simultaneously provide speakers with more complex narratives of origin and leverage new ways of viewing self and understanding the historical trials of their communities in the Western Cape. These are ways of knowing born out of struggle, what Mignolo and Walsh (2018) call 'rear guard theory', 'developed by social groups as part of their resistance against the systematic injustices and oppressions caused by capitalism, colonialism and patriarchy' (Mignolo and Walsh, 2018; Santos, 2014: x), that is, *Homo Sapiens Arrogans*. The chapter suggests that this shows how different sociolinguistic realities need to undergird the production of alter-ontologies and alternative epistemologies and that this may offer important insights into institutionalized strategies such as 'translanguaging' or the 'intellectualization of languages'.

Krog's chapter shifts the lens to how the struggles of historically oppressed and silenced voices may engage 'the mainstream Other'. She details how African language prose and poetry retranslated into English creates 'rich points', moments of linguistic and cultural juxtaposition that produce shock, surprise and awe and lead readers to an awareness of radically different worlds. The retranslations give prominence to African voices and destabilize the coloniality of our contemporary conversations, crafting powerfully new, vivid, multilingual and pluriversal spaces. In counteracting the historical invisibilization and silencing of African voices, the poems bring out the deep complicities between the logic of coloniality and rhetoric of modernity. They directly challenge the destructive arrogance of a self-centred and individualized monovocal colonial voice and reveal alternative African selves comfortably centred in a multitude of complex human, spiritual and environmental relationships.

These multilingual engagements, created through 'non-normative' practices of translation, that is translation that stays close to the (multiple) meanings of indigenous voices, are acts of Linguistic Citizenship (cf. Viveiros de Castro, 2004 on non-equivocal translations). They are about disinhabiting, stepping out of, conventional spaces of engagement at the same time as 'language' itself is redesigned.

In Stroud and Kerfoot's chapter, as well as Krog's, voicing across languages involves creating spaces of vulnerability, comprising unsettling encounters that interrupt the status quo. Senses of self may be juxtaposed and refashioned as part of the reconstruction of dominant voices and more equitable engagements with others (cf. also Du Toit, this volume). 'Spaces of vulnerability' is also a significant theme in the third chapter by Miki Flockemann, which offers a striking account of the decolonizing potential of an interventionist and reflexive pedagogy built around affect that allows for deep engagement across difference. She shows how the post-identity politics in communities of difference is brought about by students' reflexive participation (as witnesses and spectators) in theatrical performances that allow, as she puts it, the 'interleaving of sensorial and cognitive knowledge'. Witnessing a theatre performance creates a space of vulnerability where the witness (or spectator) experiences a cognitive dissonance, a disinhabiting of identity and, at the same time, an empathy for the character performed on stage. This is a dynamic process *in* and *of* the moment (cf. also Abdulatief, Guzula and McKinney, this volume, on 'third spaces'), where relationality, negotiability and the momentary becoming of the other – a strong sense of the potential of being different – encourage one of the participants to exclaim 'I am the Other I am yet to become'. Flockemann cites work that shows that empathy is triggered by neural mirroring and the alignment of one body with another. This is the experience of being self-entangled in other lives rather than the lonely habitation of distinct identities that separate and alienate. We can read Flockemann's chapter as support for the idea that decoloniality is a very local and personal experience, built out of an affinity of togetherness in difference.

In these three chapters, then, we see how the 'retooling' of languages can potentially disrupt the linguistic colonialities whereby we as *Homo Sapiens Arrogans* continue to hold ourselves captive to voicelessness. Retooling of language is imperative as the violence of the colonial language project continues to carry ramifications for the impossibility of a true meaningful exchange untainted by linguistically constructed historical division (Veronelli, 2016). This is even the case between those historically colonized who may be speakers of indigenous languages or ex-colonial varieties of metropolitan languages.

Quentin Williams's chapter takes the inevitable need for linguistic retooling as a starting point for his discussion of Hip Hop as an act of Linguistic Citizenship. Williams warns that decolonial conversations may not be easily accessible, citing Veronelli's point that we need to find alternative registers of language and emotionality in order to reinstate consensual, coordinated engagements with and across difference (cf. also Flockemann's chapter). He finds the potential for Hip Hop and the possibilities it offers for a 'corporeal connect' to other histories and other knowledges, gestures towards knowledge of self and 'love', and the reclaiming of voice. In order to account for the liberatory educational use of Hip Hop, Williams presents acts of Linguistic Citizenship in terms of a wider semiotic that goes beyond registers of language to include complex coordinations of dance, visuals and other multimodal articulations. Williams's chapter thus advances Hip Hop as a process of engagement for a mutuality and susceptibility to alternative forms of 'being together in difference' – a repair and rejuvenation of relationships to selves and others in new transformative linguistically mediated ways of relating.

The majority of the chapters discuss examples of how multilingual practices through acts of Linguistic Citizenship create new socialities and refashioned selves. Compounding 'linguistic' with 'citizenship' suggests that praxes of 'empowering language-ing' (the opportunities language carries for agency and participation) will also have sociopolitical consequences, with various implications for the knowledge project.

Marijke du Toit's chapter explores the question of how to create spaces for students to rethink – and react to – South African history agentively, by understanding how our engagement with the present entails understanding the past as contested terrain. If our futures are to break with our presents, we must seek to engage critically with those damaging pasts that continue to haunt us. Du Toit discusses how working with African texts of self-representation from the early black public sphere (cf. also Krog, this volume) in multimodal and multilingual classrooms may interrupt white settler representations of South African history and deconstruct dominant voices, while simultaneously questioning conventions of academic authority and authorship. As was the case with Flockemann's students, participants in Du Toit's classes literally become 'witnesses' to the crimes and distortions of coloniality when reading old, historical letters aloud. The use of an African language in a linguistically diverse classroom – where not even speakers of the language may feel competent in its written registers – also creates spaces of vulnerability, already familiar from Krog's discussion of rich points. Interestingly, Du Toit questions a university educational language politics that reinforces the status quo of languages while it is ostensibly designed to do otherwise, noting the need to rethink multilingualism beyond the colonial pedigree in ways that resonate with many of the other contributions to the volume (cf. Williams and Abdulatief et al. on the 'dilemma' of named languages, as well as Stroud and Kerfoot on the artificiality of intellectualization). In fact, 'non-equivocal translation' emerges in Du Toit's classroom as an important tool with which to sidestep repeating historical discourses of linguistic chauvinism.

Likewise, the chapter by Abdulatief et al. explores multilingual language use in the classroom. It recounts two case studies that use African languages in ways that enhance the confidence and participation of historically marginalized learner identities. It explores ways of decolonizing the curriculum by 'delinking' from English as the priority language of instruction. In so doing, it builds on and continues a significant tradition of anti-colonial work on language education in South Africa since at least the 1980s by local scholars working in different institutional contexts, such as the Project for Alternative Education in South Africa (PRAESA).[2] The authors detail various ways in which discipline-specific content can be negotiated multilingually, recognizing, on the one hand, that named languages, although remaining constructs of coloniality, when given recognition in educational settings, are nevertheless resources that significantly empower historically marginalized students. On the other hand, 'third spaces' of hybridity and translanguaging also open the potential for students to delink from monoglot understandings of linguistic meaning-making, thereby taking a further step away from linguistic coloniality. What we could call 'third space' strategies are particularly important for speakers of non-standardized varieties of (African) languages. Similar to the chapters by Krog and Du Toit, Abdulatief et al. emphasize how bringing African languages into the classroom creates both a moment for celebration and spaces of vulnerability. For example, English-dominant students need to rely on those speakers who have access to African language repertoires and who are able to assist in mediating content. Particularly interesting is the accompanying corporeal articulations – the embodiment – that accompany the use of languages other than English, as well as the emotional registers that find expression across the different languages (cf. also Flockemann, and Williams, both this volume). Not only do multilingual practices such as these enable students to recognize the potential of their own symbolic resources, but they also teach them how to use these resources. Thus, changing normative language practices, and the resultant shifts in power, enables a significant reconstruction of learner identities as well as what it means to learn (Heugh, 2017; Kerfoot, 2011; Stroud and Kerfoot, 2013; Stroud and Kerfoot, this volume).

Many of the chapters have noted how meanings emerge over time and across modalities and how learner identities are successively built up with evolving agency through resemiotized coordinations of selves with others. These are slow and laborious processes typical of a careful 'crafting' rather than the immediacy of the industrial mould. In their chapter, Oostendorp and colleagues illustrate how not only delivery of content but also forms of academic assessment may benefit from an approach that emphasizes emergence and multivocality. They describe how resemiotization (re-genre-ing/rematerialization) resulting in an exhibition of artefacts was used as an assessment tool in an innovative module on multilingualism. The exhibition format allowed the problematization of institutionalized conventions of knowledge and provided a decolonial framing for the deconstruction of conventional constructs of language. At the same time, while offering students a more agentive role in the assessment practice, it also created a sense of vulnerability among lecturers who had to move beyond familiar and conventional genres for articulating knowledge. An interesting by-product of the assessment format was the way in which it opened up new sites of engagement outside of the classroom when, on the day of the exhibition, homeless people entered the gallery to share food and talk around the artefacts on display. This engagement changed the nature of the artefacts by giving rise to new 'participatory spaces' (Kerfoot, 2011) that made possible interactions between very different actors in determining the significance of the module.

At the same time, this happening introduced a new ethical perspective of accountability to the wider world.

Many of the themes in the volume find a point of convergence in the penultimate chapter by Zannie Bock. Her chapter makes a clear link between the 'terms of conversation' (Mignolo, 2009) and the role of language and register in creating new author identities as a condition for curriculum change. Her analysis centres on an innovative project of textbook authorship, and she details how the 'terms of the conversation' were altered during the production of an introductory textbook to linguistics in ways that validated the linguistic and epistemic capabilities and potentialities of subaltern actors and mobilized collective agency. The work of collaborative writing, and tapping into the local knowledges that participants held about language, created 'participatory spaces' which built agency and voice – the textbook authors were legitimated as authors and knowledge producers; they became 'visibilised' and were able to imagine themselves and their linguistic knowledge differently. Bock emphasizes how the authors' ideas of 'the expert' emerged out of the many 'shifts across registers of writing', the feedback and collaborative authorship, and the polyphonia of the production process (cf. Oostendorp et al. and Stroud and Kerfoot, this volume on the unfolding of meaning and agency through re-semiotization). These circumstances led to writers gaining confidence and assurance in writing, accompanied by a sense of euphoria at managing to word and reword. Bock also underscores how change is 'emergent', slow, and the outcome of local participation and engagement. It is something that *accompanies* the simultaneous emergence of voice and agency rather than preceding or following it.

In the final chapter by Duncan Brown, the lens refocuses on the relationship of people to the broader ecology and the role of language in capturing this experience. Like Krog's chapter which seeks to make visible the experiences and 'ways of seeing' carried by poetry, Brown's chapter explores the capacity of language to mediate our relationship with our local environments. He shows how the processes of standardization (in particular, in relation to English and Shangaan[3]), undertaken as part of the colonial project of modernity, have reduced the complexity and wealth of linguistic terms previously part of these varieties and therefore their capacity to describe the nuance of landscape, weather and other ecological dimensions. He argues that this reduces not only local understandings of these phenomena, but also our capacity as human beings in general to see, feel, know and experience the ways in which humans are embedded within and interconnected to their broader ecologies.

Conclusion

In this volume, then, we bring together a number of chapters that address, from various angles, the issue of decoloniality and transformation in higher education. Although each chapter has firm roots in the South African context, we offer these studies as relevant to a wider southern endeavour. South African realities, we believe, have much to offer others in their 'quest for better worlds'.

In this chapter, we have argued that a prerequisite for an education which leads towards a 'decolonial horizon' of social justice is an adequate understanding of the role of language and, in particular, multilingualism in human relationalities. Our point of departure has been a sense of decoloniality that seeks to address the contradiction between patriarchy, competition and intolerance, on the one hand, and our humanity as loving and languaging animals, on the other. The emphasis throughout the volume is on thinking and practising language in ways that can enhance the many entanglements that bind us together across the categories of identity and language institutionalized by *Homo Sapiens Arrogans*. An important aspect of this is that new ways of knowing emerge out of emergent agentive selves and that this knowledge is what comprises the peg of structural change.

Each chapter has detailed ways in which speakers use multiple languages for conviviality, agency and participation across traditional and colonially inherited identities, creating more ethical engagements across difference. We have noted how these various uses suggest a critical take on the 'sole-named language' approach to decoloniality in favour of a notion of 'language' linked to the idea of Linguistic Citizenship and a politics of broader affinities that disengage from and disinhabit strand-based, inherited identities (such as ethnicity, race and social class) (see Chapter 2 for a fuller discussion). Linguistic Citizenship highlights the processes whereby language can be forged into a transformative tool for the attainment, or articulation, of other ways of being and other types of knowledge, what Papadopoulos (2011, 2018) calls 'alter-ontologies'. Acts of Linguistic Citizenship can make a contribution to creating conditions for the removal of patriarchal structures and their replacement with relations of empathy and conviviality, with implications for knowledge (the epistemological project) and the creation of new resources for acting in and on the world (politics and selves). Across the volume there are multiple convergences around the idea that the production of alternative ontologies – be these political or material – is a prerequisite for entertaining alternative epistemologies (cf. also Menezes de Souza, 2017). Linguistic Citizenship is an important component in an alternative politics of reality.

Maturana and Varela's (1980) understanding of 'love' as the key dynamic in the origin of the human, the essential contribution love makes to our cognition and intelligence, and the importance of love in language sets a clear agenda for (applied) linguists and educationalists. This can be stated as follows: Rethinking language is essential to reinstating our humanity, cultivating the 'love' that binds us to others, and fostering the ambiguity and multiplicity of meanings that can topple the ready and simple truths of *Homo Sapiens Arrogans* in all its guises.

Notes

1 Under Apartheid (1948–1994), all South Africans were racially classified as 'coloured', 'black', 'white' or 'Indian'. It should be noted that in South Africa, the term 'coloured' has a different meaning to the way it is used in the United States and elsewhere. Here, it refers to people of mixed heritage, many descendants of slaves from South East Asia brought here during the colonial times, or descendants of contact between the indigenous inhabitants of southern Africa and colonial settlers who began arriving nearly 400 years ago. Despite their Apartheid and colonial histories, these racial labels continue to have considerable currency as markers of social identity in contemporary South Africa.
2 For relevant forerunners here, cf. Heugh et al. (1995), Mbude-Shale et al. (2004), Nomlomo (2008) and Wababa (2004, 2009).
3 Language and group labels in the African context (as generally) are complex, problematic and contentious. Often Shangaan is used (incorrectly) to refer to all speakers of Xitsonga varieties, when it is more correct to see them as a subgroup among many. We take it that the author (Cloete) is referring to this subgroup in this context.

References

Anderson, B. (2008), 'Affective Urbanism and the Event of Hope', *Space and Culture*, 11 (2): 142–59.

Bayat, A. (2010), *Life as Politics: How Ordinary People Change the Middle East*. Amsterdam: Amsterdam University Press.

Fanon, F. (1967), *Black Skin, White Masks*. London: Pluto Press.

Heugh, K. (2017), 'Re-Placing and Re-Centring Southern Multilingualisms: A Decolonial Project', in C. Kerfoot and K. Hyltenstam (eds), *Entangled Discourses: South-North Orders of Visibility*, 209–29. New York: Routledge.

Heugh, K., P. Plüddemann and A. Siegruhn, eds (1995), *Multilingual Education for South Africa*. Johannesburg: Heinemann.

Kerfoot, C. (2011), 'Making and Shaping Participatory Spaces: Resemiotization and Citizenship Agency in South Africa', *International Multilingual Research Journal*, 5 (2): 87–102.

Lim, L., C. Stroud and L. Wee, eds (2018), *The Multilingual Citizen. Towards a Politics of Language for Agency and Change*. Bristol: Multilingual Matters.

Maturana, H. and E. Cabezon (2001), 'Values and Competencies in the School of the Future', in H. Taylor and P. Hogenbirk (eds), *Information and Communication Technologies in Education*, 239–47. Springer: International Federation for Information Processing.

Maturana, H. and F. Varela (1980), *Autopoiesis and Cognition: The Realization of the Living*. Reidel: Dordrecht.

Mbude-Shale, N., Z. Wababa and P. Plüddemann (2004), 'Developmental Research: Adual-medium Schools Pilot Project, Cape Town, 1999–2002', in Birgit Brock-Utne, Martha A. S. Qorro and Zubeida Desai (eds), *Researching the Language of Instruction in Tanzania and South Africa*, pp. 151–68. Cape Town: African Minds.

Menezes de Souza, L. M. T. (2017), 'Epistemic Diversity, Lazy Reason and Ethical Translation in Post-Colonial Contexts: The Case of Indigenous Educational Policy in Brazil', in C. Kerfoot and K. Hyltenstam (eds), *Entangled Discourses: South-North Orders of Visibility*, 189–208. New York: Routledge.

Mignolo, W. (2007), 'Delinking', *Cultural Studies*, 21 (2): 449–514.

Mignolo, W. (2009), 'Epistemic Disobedience, Independent Thought and De-colonial Freedom', *Theory, Culture and Society*, 26 (7–8): 159–81.

Mignolo, W. and C. Walsh (2018). *On Decoloniality: Concepts, Analytics, Praxis*. Durham: Duke University Press.

Milani, T. and R. Jonson (2018), 'Linguistic Citizenship in Sweden: (De)constructing Languages in a Context of Linguistic Human Rights', in L. Lim, C. Stroud and L. Wee (eds), *The Multilingual Citizen. Towards a Politics of Language for Agency and Change*, 221–46. Bristol: Multilingual Matters.

Nomlomo, V. (2008), 'IsiXhosa as a Medium of Instruction in Science Teaching in South Africa: Challenges and Prospects', in M. Qorro, Z. Desai and B. Brock-Utne (eds), *LOITASA Reflecting on Phase 1 and Entering Phase II*, 81–102. Dar es Sallam: E&D Vision Publishing Ltd.

Papadopoulos, D. (2011), 'Alter-ontologies: Towards a Constituent Politics in Technoscience', *Social Studies in Science*, 41 (2): 177–201.

Papadopoulos, D. (2018), *Experimental Practice: Technoscience, Alterontologies and More-than-Social Movements*. Durham: Duke University Press.

Rampton, B., M. Cooke and S. Holmes (2018), *Promoting Linguistic Citizenship: Issues, Problems, Possibilities, Working Papers in Urban Language and Linguistics*, Paper 233, Kings College London.

Santos, B. de S. (2014), *Epistemologies of the South: Justice against Epistemicide*. Boulder, CO: Paradigm Publishers.

Savransky, M. (2017), 'A Decolonial Imagination: Sociology, Anthropology and the Politics of Reality', *Sociology*, 51 (1): 11–26.

Soudien, C. (2014), 'Bodies of Language and Language of Bodies: South African Puzzles and Opportunities', in M. Prinsloo and C. Stroud (eds), *Educating for Language and Literacy Diversity: Mobile Selves*, 206–15. London: Palgrave Macmillan.

Stroud, C. (2001), 'African Mother-Tongue Programmes and the Politics of Language: Linguistic Citizenship versus Linguistic Human Rights', *Journal of Multilingual and Multicultural Development*, 22 (4): 339–55.

Stroud, C. (2009), 'A Postliberal Critique of Language Rights: Toward a Politics of Language for a Linguistics of Contact', in J. E. Petrovic (ed.), *International Perspectives on Bilingual Education: Policy, Practice, and Controversy*, 191–218. Charlotte, NC: Information Age Publishing.

Stroud, C. (2018), 'Linguistic Citizenship', in L. Lim, C. Stroud and L. Wee (eds), *The Multilingual Citizen: Towards a Politics of Language for Agency and Change*, 17–39. Bristol, UK: Multilingual Matters.

Stroud, C. and C. Kerfoot (2013), 'Towards Rethinking Multilingualism and Language Policy for Academic Literacies', *Linguistics and Education*, 24 (4): 396–405.

Stroud, C. and K. Heugh (2004), 'Linguistic Human Rights and Linguistic Citizenship'. in D. Patrick and J. Freeland (eds), *Language Rights and Language Survival: A Sociolinguistic Exploration*, 191–218. Manchester: St Jerome.

Veronelli, G. (2016), 'A Coalitional Approach to Theorizing Decolonial Communication', *Hypatia*, 31 (2): 404–20.

Viveiros de Castro, E. (2004), 'Perspectival Anthropology and the Method of Controlled Equivocation', *Tipití: Journal of the Society for the Anthropology of Lowland South America*, 2 (1): 3–22.

Wababa, Z. (2004), 'Teaching Grade 6 Natural Science in isiXhosa to African Language Learners', in *Making Multilingual Education a Reality for All*, 260–70. Centre for Language Studies, University of Malawi: Zomba, Malawi.

Wababa, Z. (2009), 'How Scientific Terms Are Taught and Learnt in the Intermediate Phase'. Doctoral dissertation, Stellenbosch: University of Stellenbosch.

Walsh, C. (2014), 'Pedagogical Notes from the Decolonial Cracks', *Decolonial Gesture*, 11 (4). Available online: http://hemisphericinstitute.org/hemi/en/emisferica-111-decolonial-gesture/walsh (accessed 12 May 2016).

Williams, Q. (2019), 'Let's Reinvent Afrikaans (and Ourselves) Together', *Mail and Guardian*, 17 September.

Williams, Q. and C. Stroud (2015), 'Linguistic Citizenship. Language and Politics in Postnational Modernities', *Journal of Language & Politics*, 14 (3): 406–30.

2

Decolonizing Higher Education: Multilingualism, Linguistic Citizenship and Epistemic Justice

Christopher Stroud and Caroline Kerfoot

Introduction

Long-simmering calls to decolonize South African universities gained explosive new energy from the #RhodesMustFall and #FeesMustFall student movements in 2015. This surge of interest in decoloniality could be explained by a mix of factors. One factor was surely a critical mass of black scholars after twenty-one years of democracy and an increase in the number of black graduates from about 3,400 in 1986 to more than 63,000 in 2012 (Van Broekhuizen, 2016). At the same time, retention and throughput rates for black students were tied to material inequalities in socio-economic status and education quality (Nyamnjoh, 2016; Van Broekhuizen et al., 2016). Other factors were the substantial decline in state funding for the public universities, from 49 per cent of institutions' total income in 2000 to 39 per cent in 2015 (Africa Check, 2016), and despair and anger over deepening poverty and unemployment after almost nine years of ineffective and often predatory state management (2009–18) combined with continuing immense disparities in wealth among groups.

All of these factors underscored the significant challenges facing post-Apartheid reform attempts. It was not surprising, then, when under these circumstances, student movements called for free and decolonized education, democratized access, and Afrocentric institutions and curricula. What might be surprising, however, is that the issue of language in decolonial deconstruction

---

This research was supported by the Riksbankens Jubileumsfond of Sweden under project no. SAB17-1020:1 (Caroline Kerfoot) and project no. SAB19-1031:1 and the South African National Research Foundation project no. IFR180308316420.

has largely been absent from recent student and academic debates related to these calls (see, for example, Langa et al., 2017). An exception is Mayaba et al. (2018).[1]

Both within and outside of universities worldwide, and South Africa in particular, languages and languaging practices continue to be ranked and regulated in ways that privilege communication and knowledge production through European languages – with insidious consequences such as educational failure. Just as important, an even more insidious consequence of exclusionary language policies remains unaddressed, namely that epistemic authority is removed from speakers of other, non-metropolitan languages (Alexander, 1989; Ngũgĩ wa Thiong'o, 1994; Santos, 2014). This raises deep concerns about 'epistemic injustice' (e.g. Miranda Fricker, 1998, 1999, 2007) and the need for epistemic justice, an 'ethical project of reversing epistemic exclusions, mitigating epistemic exploitation, and seeking parity of epistemic authority for the historically oppressed' (Kerfoot and Bello-Nonjengele, 2021).

In this chapter, we explore some of the ways we need to rethink language – and multilingualism in particular – in order to further epistemic justice. We take our departure in a critical review of some of the existing strategies or remedies proposed to overcome epistemic *in*justice in the last thirty years in order to situate the question of language in a broader decolonial project. We argue that the role of language/multilingualism in furthering epistemic justice is compromised by the understandings of language inherited from the colonial project, an inheritance that Veronelli (2015) refers to as the 'coloniality of language', that is, the specific, linguistic instantiation of the more general phenomenon of 'coloniality'. 'Coloniality', which should not be confused with colonialism, refers to the patterns of power, control and hegemonic systems of knowledge that rationalized colonial domination. It has been kept alive in contemporary systems of oppression and dispossession, even after the demise of colonialism as a military or economic order (e.g. Grosfoguel, 2011; Maldonado-Torres, 2007; Ndlovu-Gatsheni, 2013, 2018). Pursuing epistemic justice means 'going beyond' colonialities of language and critically engaging with contemporary ideas of multilingualism and the very notion of language itself.

In the second half of this chapter, we advance the notion of Linguistic Citizenship (see Stroud, 2001, 2009, 2018; Stroud and Heugh, 2004; Williams and Stroud, 2015) as a conceptual framing with which to disengage coloniality. We argue that Linguistic Citizenship can inform epistemic justice by focusing on the potential carried by language(s) for 'ontological refashioning' of selves, socialities and concomitant knowledges and that it may offer a way to rethink multilingualism 'as a transformative epistemology and methodology of difference' (cf. Stroud and Kerfoot, 2013) rather than a conserving, and even reproductive, force. The chapter concludes with the proposal that creating spaces for the exercise of Linguistic Citizenship could be a key component in the decolonization of South African universities.

Epistemic (in)justice and the coloniality of language

The question of the role of language in epistemic justice cannot be detached from the uses to which both language and knowledge are, and have been, put in a politics of globalized inequity and dispossession. Vasquez (2011: 27) remarks on how global social inequality is far from merely a 'consequence of an incomplete modernity' and that inequalities of knowledge and an epistemic monoculture have contributed greatly to modern systems of oppression and destitution, comprising one essential bulwark in propping up an unjust world.[2] Grosfoguel (2011: 6) notes that this is the case even today as 'the success of the modern/colonial world-system consists precisely in making subjects that are socially located in the oppressed side of the colonial difference, think epistemically like the ones on [sic] dominant positions'. An epistemic monoculture is a form of (epistemic) oppression, the 'situation in which the social experiences of the powerless are not properly integrated into collective understandings of the social world' (Fricker, 2007: 207) but are in fact deliberately excluded from it. Epistemic justice requires a form of life that is informed by the social experience of everyone and freed of the narrow interpretive practices of a privileged minority (Fricker, 2007).

Universities are traditionally powerful spaces for the reproduction of colonial knowledge projects (Connell, 2013) and the privileging of minority interpretive frames characteristic of epistemic oppression. Epistemic justice requires that priority be given to the question of how to capture a broader spectrum of voices if universities are to truly decolonize and transform (Andreotti et al., 2011, 2015; Mbembe, 2016; Mungwini, 2013; Ogone, 2017). This means creating an inclusiveness and generosity of dialogue with those who live and speak from the other side of the 'abyssal line' that for Santos (2014) separates 'modern' from other knowledges, that side of the line of non-being where 'reality becomes non-existent and is produced ... as not existing in any comprehensible way' (Santos, 2014: 118). To think and engage with the incommensurable, so as to validate epistemic authority for subaltern actors and mobilize collective knowledge production requires attention to how students' and lecturers' multilingual and multimodal semiotic resources might significantly enhance the audibility and affirmation of voices less heard.

In the South African higher education (HE) landscape, there have been roughly three different, but complementary, remedies or strategies for getting to grips with the problems of language in access to knowledge. These are (i) a continuation of the Apartheid era status quo with the use of the old and established languages of power, English and to a lesser extent Afrikaans, as the main languages of teaching and learning, complemented with a variety of scaffolding supports; (ii) the (minimal) introduction of African languages, bolstered by new and increasingly 'urgent' government (and revised university) language policies; and (iii) the use of translanguaging, which purportedly allows 'the first languages of the learners into the L2 classroom as linguistic and cognitive resources, while retaining the focus on the target language' (Carstens, 2016) (for overviews, see Antia and Dyers, 2017; Hibbert and van der Walt, 2014; Stroud and Kerfoot, 2013).

We look critically at each of the three main remedies identified above in turn – aware that the studies we discuss, conducted under conditions of severe resource constraint, are all rigorously conceptualized and implemented attempts to improve students' chances of conceptual engagement and overcome histories of exclusion and discrimination.

Colonial metropolitan languages: The absent self

A large body of work has been done on ways of improving students' access to English and Afrikaans to facilitate epistemic access. However, these attempts have tended to underestimate the extent and complexity of (linguistic) coloniality layered into the historical formation of these languages. Veronelli, the Argentinian linguist and philosopher, describes how 'the communicative conditions created by coloniality ... restrict building ... connections of dialogue' even in what is ostensibly labelled the 'same language' (2016: 408). Historically, colonial ideologies and practices of languages played an important role in building the 'subjectivities' and knowledge frameworks whereby the cruelties of colonial dispossessions were rationalized as just and benevolent. Colonial languages were the foremost tool in the interpellation of a colonial Other: they displaced indigenous languages in public spaces, served to discipline the 'native' and determine legitimate forms of interaction and engagement among the colonized and colonial masters (Stroud, 2007). They shaped and were, in turn, moulded by the tangible, physical conditions of the moments of communication between Europeans and Africans (cf. Fabian, 1986; Gilmour, 2006; Stroud, 2007). Importantly, colonial languages were cultivated as repositories of indigenous knowledge through tools of translation. Translation selectively 're-wrote' indigenous knowledge in idioms that made available to colonizers powerful frames for making sense of, interacting with and managing worlds of difference. As modernity expanded, translation laid the foundation for a Western monovocality and monomodality of voice, as, with few exceptions, only forms of indigenous knowledge that could be written down, lexicalized and articulated discursively in ways that made sense to missionary linguists were accommodated in colonial languages. In Vasquez's words (2011: 27), translation rendered invisible everything that did not fit into the 'parameters of legibility' of modernity's epistemic territory, thereby laying the basis for claims to the universality of European knowledge. This was not without deep and inherited trauma. Fanon (1967) noted how immersion in imposed alien structures and meanings, and the revoicing of local knowledge, produced in the colonial subject a sense of existing 'absolutely for the other': a psychic split characterized by feelings of disconnect from an agentive sense of self and human value.

There are countless examples of how metropolitan languages still have 'the potential to disempower those of us who are just learning to speak, who are just learning to claim language as a space where we make ourselves subjects' (hooks, 1994: 168), Botsis (2017), Heugh (2017), Makoe and McKinney (2014) and Veronelli (2015, 2016). A telling, recent, example of how the monovocality of metropolitan languages continues to engage black bodies in a Fanonian echo is the recent #OpenStellenbosch movement at Stellenbosch University, an off-shoot of the #FeesMustFall movement documented in the video 'Luister' (Contraband Cape Town, 2015). In the documentary, African language–speaking students express a strong sense of distress and dehumanization both inside and outside of the lecture hall when required to engage with Afrikaans.[3] In encounters with white Afrikaans speakers in the cafes and on the streets of Stellenbosch, they experienced the language to be a powerful tool in interactionally reinforcing an injurious form of black-white relationship. And, they lament the genuine physical pain brought on in the lecture hall when listening to Afrikaans through different forms of simultaneous, whispered translation that removed them both physically and temporally (resulting from translation lag) from the physical presence of their colleagues in class (cf. Stroud and Williams, 2017). Their affective and corporeal engagements with Afrikaans suggest that the contemporary resonances of linguistic coloniality on subject formation go far beyond the mere formal repertoires of language; they engage deeply divisive historical chronotopes of affect and interpellation that are as yet poorly understood.

Part of the rationale for the continued widespread appeal of metropolitan languages is their supposed communicative efficacy and universality, and the presumption that speaking the 'same' language implies an 'essential similarity between what the Other and We are saying' (Viveiros de Castro, 2004: 10). However, as Veronelli (2016: 408) has argued, the myth that metropolitan languages are conduits to global, regional understanding and mutuality of encounter does not take into account the way in which metropolitan languages shore up semiotic borders and temper multivocality. There is a wealth of literature on how metropolitan languages (in particular English) are a force in the production of global disadvantage (e.g. Tollefson, 1995). The question, then, is whether indigenous languages better allow a more equitable participation of different voices.

African languages: Discourses of the past

The use of African languages faces great challenges in offering solutions to the impasse of epistemic justice in the foreseeable future, given how they have been discursively constituted through linguistic coloniality. Material artefacts such as grammars, dictionaries and language-teaching materials, tools in the reorganization of the languages of the local people, aided in dividing and controlling their social interactions (Makoni, 1998; Maseko, 2017; Veronelli, 2015) and provided colonial officials and missionaries with the tools of nation-state governance (see Blommaert, 2008; Errington, 2008; Gilmour, 2006; Heugh, 2017; Irvine, 2008). An important dimension of the coloniality of language was the discursive construction of African languages as vessels of the past. Hountondji (1997) has remarked on how Africa has generally been construed as residing in the past, and the speakers of its languages no less so. Discourses of pastness have provided a powerful rationale for the depiction of African language speakers as 'simple communicators', removed from the complexities of thought and expression necessary for life in modernity and requiring patronage and government.

Discourses of 'past-ness' underlie two ostensibly very different approaches to African languages as knowledge projects, namely so-called intellectualization (see, for example, Kaschula and Maseko, 2014; Prah, 2017) and 'endogenization'. The essence of intellectualization is found in the words of Kwesi Prah (2017: 215–16), one of its foremost African proponents, who contends that 'the real challenge is how to bring African languages ... up to speed with the linguistic techniques of modernity and advanced contemporary thought' (cf. Alexander, 1997, 2003). Contrary to intent, intellectualization poses a number of problems for epistemic justice. One of these is captured in a forthright critique of African education more generally by Nyamnjoh (2012: 129), which he sees as a 'victim of a resilient colonial and colonizing epistemology', justified by a postcolonial African elite through rhetoric on the need to be competitive internationally. The outcome is often a devaluation of African 'creativity, agency and value systems, and an internalized sense of inadequacy', where the subjugated, alternative and contemporary knowledges of the everyday remain sadly invisibilized. In a pluriverse of knowledges, epistemic justice cannot mean only equipping African languages with parity of expression in reproducing the 'abstract rationality of the canonic philosophy of the North' (Santos, 2018).

'Endogenization', which refers to the expansion of epistemic registers with more home-grown knowledge systems, would at first glance appear to offer better recourse to the 'creativity, agency and value systems' of African thought that intellectualization elides. Nevertheless, although ostensibly tapping into local knowledge systems, endogenization also builds on discourses of 'pastness'. To the extent that the knowledge sought through endogenization is to be found in African pasts with little bearing on contemporary struggles, it also risks minimal engagement with the concerns of epistemic justice. The problem is compounded by the realization that any diversity of thought in precolonial societies may have gone undocumented, and even suffered attrition, and that what is considered as 'endogenous' knowledge may also have a colonial and elite pedigree that has selectively silenced subaltern voices through time (cf. Hountondji, 1997; Mudimbe, 1988, 1995). Mkhize (2016: 146) makes a similar point when referencing in particular literary use of African languages, when she calls for a 're-framing of the kind of "native subject" or "implied reader", what she calls, the "good Bantu", inherited from the African language literary tradition. She suggests that the "institutionalization model" of promoting African languages fails because it reproduces conservative scholarly practices associated with African languages teaching and literary culture' (Mkhize, 2016: 147). These practices include the close linkage between ethnic identity and language, the use of African language as cultural reclamation, and lack of inventiveness in literary production. She argues for a move away from 'conservative themes, in which cultural pride, propriety and identity take centre stage' (Mkhize, 2016: 146) and for new forms that 'can handle plurality and intersectionalism' and that 'boldly use vernacular idiom to theorise the transgressive' (Mkhize, 2016: 150).

Most problematic is the question to what extent endogenous knowledge systems – in whatever condition – are even minimally functional in local ecologies and social systems that have undergone extensive colonial destruction. Without an understanding of 'endogenous' as indexing the contemporary 'dynamism, negotiability, adaptability and capacity for autonomy and interdependence, creativity and innovation in African societies and beyond' (Nyamnjoh, 2012: 136), the potential of endogenization for transforming the academy is limited.

Thus, a key shortcoming of both intellectualization and endogenization for present-day speakers of African languages is that they risk the continuing exclusion of certain voices from participation in the knowledge project, those voices which cannot be accommodated within existing frameworks. In this sense, both strategies continue to select the same 'ontological subjects' and to return or keep captive those dispossessed and invisibilized subjects traditionally held hostage to colonialism on the 'native' side of the abyssal line. Subjugated voices have yet to be heard in all their complexity in ways that shift the perceptions of what constitutes knowledge and creates the necessary conditions for engaging with it. The third remedy, translanguaging, claims to address these shortcomings.

Translanguaging: A modality of social change?

'Translanguaging' is the third, and most recent, linguistic remedy for the ills of the colonial language project. It claims to transcend the limitations of bordered languages by incorporating multiple identities in the learning process in order to accommodate subjugated knowledges. It is said to be able to 'offset the symbolic violence of monoglossic ideologies' (Makalela, 2014: 668) (and thereby address a shortcoming of metropolitan languages noted earlier) by allowing the students' use of 'highly complex identifying processes that mark fluid, multiple affiliations and mobile and creative negotiation of an identity matrix through hybrid language forms' (thereby tapping into endogeneity). Especially, in recent years, approaches built on translanguaging have sought to make space for (linguistic) difference and to shift racialized attributions of symbolic value in order to thereby improve epistemological access (see for example Antia and Dyers, 2016, 2019; Makalela, 2014; Plüddemann et al., 2010). Ultimately, claims are made that translanguaging is a force in social transformation, able 'to give back voice, transform cognitive structures, raise well-being and attainment levels and eventually transform an unequal society into a more just world' (Jaspers, 2018: 3, citing García and Li Wei, 2014).

There are a host of complexities in the debate around translanguaging (Block, 2018; Charalambous et al., 2016; Heugh, 2017, 2019; Jaspers, 2018). One is that translanguaging focuses on 'bordering', on moving between 'named' languages or codes, without engaging the powerful role this 'technology' has played in coloniality. It thereby risks replicating modernist ideas of language as a self-contained, logocentric system together with epistemologies of exclusion. Linguistic borders often served to consolidate core linkages between (ethnic) identities and language. In the South African context, the roots of bordering lie in the reconstructive work on African languages carried out to find the origins of languages and peoples that were perceived by colonialists to have been dispersed and mixed through warfare and migration (Harries, 2007). Determining the provenance and pedigree of languages aided the import by colonial managers of social categories such as 'tribe' and 'kingdom', social units of a type familiar to colonial administrators and missionaries that lent themselves readily to bringing order to a seemingly chaotic reality.

The claim that translanguaging moves 'beyond' named languages and creates 'new language practices' that are different from 'a synthesis of different language practices' or 'a hybrid mixture' is not empirically supported (Bhatt and Bolonyai, 2019: 19). Furthermore, translanguaging 'certainly does not enhance any theoretical understanding of bilingual language use beyond what the sociolinguistic studies of code-switching have offered' (ibid. 1). In fact, as a number of authors have pointed out, there is little to distinguish translanguaging from code-switching. Both paradigms, as evident in research documenting contemporary classroom practices, assume languages as structural entities between which speakers move, thus replicating the structural notion of language in modernist linguistics. Thus, to the extent that translanguaging as implemented pedagogically implicitly or explicitly relies on 'named' languages and their varieties, it cannot counter the critique that metropolitan and local languages remain captive to coloniality.[4]

Thus, rather than being transformative of the status quo, translanguaging could arguably be seen as one more version of the distinctions made in modernist ideologies of language between centrifugal versus centripetal dynamics of (standard) languages, between normativity and constraint in different language practices (cf. Jaspers, 2018: 8 on purity and hybridity). It is fundamentally an appeal to temporarily suspend a requirement of standard so that speakers on the margins may gradually become inculcated to normativity. For translanguaging to have a place in furthering epistemic justice as part of an agenda for social change, it would need to engage more extensively with concepts such as 'transknowledging' or the two-way exchange of knowledge (Heugh, 2019) and 'intercultural/equivocal translation' (Santos, 2018) as part of an agenda for social change as an ethical relationship necessary in relating to epistemic difference, even when total mutual illegibility is not possible[5] (Vivieros de Castro, 2004). This would involve a sense of translanguaging as engaging new ontologies of speakers and languages (Heugh, 2017) where the idea of language itself is shifted in the process.

Summary

The three remedies discussed in this section can be seen as related but distinct aspects of what Andreotti et al. (2015) have called 'radical-reform' strategies. These are approaches to inclusivity that use notions of equity, access, voice, recognition, representation or redistribution to facilitate access to the knowledge system. They are affirmative strategies in Nancy Fraser's (1995) sense, premised on the institutional status quo and defining the problem of epistemic justice as one of diversity and access within existing educational formats and tweaked institutional arrangements.[6] This is not to deny in any way the enormous value of this approach. It is important to note that there have been a handful of programmes which go much further in their attempt to legitimate and develop African languages as epistemic resources. See, for example, the bilingual teacher education programme by the University of the Western Cape with the NGO PRAESA (Plüddemann et al., 2010) and the sustained work of Esther Ramani and Michael Joseph which resulted in the first bilingual humanities degree at the University of Limpopo (Ramani and Joseph, 2002). More recently, the work of Bassey Antia and Charlyn Dyers (2016, 2019) has sought to enhance epistemological access and decolonize the languages of the academy through multimodal lectures using several language varieties, including urban vernaculars.

Although radical-reform approaches offer some valuable, gap-stopping, remedies, they do not change ontological dominance. In fact, as we have argued above, the effect of using metropolitan languages is to perpetuate exclusion; processes such as intellectualization and endogenization reproduce ideas of pastness and the temporal disconnect between African languages and their speakers; and translanguaging as implemented pedagogically in contemporary classrooms tends to reinforce in different terms the very notion of modernist colonial linguistics shared by all remedies.[7] In other words, not one of the remedies can easily re-form language for epistemic justice unless the workings of language as a contemporary resonance of coloniality are addressed. This requires that linguistic issues be approached as one component in a broader project of transformative social change.

Each of the remedies is an instance of what we can call a 'zero-point multilingualism', reflecting what Castro-Gómez (2007) terms the 'hubris of the zero point' of observation, apparently unlocated but in fact masking a set of ethnocentric assumptions assumed to have universal validity. This is a multilingualism of monovocality that has little place for pluriversality. It is thus unable to articulate subaltern knowledges and redraws the abyssal line by reaffirming conventional fault lines of what can be said (and known) in a semiotic imaginary of the one-world of coloniality-modernity.

Andreotti and colleagues (2015) are emphatic that while it is important and necessary, in the short term, to value remedies that are not ontologically transformative, there needs to be something 'beyond-reform', which goes beyond advocating for inclusion in a system of exclusion. To avoid treading the fault lines of linguistic coloniality and so as to engage subjugated selves in pursuit of epistemic justice, a radically different conceptualization of language and language use, ultimately, a very different construct of multilingualism, is required (Heugh, 2017). This is one that would be able to attend to a multitude of meanings (pluriversality) in ethical engagements with different others in ways that acknowledge their subjecthood and agency and that admit of forms of 'subjugated' knowledges emerging out of contemporary conditions of existence. We turn in the next section to the idea of Linguistic Citizenship as such a 'beyond-reform' strategy to explore under what conditions we might build multilingualism as a transformative dynamic for epistemic justice.

Transformative/decolonial multilingualism through Linguistic Citizenship: Reconfiguring language

Santos (2014) writes on the importance of everyday struggle against colonialism – against the inequities and unjustness of the capitalist modes of existence – as a decolonial epistemological event, where a plurality of alternative, complex and competing voices emerges on the back of a politics for social change. However, struggle alone can never be sufficient. Struggle needs to be acknowledged as such by an invested community of actors and be part of an emerging sociality, communion or an alternative citizenship, a necessity recognized by Fanon – and later Mbembe for South Africa – in their emphasis on new socialities for a new humanity. 'Citizenship' in this sense is understood as **acts** of engagement that make visible/audible subjects and their claims. This should not be understood as only claims to 'recognition' (cf. Isin, 2008) or for the betterment of lives, but rather demands for the fundamentals of existence to be met, to a 'being or "becoming"' and to 'count' in ways not previously recognized or imagined possible by institutions. The significance of acts of citizenship in this sense is as a modality of action that seeks to radically transform the conditions for 'legitimate' political actorhood – to repopulate the political arena and its priorities and to offer new ways of seeing, being in, and understanding the world for those hitherto existing outside of it on the other side of Santos's abyssal line (Fanon, 1967; Fraser, 1995). Such acts of citizenship have conceptual affinities with other acts of citizenship (Isin, 2008) meant to expand the scope of legitimate political subjectivity and its material consequences and to introduce alternative forms of knowledge in the process (such as feminist citizenship, ecological citizenship) as new collective identities (Alcoff, 2011). This is a sense of citizenship 'permitting' new ontologies of self and others, living in a sociality that is ontologically populated by possibility and the (engaged) human means for its actualization.

Language is at the centre of citizenship struggles; ontologically 'refashioned selves' require 'refashioned languages', just as in like manner, the refashioning of languages needs new speakers. Linguistic Citizenship (Stroud, 2001; Stroud and Williams, 2017) refers to acts of language, frequently and of necessity, performed outside of the institutional status quo, that engage with voices on the margins to create conditions for a transformative agency. It is a modality of struggle that seeks to capture the close, material links between language and the struggles of everyday politics. Linguistic Citizenship is about people using language to build alternative, caring relationships with Others (the 'new' socialities of Fanon, 1967). In turn, these relationships allow for the possibility of crafting alternative selves and ultimately contributing to grounding new ways of thinking and changing the world and its politics. It attempts to accommodate the unintelligible or incommensurable by according voice and epistemological authority to the poor and to the marginalized, that is, those whose lives and experiences as 'abyssal subjects' lie beyond, or are marginalized, by the 'dialectic of intelligible possibilities' (Alcoff, 2011: 3). In like manner to the way feminist and ecological citizenships have shifted the meaning and political import of sexuality, gender, nature and other social categories, Linguistic Citizenship carries the potential to move the linguistic centre of gravity away from a constraining colonial construct of language towards one that affirms decolonial modalities of interaction and engagement. Linguistic Citizenship, then, as exemplified by Afrikaaps later in this chapter, is about the way languages are used and re-formed in struggle to introduce and make audible neglected subjectivities. In the process, it generates new understandings of the potential of self and other and the possibility of epistemic justice. Importantly, at the same time, the meaning of language is also resignified.

The workings of acts of Linguistic Citizenship are nicely illustrated in the following example of a contemporary emerging movement in South Africa to reconfigure Kaaps, a stigmatized variety of Afrikaans spoken predominantly among the so-called 'coloured' population in the townships of the Cape Flats, into Afrikaaps (cf. Hendricks and Dyers, 2016). Afrikaaps is the 'struggle name' given by activists to this emerging decolonial Afrikaans, the language that together with English was one of the two official languages of pre-democratic South Africa. Afrikaans, as the politically engineered language of the Apartheid regime, was sanitized in the 1940s of any remnants of its complex colonial contact heritage and given a full-bloodied European ancestry as a direct descendant of Dutch. It remains today in many circles a language associated with the Apartheid past. Kaaps, the Afrikaans of the so-called Cape Coloureds in pre-democracy South Africa, was considered an imperfect system, a bastardized variety, *gamtaal*, the language of Gam, 'kitchen Afrikaans',[8] subject to its own laws and trajectories of change. In post-Apartheid South Africa, it remains a salient marker of racial and socio-economic disadvantage, indexing dispossession, 'victimhood', gross inequity and the violence and social deprivation of contemporary South Africa in general, and the Cape Flats in particular. Given this history, the politically named language Afrikaaps encapsulates a clear politicization of Kaaps, a construct of language firmly anchored in the ambition of its speakers for historical redress, and privileging the perspective of 'the poor' and the excluded. The momentum of the Afrikaaps movement has until now been carried by a troupe of young rappers intent on decentring the official, dominant, narrative of Afrikaans and its fictional claims to universality but is rapidly gaining purchase among a wider demographic.

Acts of Linguistic Citizenship around Afrikaaps speak to the concerns raised in the previous section, namely the problem of language and subjectification, the question of engaging local and contemporary voice in struggle, and a construct of 'language' that goes beyond its conventional coloniality. Most importantly, the knowledge that emerges out of the acts of Linguistic Citizenship – a struggle knowledge – is what directly mobilizes speakers into a 'community' with the potential for increasingly sophisticated and far-reaching claims to historical redress and its material consequences. As such, the example addresses many of the issues around language and HE noted above, that is, how to engage the political realities of different voices – and disengage from historical disadvantage – through a reworked notion of language in conjunction with the decolonial knowledge project.[9]

Linguistic Citizenship: Language and subjectification

Earlier, we noted how metropolitan languages created a crisis of identity and belonging, a sense of dissonance and alienation, as a result of their imposition under circumstances of Apartheid-stymied subjectification. In contrast, Afrikaaps was literally born out of the lives of speakers and is made up of a multitude of registers through which speakers 'feel at home'. In fact, an essential feature in the emergence of Afrikaaps is the recognition its speakers accord to a manifold of 'voices', manners and modes to be 'legitimate' speakers of the variety. Acknowledgement of the colourful and diverse local voices that contribute to the complex, unfolding of its history in musical genres, street performances, criminal argots, slave dances, and in contemporary local neighbourhood voices is a hallmark of present-day Afrikaaps (Stroud and Williams, 2017; Williams, 2017). It is a variety that admits to having many roots and that interrupts any account of Afrikaans as a homogenous European lineage or any one social, imposed and estranging, identity or alignment. Rather Afrikaaps emerges out of a web and multiplicity of relations and histories, encounters and entanglements as a repertoire of 'practices attuned to a multitude of identities, subject positions and positions of interest' (Stroud, 2009: 213).

In this respect, Afrikaaps illustrates an important dimension of Linguistic Citizenship, namely what the philosopher Hanna Arendt (1958) calls 'plurality' (and that we choose to refer to as 'pluriversality' (cf. also Veronelli, 2016)), the many voices that are the necessary condition of actorhood. To be recognized in the voices and eyes of others, and, in turn, to mutually recognize ourselves in this recognition, is what gives individuals 'unique identities' and interpellates individuals as agents/actors; it is out of the plural recognition of the active appearance of participants in the public space that selves are constituted. Acts of Linguistic Citizenship engage plurality/pluriversality by lifting forth the voices of those 'exterior' to official Afrikaans in non-normative systems of meaning and creating opportunities for individuals and groups historically captured in circuits of invisibilization, to demand recognition and lay claims to dignity. Afrikaaps illustrates Linguistic Citizenship as a 'struggle' notion, referring to acts that transgress conventional semiotic normativities in order to give voice to those who have historically inhabited the other side of the 'abyssal line'. The many different voices around Afrikaaps lend nuance and novelty to what it means to speak it, in the process interpellating new senses of self as speaker and a new agency. These news selves offer an alternative perspective on familiar and conventionalized worlds of coloniality. Their becoming visible in plurality/pluriversality is also an important dynamic in what re-forms stigmatized Kaaps into Afrikaaps; concurrent with the import of what it means to be a speaker of Afrikaaps is the refashioning of the significance of the variety itself in claims to 'language-hood'.

Linguistic Citizenship: Local and contemporary voice

As we have argued above, African languages and speakers have been figured as 'out of time', and we have traced discourses of 'pastness' in practices of both intellectualization and endogenization that do not engage with the contemporary voices of subjugated populations. Rather than risk voices undergoing reduction through intellectualization and endogenization as in the case with African languages, Afrikaaps intellectualizes out of a broad constituency of speakers and reaches into endogenous knowledges relevant to the contemporary struggles of its speakers (cf. Nyamnjoh, 2012). Again, we identified this above as a central challenge for HE. Many of the activities profiling Afrikaaps as a struggle variety lift forward the historical context around the genesis of the language during the Apartheid years. During this time specifically, what was to become official Afrikaans underwent extensive linguistic purification, where the many early influences on the language from Malay, Tamil and Khoi were expunged from the language to give it a whiter and more European pedigree. The processes behind what was to become 'Kaaps', 'gamtaal', etc. were those of bordering and exclusion and other co-temporaneous forms of exclusion and purification, such as forced removals, and prohibition against mixed marriages. There is extensive local knowledge of these historical events, which continue to impact on the community in many ways and where the sociopolitics of the genesis of Afrikaaps engage contemporary political arenas, such as education.

Intellectualization **of** and **in** Afrikaaps is also underway with initiatives from academics and NGOs to work in concert to 'vitalize' Afrikaaps registers (cf. Williams, 2017). In contradistinction to Afrikaans and the critique levelled against 'revitalization' practices for African languages generally, these activities emerge out of the engagement of Afrikaaps' speakers with 'standard Afrikaans' and its forms. Viveiros de Castro (2004) has called such processes of engagement 'equivocation', where one voice does not silence the other 'by presuming a univocality' and reducing the terms of engagement to 'sameness' but works with difference and indeterminacy. 'Equivocal translation' (Viveiros de Castro, 2004) is a highly productive strategy in the reconstitution of Afrikaaps, where hegemonic and subjugated knowledges are brought into contrast and allowed to 'play out' at the border of languages. The juxtapositions of Afrikaaps and Afrikaans produce novelty and indeterminacy of meaning and expression, flaunting opacity, the ontological and aesthetic condition of irreducible difference (see Glissant, 1997).

Lugones (2006: 75) characterizes the border as the 'limen', the space 'at the edge of hardened structures, a place where transgression of the reigning order is possible', with Blaser remarking on how equivocal translation in contexts of coloniality necessarily involves addressing power and overcoming epistemic racism (Blaser, 2016). Afrikaaps illustrates well how the 'borders' between 'modernist Afrikaans' and Kaaps constitute such sites of rebellion where the coloniality of language is starkly revealed, and insights offered into how historical invisibilities can be linguistically made visible for present-day concerns.

Linguistic Citizenship: Decolonial constructs of language

Our brief discussion of translanguaging above suggested that despite claims to the contrary, translanguaging risks reinstating a modernist and colonial construct of language as a self-contained system. However, as noted above, linguistic borders are sites of potential contest and a significant part of social struggle which can 'challenge and redefine the oppressive grammars of power', displacing and re-signifying terms (Vasquez, 2011: 41). This is the case in the processes of 'bordering' in Afrikaaps, where the meaning and significance of Afrikaaps emerge simultaneously with the unfolding of social processes; the movement across varieties is not just a formal exercise in structure, but an essential part of a changing landscape of power relations. What we also find in Afrikaaps is that bordering work goes beyond the formalia of the linguistic system to involve a variety of semioses across different modalities, media and spaces of engagement, what we could call 'trans-semioticity' or inter-mediality. These trans-semioticities offer expressive possibilities beyond normed codes or registers (cf. Heugh, 2019; Kerfoot, 2011). In fact, given the silenced and invisibilized position of the subjugated/abyssal subject, overcoming linguistic exclusion, of necessity, requires forms of meaning-making able to transcend the constraints of fixed understandings of legitimized language. The meaning of Afrikaaps is literally fashioned across a series of modes and modalities –

poetry, Hip Hop, song, dance and styles of speaking in character sketches (the gangster, the traditional healer, the Spaza store keeper) and everyday, mundane interactions.

As social processes and linguistic forms unfold synergistically, flows of power are altered through 'resemiotization' (Iedema, 2001), so that silenced voices and invisibilized knowledges in one variety, modality or mode find space to be heard in other varieties, modalities or modes (Kerfoot, 2011). Through resemiotization, the terms of the conversation emerge, are negotiated and/or contested differently in each space, permitting speakers to claim an authoritative voice, unconventionally articulated, that goes beyond standard accounts of what it means to know a language. These different genres give different speakers opportunity to step forward and contribute their own stories and experiences of speaking Afrikaaps. Thus, the multiple modes of articulating knowledge of Afrikaaps are acts of Linguistic Citizenship that also broaden participation and allow for the legitimate recognition of novel agencies at the same time as the meaning of Afrikaaps takes on new dimensions.

Summary

We have offered Linguistic Citizenship as a blueprint for getting to grips with some of the shortcomings of the radical reform remedies we have pointed to above. Firstly, it offers a model of how subjugated speakers can 'appropriate' (indigenized) ex-colonial languages (Afrikaans) in ways that reconnect self and language and avoid replicating the colonial experience of a Fanonian 'linguistically induced psychic split'. In Afrikaaps, we have a community of speakers establishing syncretic language and knowledge projects in a collective process of struggle. Secondly, the example of Afrikaaps speaks to issues of indigenous language 'intellectualization' and endogenization with potential lessons for how to revitalize or reconfigure local languages and to build registers for epistemic justice 'bottom-up'. Finally, the manner with which speakers of Afrikaaps negotiate various forms of bordered, 'inter-lingual' negotiation with Afrikaans in conjunction with the unfolding of social processes may carry insights into ways of rethinking translanguaging as a force in linguistic re-formation and concomitant social transformation. By interrupting and reshaping forms of speech and practices of speakerhood, the construct of Afrikaaps unsettles existing power relations bound up in its forms. It means that authority over the language and its ownership is momentarily at least 'shifted away' from the grammarians and lexicographers of institutionalized Afrikanerdom to the speakers of Afrikaaps, allowing hitherto unscripted knowledges to become visible.

As with the politics of sexuality and gender citizenship, a focus on the politics of the 'linguistic' opens up new vistas for living language and life differently. The gradual emergence of a different construct of language is in itself a precondition for, as well as a consequence of, the knowledge project and goes some way to addressing the shortcomings of radical-reform approaches to questions of language and epistemic justice. The work that Linguistic Citizenship does of crafting 'forms of life' that are informed by – and simultaneously inform – the social experience of everyone speaks to its suitability in the pursuit of a decolonial approach to epistemic justice.

By way of introduction to this chapter, we argued that multilingualism can be re-conceptualized as a transformative epistemology and methodology of difference. What, then, are the more direct implications of the discussion here for a revised view of multilingualism?

Multilingualism as transformative

In the South African context, conditions for an epistemic justice cannot be delinked from strategic considerations towards a new non-racialized order. This requires an ontological (non-racial) refashioning of selves and others and engagements across difference characterized by openness, imagination and wonder. In unleashing restorative social processes and the generation of new knowledge frameworks to engage with the racial constructions still rife in South African society, multilingualism refigured through acts of Linguistic Citizenship offers the terrain for the creation of new relations, ethical and knowledge systems. A decolonial perspective on Afrikaaps has shown how linguistic technologies of classification and control can be muted and the coloniality of hierarchical arrangements of bordered languages and persons delinked. In effect, the restoration of Afrikaaps is nothing less than an event of 'transformative multilingualism' (cf. Stroud and Kerfoot, 2013). It is the outcome of acts of citizenship (Isin, 2008) characterized by bottom-up pluriversality, an unfolding of voices across spaces and multimodal representations that generate unpredictable significance and a multiplication of agencies. The new construct of Afrikaaps emerges out of speakers' 'capacity to act in relation' (Osborne and Rose, 1999: 758) on the cusp and in the fissures of normative, institutionalized regimes, across conventionalized identities. It also reveals how re-borderings, processes of equivocal translation, and resemiotizations across bounded languages can be redeployed in creative ways to produce new forms of actorhood, sociality and ways of knowing. All of this suggests a vantage point on multilingualism as a 'semiotic of relationality', that is, multilingualism as a mode of engaging with difference, as the process of ordering encounters linguistically.

A central feature of these processes, equivocation, points to how a multilingualism conceived in such terms as a semiotic of relationality could work as a transformative dynamic in recalibrating the racial order. Lugones's (2006: 75) notion of 'complex communication' captures a key feature of equivocation when she speaks about 'praxical awareness of one's own multiplicity and a recognition of the other's opacity that does not attempt to assimilate it into one's own familiar meanings'. One of the consequences of equivocal translation – not necessarily understanding the other, not being able to assume knowledge of the other – is uncertainty and vulnerability. Vulnerability is a useful lens with which to approach 'ontological refashioning'. On the one hand, being vulnerable opens to discomfort, while simultaneously comprising a condition of openness to others, and therefore carries the potential for alternative engagement with selves. The notion of vulnerability also finds resonance with Arendt's notions of plurality/pluriversality, as it is the human capacity for action that continually brings forth newness and makes the world unpredictable, and its inhabitants subsequently vulnerable. Thinking about vulnerability in conjunction with plurality and pluriversality highlights the relational aspects of mutual dependence, as conditions of vulnerability require joint, 'collaborative' interventions to ameliorate and benefit from change. Linguistic Citizenship is an approach to a politics of language and multilingualism that starts from a notion of vulnerability, in the sense of the emergent and sensitive process of 'disinhabiting', that is, stepping out of, imposed and entangled subjectivities.

Equivocation in acts of Linguistic Citizenship is found in epistemologies of the exteriority (Dussel, 1977/2003) and of the borders (Mignolo, 2011) and ethical translation (Santos, 2014) and is enhanced by understanding pedagogic encounters as 'spaces of equivocation' where qualitatively and hegemonically different sets of knowledge and culture are in contact and require equivocal translation. 'To translate is to emphasize or potentialize the equivocation, that is to open and widen the space imagined not to exist between the conceptual languages in contact' (Viveiros de Castro, 2004: 10), simultaneously establishing the ethical relationship necessary in relating to epistemic difference, an ethics of 'becoming with others'.

There are a number of pedagogical frameworks that could accommodate working around multilingual vulnerabilities and provide spaces of experimentation for epistemic justice (for overviews cf. Bozalek et al., 2018; Bozalek and Zembylas, 2017; Stroud and Kerfoot, 2013). All of these pedagogical initiatives interrogate legitimized 'representational resources' (Kress, 1996: 18) or routinely accepted ways of using language and other forms of semiosis in tertiary educational spaces.

One such approach that directly engages language in the formation of new subjectivities is the pedagogical use of Deleuzian 'fabulation' and 'people-becoming' (cf. Kruger and Le Roux, 2017).[10] Also of interest here are 'pedagogies of discomfort' (Boler and Zembylas, 2003; Leibowitz and Bozalek, 2016)[11] that attend to the question of developing new empathetic and response-able Others (cf. also 'unquiet pedagogies' in Berthoff, 1987). What Bozalek and Zembylas (2017: 62) term 'response-able pedagogies' are pedagogies that nurture 'ethico-political practices such as attentiveness, responsibility, curiosity, and rendering each other capable' and that 'incorporate a relational ontology into teaching and learning activities' (ibid. 64). Chapters in this book offer further excellent examples of 'decolonising methodologies' (Smith, 1999) and creative pedagogical innovation. There are also a number of enticing approaches where languages are negotiated to articulate the contemporary and everyday concerns of students. Antia's (2017) research on the classroom use of invisibilized practices such as 'hushed translanguaging' is particularly promising here.

It would be desirable to interrogate the potential of these pedagogical framings as epistemic resources and, beyond this, to trace students' processes of resemiotization across spaces of learning both formal and informal, physical and virtual, to uncover the vectors along which knowledge flows. As meanings are translated from one mode to another, resemiotization offers the analytical means for tracking processes of engagement among multilingual speakers, knowledges and values in the potential emergence of new ecologies of knowledge (Santos, 2014).

Conclusion

We have argued that there are deep colonial relationalities that remain embedded in our view of language as a pedagogical resource and that these are reaffirming of colonial and Apartheid identities and ways of understanding the world. Afrikaaps is born out of struggle as part of a more general transformative dynamic in contemporary South Africa contesting deep historical and racialized tensions. Although this chapter has used Afrikaaps as an example of potentialities, this argument would apply to many urban metropolitan registers. We have exemplified how Linguistic Citizenship in struggles over the legitimization of a subjugated linguistic 'variety' rejuvenated this variety in the process of building a new convivial community with transformative implications for the dignity, visibility and material benefit of its speakers.

We have underscored how epistemology and language both emerge simultaneously in the ontological construction of the self and that these constructs of self and other are what open and close for 'ways of knowing' (Papadopoulos, 2018). This allows for alternative understandings of what there *is*, unlocking elements of history, culture, aesthetics – a new ontology and epistemology – simultaneous with the reworkings of language and the problematization of linguistic borders. The conclusion is that a reconstructed notion of multilingualism must be part and parcel of the specific epistemological/ontological work that goes into rethinking and engaging with knowledge areas. While the implications for educational contexts, including teacher education, are significant, the consequences of this approach offer multilingualism as a transformative and decolonial instrument of social change and epistemic justice more broadly.[12]

Notes

1   Language was, however, extensively discussed as part of decolonization debates under Apartheid, for example, in the 1980s by the National Language Project, Neville Alexander, Kathleen Heugh, Es'kia Mphahlele and others.
2   This is, of course, not to deny the all-important role of military might and land dispossession in the colonial oppression of peoples but to draw attention to the important role of language and knowledge as ways of rationalizing these other forms of oppression.
3   The imperative to 'transform' has meant that South African Higher Education institutions have opened their doors to students who are historically not speakers of English or Afrikaans. This has meant considerable demands on workable language policies. The University of the Western Cape is perhaps the institution that has shown the greatest ingenuity in developing a flora of alternative language provisions for these students.
4   Yet see work by Antia and Dyers for some interesting exceptions to this generalization.

5 'To translate is to presume that an equivocation always exists; it is to communicate by differences, instead of silencing the Other by presuming a univocality – the essential similarity – between what the Other and what We are saying' (Viveiros de Castro, 2004: 10).
6 This overview does not cover the significant work done by many scholars under the umbrella of 'Academic Development' over the past few decades – work which sought to enable academic access to the historically dominant disciplinary conversations and institutional spaces, albeit through the dominant language/ English (e.g. Leibowitz and Volbrecht, 1995; Thesen and van Pletzen, 2006).
7 Exceptions are, for example, Antia and Dyers (2019) and Makalela (2014).
8 Gamtaal [gam language] is an appropriation of the term *gam*, a reference to the curse of Ham in the Bible and its use as a justification for slavery (Adhikari, 2006).
9 For a more extensive body of work on Afrikaaps in this framework, see Stroud and Williams (2017) and Williams and Stroud (2015).
10 For Deleuze (1989) 'fabulation' is a beneficial artistic force that enables the invention of 'a people to come'. For Kruger and Le Roux (2017: 54) operationalizing fabulation in pedagogy is about 'short-circuiting impasses' of thought and expression in order to create 'new opportunities for experimenting with emerging social collectivities'.
11 For Boler and Zembylas (2003: 108), a pedagogy of discomfort 'emphasizes the need for both the educator and students to move outside of their comfort zones.... [It] recognizes and problematizes the deeply embedded emotional dimensions that frame and shape daily habits, routines, and unconscious complicity with hegemony. ... By closely examining emotional reactions and responses ... one begins to identify unconscious privileges as well as invisible ways in which one complies with dominant ideology.'
12 We recognize that our structural location as white limits our right to suggest how transformation might take place.

References

Adhikari, M. (2006), 'Hope, Fear, Shame, Frustration: Continuity and Change in the Expression of Coloured Identity in White Supremacist South Africa, 1910–1994', *Journal of Southern African Studies*, 32: 467–87.

Africa Check (2016), 'Factsheet: Funding and the Changing Face of South Africa's Public Universities', 26 October. Available online: https://africacheck.org/factsheets/factsheet-funding-changing-face-sas-public-universities/ (accessed 8 December 2018).

Alcoff, L. M. (2011), 'An Epistemology for the Next Revolution', *Transmodernity: Journal of Peripheral Cultural Production of the Luso-Hispanic World*, 1 (2): 67–78.

Alexander, N. (1989), *Language Policy and National Unity in South Africa/Azania: An Essay*. Cape Town: Buchu Books.

Alexander, N. (1997), 'Language Policy and Planning in the New South Africa', *African Sociological Review*, 1: 82–92.

Alexander, N. (2003), 'Language Policy, Symbolic Power and the Democratic Responsibility of the Post-Apartheid University', *Pretexts: Literary and Cultural Studies*, 12 (2): 179–90.

Alexander, N., ed. (2005), *The Intellectualisation of African Languages*. Cape Town: PRAESA/University of Cape Town.

Andreotti, V., C. Ahenakew and G. Cooper (2011), 'Epistemological Pluralism: Ethical and Pedagogical Challenges in Higher Education', *AlterNative: An International Journal of Indigenous Peoples*, 7 (1): 40–50.

Andreotti, V., S. Stein, C. Ahenakew and D. Hunt (2015), 'Mapping Interpretations of Decolonization in the Context of Higher Education', *Decolonization: Indigeneity, Education & Society*, 4 (1): 21–40.

Antia, B. E. (2017), 'Shh, Hushed Multilingualism! Accounting for the Discreet Genre of Translanguaged Siding in Lecture Halls at a South African University', *International Journal of the Sociology of Language*, 243: 183–98.

Antia, B. E. and C. Dyers (2016), 'Epistemological Access through Lecture Materials in Multiple Modes and Language Varieties: The Role of Ideologies and Multilingual Literacy Practices in Student Evaluations of Such Materials at a South African University', *Language Policy*, 15 (4): 525–45.

Antia, B. E. and C. Dyers (2017), 'Affirming the Biliteracy of University Students: Provision of Multilingual Lecture Resources at the University of the Western Cape, South Africa', in D. M Palfreyman and C. van der Walt (eds), *Academic Biliteracies: Multilingual Repertoires in Higher Education*, 113–41. Bristol: Multilingual Matters.

Antia, B. E. and C. Dyers (2019), 'De-Alienating the Academy: Multilingual Teaching as Decolonial Pedagogy', *Linguistics and Education*, 51: 91–100.

Arendt, H. (1958), *The Human Condition*. Chicago, IL: University of Chicago Press.

Berthoff, A. E. (1987), 'Foreword', in P. Freire and D. Macedo (eds), *Literacy: Reading the Word and the World*, xi–xxv. South Hadley, MA: Praeger.

Boler, M. and M. Zembylas (2003), 'Discomforting Truths: The Emotional Terrain of Understanding Difference', in P. Trifonas (ed.), *Pedagogies of Difference: Rethinking Education for Social Change*, 110–36. London: Routledge Falmer.

Bhatt, R. M. and A. Bolonyai (2019), 'On the Theoretical and Empirical Bases of Translanguaging', *Working Papers in Urban Language & Literacies*, Paper 254.

Blaser, M. (2016), 'Is Another Cosmopolitics Possible?', *Cultural Anthropology (Society for Cultural Anthropology)*, 31 (4): 545–70.

Block, D. (2018), 'The Political Economy of Language Education Research (or the Lack Thereof): Nancy Fraser and the Case of Translanguaging', *Critical Inquiry in Language Studies*, 15: 237–57.

Blommaert, J. (2008), *Grassroots Literacy: Writing, Identity and Voice in Central Africa*. London: Taylor & Francis.

Botsis, H. (2017), *Subjectivity, Language and the Postcolonial: Beyond Bourdieu in South Africa*. London: Routledge.

Bozalek, V. and M. Zembylas (2017), 'Towards a Response-Able Pedagogy across Higher Education Institutions in Post-Apartheid South Africa: An Ethico-Political Analysis', *Education as Change*, 21 (2): 62–85.

Bozalek, V., R. Braidotti, T. Shefer and M. Zembylas, eds (2018), *Socially Just Pedagogies: Posthumanist, Feminist and Materialist Perspectives in Higher Education*. London: Bloomsbury Academic.

Carstens, A. (2016), 'Designing Linguistically Flexible Scaffolding for Subject-Specific Academic Literacy Interventions', *Per Linguam: A Journal of Language Learning*, 32 (3): 1–12.

Castro-Gómez, S. (2007), *La Hybris Del Punto Cero: Ciencia, Raza E Ilustracion En La Nueva Granada (1750–1816) [The Hubris of the Zero Point: Science, Race and Illustration in New Granada]*. Bogotá: Editorial Pontificia Universidad Javeriana.

Charalambous, P., C. Charalambous and M. Zembylas (2016), 'Troubling Translanguaging: Language Ideologies, Superdiversity and Interethnic Conflict', *Applied Linguistics Review*, 7: 327–52.

Connell, R. (2013), 'Using Southern Theory: Decolonizing Social Thought in Theory, Research and Application', *Planning Theory*, 13 (2): 210–23.

Contraband Cape Town (2015), Luister. Available online: https://www.youtube.com/watch?v=sF3rTBQTQk4 (accessed 9 September 2019).

Deleuze, G. (1989), *Cinema 2: The Time-Image*, trans. H. Tomlinson and R. Galeta, Minneapolis: University of Minnesota Press.

Dussel, E. (2003), *Philosophy of Liberation*, trans A. Martinez and C. Morkovsky, Eugene, Or.: Wipf & Stock Pub. Orig. Publ. 1977.

Errington, J. (2008), *Linguistics in a Colonial World: A Story of Language, Meaning, and Power*. London: John Wiley & Sons.

Fabian, J. (1986), *Language and Colonial Power*. Cambridge and New York: Cambridge University Press.

Fanon, F. (1967), *Black Skin, White Masks*, trans R. Philcox. London: Grove Press.

Fraser, N. (1995), 'From Redistribution to Recognition? Dilemmas of Justice in a "Post-Socialist" Age', *New Left Review*, 1: 212.

Fricker, M. (1998), 'Rational Authority and Social Power: Towards a Truly Social Epistemology', *Proceedings of the Aristotelian Society*, 98: 159–77.

Fricker, M. (1999), 'Epistemic Oppression and Epistemic Privilege', *Canadian Journal of Philosophy*, 29 (sup1): 191–210.

Fricker, M. (2007), *Epistemic Injustice: Power and the Ethics of Knowing*. New York: Oxford University Press.

Garcia, O. and Li Wei (2014), *Translanguaging: Language, Bilingualism and Education*. Basingstoke, Hampshire: Palgrave Pivot.

Gilmour, R. (2006), *Grammars of Colonialism: Representing Languages in Colonial South Africa*. Basingstoke, England and New York: Palgrave Macmillan.

Glissant, E. (1997), *Traité du Tout-Monde*. Paris: Gallimard.

Grosfoguel, R. (2011), 'Decolonizing Post-Colonial Studies and Paradigms of Political-Economy: Transmodernity, Decolonial Thinking, and Global Coloniality', *Transmodernity: Journal of Peripheral Cultural Production of the Luso-Hispanic World*, 1 (1): 1–38.

Harries, P. (2007), *Butterflies & Barbarians: Swiss Missionaries and Systems of Knowledge in South-East Africa*. Athens: Ohio University Press and Oxford: James Currey.

Hendricks, F. and C. Dyers, eds (2016), *Kaaps in fokus*. Stellenbosch: Conference Rap.

Heugh, K. (2017), 'Re-Placing and Re-Centring Southern Multilingualisms: A De-Colonial Project', in C. Kerfoot and K. Hyltenstam (eds), *Entangled Discourses: South-North Orders of Visibility*, 209–29. New York: Routledge.

Heugh, K. (2019), 'Multilingualisms, Translanguaging and Transknowledging', Keynote presentation. The Various Guises of Translanguaging, Symposium in Ghent, 1 July.

Hibbert, L. and C. van der Walt (2014), *Multilingual Universities in South Africa: Reflecting Society in Higher Education*. Bristol: Multilingual Matters.

hooks, b. (1994), *Teaching to Transgress: Education as the Practice of Freedom*. New York: Routledge.

Hountondji, P. J. (1997), *Endogenous Knowledge: Research Trails*. Oxford: African Books Collective.

Iedema, R. (2001), 'Resemiotization', *Semiotica*, 137 (1/4): 23–39.

Irvine, J. T. (2008), 'Subjected Words: African Linguistics and the Colonial Encounter', *Language and Communication*, 28 (4): 323–43.

Isin, E. F. (2008), 'Theorizing Acts of Citizenship', in E. F. Isin and G. M. Nielsen (eds), *Acts of Citizenship*, 15–43. London: Palgrave Macmillan.

Jaspers, J. (2018), 'The Transformative Limits of Translanguaging', *Language & Communication*, 58: 1–10.

Kaschula, R. and P. Maseko (2014), 'The Intellectualisation of African Languages, Multilingualism and Education: A Research-Based Approach', *Alternation*, 13: 8–35.

Kerfoot, C. (2011), 'Making and Shaping Participatory Spaces: Resemiotization and Citizenship Agency in South Africa', *International Multilingual Research Journal*, 5 (2): 87–102.

Kerfoot, C. and B. O. Bello-Nonjengele (2021), 'Towards Epistemic Justice: Constructing Knowers in Multilingual Classrooms'. Manuscript in preparation.

Kress, G. R. (1996), *Before Writing: Rethinking the Paths to Literacy*. London and New York: Routledge.

Kruger, F. and A. Le Roux (2017), 'Fabulation as a Pedagogical Possibility: Working towards a Politics of Affirmation', *Education as Change*, 21 (2): 45–61.

Langa, M., S. Ndelu, Y. Edwin and M. Vilakazi (2017), '# Hashtag: An Analysis of The# FeesMustFall Movement at South African Universities'. Johannesburg: Centre for the Study of Violence and Reconciliation.

Leibowitz, B. and T. Volbrecht, eds (1995), *Language in Development. AD Dialogues*, Vol. 4, 65–94. Bellville: University of the Western Cape Academic Development Centre.

Leibowitz, B. and V. Bozalek (2016), 'The Scholarship of Teaching and Learning from a Social Justice Perspective', *Teaching in Higher Education*, 21 (2): 109–22.

Li, W. (2018), 'Translanguaging as a Practical Theory of Language', *Applied Linguistics*, 39: 9–30.

Lugones, M. (2006), 'On Complex Communication', *Hypatia*, 21 (3): 75–85.

Makalela, L. (2014), 'Fluid Identity Construction in Language Contact Zones: Metacognitive Reflections on Kasi-Taal Languaging Practices', *International Journal of Bilingual Education and Bilingualism*, 17 (6): 668–82.

Makoe, P. and C. McKinney (2014), 'Linguistic Ideologies in Multilingual South African Suburban Schools', *Journal of Multilingual and Multicultural Development*, 35: 658–73.

Makoni, S. (1998), 'African Languages as European Scripts: The Shaping of Communal Memory', in S. Nuttall and C. Coetzee (eds), *Negotiating the Past: The Making of Memory in South Africa*, 242–48. Cape Town: Oxford University Press.

Maldonado-Torres, N. (2007), 'On the Coloniality of Being', *Cultural Studies*, 21 (2/3): 240–70.

Maseko, P. (2017), 'Exploring the History of the Writing of isiXhosa: An Organic or an Engineered Process?', *International Journal of African Renaissance Studies – Multi-, Inter- and Transdisciplinarity*, 12: 81–96.

Mayaba, N. N., K. R. Monwabisi and P. Angu (2018), 'Student Voice: Perspectives on Language and Critical Pedagogy in South African Higher Education', *Educational Research for Social Change*, 7 (1): 1–12.

Mbembe, A. (2016), 'Decolonizing the University: New Directions', *Arts and Humanities in Higher Education*, 15 (1): 29–45.

Mignolo, W. (2011), *The Darker Side of Western Modernity: Global Futures, Decolonial Options*. Durham: Duke University Press Books.

Mkhize, N. (2016), 'Away with Good Bantus: De-Linking African Language Literature from Culture, "Tribe" and Propriety', *Arts and Humanities in Higher Education*, 15 (1): 146–52.

Mudimbe, V. Y. (1988), *The Invention of Africa: Gnosis, Philosophy, and the Order of Knowledge*. Bloomington: Indiana University Press.

Mudimbe, V. Y. (1995), *The Idea of Africa*. Oxford: James Currey.

Mungwini, P. (2013), 'African Modernities and the Critical Reappropriation of Indigenous Knowledges: Towards a Polycentric Global Epistemology', *International Journal of African Renaissance Studies – Multi-, Inter- and Transdisciplinarity*, 8 (1): 78–93.

Ndlovu-Gatsheni, S. J. (2013), *Coloniality of Power in Postcolonial Africa: Myths of Decolonization*. Dakar: Codesria.

Ndlovu-Gatsheni, S. J. (2018), *Epistemic Freedom in Africa: Deprovincialization and Decolonization*. London: Routledge.

Ngũgĩ wa Thiong'o (1994), *Decolonising the Mind. The Politics of Language in African Literature*. Oxford: James Currey.

Nyamnjoh, F. B. (2012), '"Potted Plants in Greenhouses": A Critical Reflection on the Resilience of Colonial Education in Africa', *Journal of Asian and African Studies*, 47 (2): 129–54.

Nyamnjoh, F. B. (2016), *#RhodesMustFall. Nibbling at Resilient Colonialism in South Africa*. Oxford: African Books Collective.

Ogone, J. O. (2017), 'Epistemic Injustice: African Knowledge and Scholarship in the Global Context', in A. Bartels, L. Eckstein, N. Waller and D. Wiemann (eds), *Postcolonial Justice: Common Skies, Divided Justice*, 17–36. Amsterdam and New York: Brill Rodopi.

Osborne, T. and N. Rose (1999), 'Governing Cities: Notes on the Spatialisation of Virtue', *Environment and Planning D: Society and Space*, 17 (6): 737–60.

Papadopoulos, D. (2018), *Experimental Practice: Technoscience, Alterontologies, and More-Than-Social Movements*. Durham, NC: Duke University Press.

Plüddemann, P., V. Nomlomo and N. Jabe (2010), 'Using African Languages for Teacher Education', *Alternation*, 17 (1): 72–91.

Prah, K. K. (2017), 'The Intellectualisation of African Languages for Higher Education', *Alternation*, 24 (2): 215–25.

Ramani, E. and M. Joseph (2002), 'Breaking New Ground: Introducing an African Language as Medium of Instruction at the University of the North: New Developments and Research', *Perspectives in Education*, 20 (1): 233–40.

Santos, B. de S. (2014), *Epistemologies of the South: Justice against Epistemicide*. Boulder, CO: Paradigm Publishers.

Santos, B. de S. (2018), *The End of the Cognitive Empire: The Coming of Age of Epistemologies of the South*. Durham: Duke University Press Books.

Smith, L. T. (1999), *Decolonizing Methodologies: Research and Indigenous Peoples*. London: Zed Books.

Stroud, C. (2001), 'African Mother-Tongue Programmes and the Politics of Language: Linguistic Citizenship versus Linguistic Human Rights', *Journal of Multilingual and Multicultural Development*, 22 (4): 339–55.

Stroud, C. (2007), 'Bilingualism: Colonialism and Postcolonialism', in M. Heller (ed.), *Bilingualism: A Social Approach*, 25–49. Basingstoke: Palgrave Macmillan.

Stroud, C. (2009), 'A Postliberal Critique of Language Rights: Toward a Politics of Language for a Linguistics of Contact', in J. E. Petrovic (ed.), *International Perspectives on Bilingual Education: Policy, Practice, and Controversy*, 191–218. Charlotte, NC: Information Age Publishing.

Stroud, C. (2018), 'Linguistic Citizenship', in L. Lim, C. Stroud and L. Wee (eds), *The Multilingual Citizen: Towards a Politics of Language for Agency and Change*, 17–39. Bristol, UK: Multilingual Matters.

Stroud, C. and K. Heugh (2004), 'Linguistic Human Rights and Linguistic Citizenship', in D. Patrick and J. Freeland (eds), *Language Rights and Language Survival: A Sociolinguistic Exploration*, 191–218. Manchester: St Jerome.

Stroud, C. and C. Kerfoot (2013), 'Towards Rethinking Multilingualism and Language Policy for Academic Literacies', *Linguistics and Education*, 24 (4): 396–405.

Stroud, C. and Q. Williams (2017), 'Multilingualism as Utopia: Fashioning Non-Racial Selves', *AILA Review*, 30: 167–88.

Thesen, L. and E. van Pletzen, eds (2006), *Academic Literacy and the Languages of Change*. London: Continuum.

Tollefson, J. W. (1995), *Power and Inequality in Language Education*. Cambridge: Cambridge University Press.

Van Broekhuizen, H. (2016), 'Graduate Unemployment and Higher Education Institutions in South Africa', *Working Papers* 08/2016, Department of Economics, Stellenbosch University.

Van Broekhuizen, H., S. van der Berg and H. Hofmeyr (2016), 'Higher Education Access and Outcomes for the 2008 National Matric Cohort', *Working Papers* 16/2016, Department of Economics, Stellenbosch University.

Vázquez, R. (2011), 'Translation as Erasure: Thoughts on Modernity's Epistemic Violence', *Journal of Historical Sociology*, 24 (1): 27–44.

Veronelli, G. (2016), 'A Coalitional Approach to Theorizing Decolonial Communication', *Hypatia*, 31 (2): 404–20.

Veronelli, G. A. (2015), 'The Coloniality of Language: Race, Expressivity, Power, and the Darker Side of Modernity', *Wagadu: A Journal of Transnational Women's & Gender Studies*, 13: 108–34.

Viveiros de Castro, E. (2004), 'Perspectival Anthropology and the Method of Controlled Equivocation', *Tipití: Journal of the Society for the Anthropology of Lowland South America*, 2 (1): 3–22.

Williams, Q. (2017), *Remix Multilingualism: Hip Hop, Ethnography and Performing Marginalized Voices*. London: Bloomsbury Academic.

Williams, Q. and C. Stroud (2015), 'Linguistic Citizenship. Language and Politics in Postnational Modernities', *Journal of Language & Politics*, 14 (3): 406–30.

3

Indigenous Texts, Rich Points and Pluriversal Sources of Knowledge: *Siswana-sibomvana*

Antjie Krog

While working on a text with an experienced isiXhosa translator some time ago, there was a magical moment. 'The word s*iswana-sibomvana* in the poem means whites, or you-white-people,' he said, 'but literally the word means those-with-the-red-stomachs (or sunburnt bellies), and if you want to look into its idiomatic use, according to the dictionary, the stomach is red because of gluttony'. And there it was: the word broken up into its various possibilities, a hermeneutics of interpretation that explores the literal and figurative, cultural and ethical.

As this illuminating personal experience and several projects involve translating Indigenous poems with mother tongue speakers, I have included two Indigenous poems in my creative writing and other courses. At times, the self-possessed confidence of the American or German students doing the course has an intimidating effect on others in the lecture room. But when a poem in an Indigenous language is given to the class and a mother tongue speaker is asked to read the original text aloud, the power hierarchy is inverted. The speakers of the Indigenous languages find they have an authority which none of us non-speakers can claim. I, as a lecturer, and all of the non-speakers of Indigenous languages are then open to being sharply corrected and challenged by the insights and knowledge the others have.

A similar shift in power occurred when Indigenous language texts from the archives were used in a class at the University of KwaZulu-Natal. Marijke du Toit found that introducing texts written in isiZulu with their translations enabled isiZulu students to make academic use of their fluency in an African language for the first time (see Du Toit, this volume). When the archival texts posed challenges even to isiZulu students, this was even more stimulating and exciting. At the same time, the systematic inclusion of translations into English means that while the students who do not speak isiZulu are largely able to participate, first-language speakers find themselves in a strong position to contribute their particular skills (2016: 17).

This kind of multilingual context described above has been textured for quite some time by some of the formulators of Linguistic Citizenship. They describe a 'space of vulnerability' where 'speakers meet different others in disruptive and unsettling encounters that interrupt the status quo (Pinchevski, 2005); where senses of self may be juxtaposed and refashioned as part of the deconstruction of dominant voices and more equitable linguistic engagement with others' (Stroud, 2018: 20).

Baker (2012: 11) talks about the 'creation of a transmodern world where many different worlds can coexist without an imposed assimilation ethos into a dominant culture'. His argument probes deeply into the concept of decoloniality, which he sees as an epistemic revolution: 'A central theme in decolonial education is the equal recognition and democratic and pragmatic inclusion of the epistemological diversity of the world.'

Whether through comparative analysis, translation, translanguaging, cultural translation and/or code-switching, the multilingual practices explored in Linguistic Citizenship put speakers more firmly in control in their everyday sociopolitical strivings for agency and transformation. Incorporating texts in the original Indigenous South African languages, with or without translation, could change the current education curricula in interesting ways, constructing powerfully vivid, new and multivocal spaces.

Inspired by the idea that multilingual commitment presents an approach that one could use to 'engage *ethically* with others across encounters of difference' (my emphasis, Stroud, 2018: 17) this chapter points to possible ways in which Indigenous texts can be used to destabilize current epistemologies through decolonial interventions.

Some remarks on Indigenous languages

The outstanding metaphorical quality of African languages was noted more than a century ago by French missionary, Eugéne Casalis:

> The language (Sesotho), from its energetic precision, is admirably adapted to the sententious style, and the element of metaphor has entered so abundantly into its composition, that one can hardly speak it without unconsciously acquiring the habit of expressing one's thoughts in a figurative manner.
>
> ([1861] 1965: 307)

In his book *The Basutos* (1965) Casalis provided lists of single words carrying metaphoric meaning, such as the following:

ndiyazidla – I eat myself (literal); I am proud (figurative);
ukutshona – to set (sun); to drown/go down (literal); to die (figurative);
letlokoa – straw (literal); vanity (figurative);
pelu ea ithatha – my heart loves itself (literal); I am happy (figurative).

The isiXhosa translator that I referred to earlier has recently provided another example: Rolihlahla Nelson Mandela. The name Rolihlahla figuratively means 'Troublemaker.' (It is rumoured that former state president PW Botha famously once said: 'How can I release a man whom his own people call a troublemaker?') Literally *rhola* means 'to pull out' and *ihlahla* means 'branch'. In the poem delivered at Mandela's inauguration in 1994, imbongi S'thembile Mlangeni exploited the sounds in the word "Rolihlahla" as well as its literal and figurative meaning to create a metaphoric area resounding with hypnotic l-, r- (pronounced as a rasping g) and hl-sounds:

Yiyo leyo Rolihlahla/eli hlahla larholwa mhlamnene/larholw'ezizweni/larholw'e Zambiya.

Figuratively it could be translated as 'Here is the Troublemaker, / he made his mark long ago / and reached many nations / even in Zambia.' Or it can be translated as 'Here he stands (before us), Rolihlahla, the true Troublemaker / Pulled-branch pulled long ago / Trails-of-his-leaves lie among many nations / Trails-of-his-leaves even lie in Zambia.'

By using both literal and figurative meanings in the second translation, the notion of troublemaker is powerfully enhanced. The image is created of a Mandela rooted within a solid tree: genealogically he is of royal blood but is also guided by the ancestors who have pulled (selected/chosen) him since birth. When he visits other places, he is not merely one person but brings with him a whole tree of culture, wisdom and blessings. In other words the trouble he engenders, of which the leaves leave so much evidence, is a blessed kind of trouble that is rooted in Mandela himself. The name Rolihlahla can therefore be regarded as a 'rich point'.

The challenge of rich points

North American anthropologist, Michael Agar, introduced the concept of 'rich points'. According to Agar, culture is 'not something that people have;

it is something that fills the spaces between them'. These cultural boundaries are marked by rich points, which are differences in cultural make-up, causing bewilderment or even a breakdown in communication between communities in contact:

> When you encounter a new language, some things are easy to learn ... Other things are more difficult ... but some things that come up strike you with their difficulty, their complexity, their inability to fit into the resources you use to make sense of the world. These things – from lexical items through speech acts up to fundamental notions of how the world works – are called rich points.
>
> (Agar, 1991: 168)

These rich points seem to be the very places to start the destabilizing conversation. I use a few examples to illustrate the point.

1. Rich point of listing names

African poetry is filled with long lists of names. This is often regarded as boring or irrelevant by readers of Western poetry, but Debra Walker King emphasizes that naming is an important act in African culture as it

> imbues the act of naming with generative power .... Although the exact mechanics of the incantatory properties of naming differ slightly between various regional cultures, the core idea is essentially equivalent and is most precisely articulated in the West African concept of nommo. Loosely translated as 'the word,' nommo is the spiritual-physical energy [...] that conjures being through naming, [...] the seed of word, water and life that brings to the body its vital human force.
>
> (1998: 37)

There seems to be consensus among most scholars that the concept of 'nommo' reflects the singular importance of naming and names to 'traditional African ways of knowing and being'. McPhail suggests that the prominence of nommo as a guiding principle in African epistemology and ontology serves to underscore 'the juxtaposition of what is essentially African ... contrasting the utilitarian and pragmatic dimensions of traditional Western rhetoric with the complementary and integrative aspects of traditional African philosophy that views the word as generative' (1998: 119). In other words, names are not static labels that simply distinguish one object or person from another but are in fact the spiritual force that shapes and compels the object or person.

2. Rich point of whiteness

Through the centuries of contact between southern Africa and Europe, most Indigenous languages coined a variety of words to denote whiteness. One of the early, and most denouncing, definers of whiteness was the celebrated Samuel Edward Krune Mqhayi. In his famous poem about distributing the stars, which he also performed at Mandela's school when the latter was a boy (see Mandela, 1994: 38–40), Mqhayi identified selfishness as the main trademark of Britishness:

> *Nina baseBritani thathan' iKhwezi, / Niya kubambana namaJamani namaBhulu, / Noko nibantu bangakwaziy' ukwabelana / Nisuke nenz' imfazwe yamaBhulu neyamaJamani*
>
> You from Britain, take Venus, / And share it with the Germans and the Boers. / You-with-an-inability-to-share-anything / Learn to share it with the Boers and the Germans

In this well-known poem, Mqhayi greets the Prince of Wales with the words *Nyashaz' ekad' inyashaza* (Trasher-with-the-feet) and *Ndlalifa yelakowethu* (The-one-who-feasts-on-our-inheritance).

In Setswana white people are described as having red clay-baked faces: 'redfaced people with jutting noses (that cast shadows)' (*Makgakwana borranko-emoriti*) (Comaroff and Comaroff, 1992: 194). Instead of simply using the term 'whites' or 'white people' to translate terms such as *Makgakwana borranko-emoriti* we need to realize that they are rich points that reveal to us the about Indigenous languages' view of whiteness.

3. Rich point of indexing

It is often impossible to classify Indigenous poems under the 'standard' rubrics such as nature poems, love or political poems. Love poems often have strong references to the history of the area or the families involved, the role of the ancestors in choosing the girl, or the extent to which the beloved ruptures the relationship between lover and family, thereby disturbing his being-ness within his community. The war poems assess the role of humanity in war and the characteristics of a humane ruler, but also deal with the domestic crisis wars generate. The interconnectedness of many of the Indigenous poems does not allow for easy theme-ing. This 'unfocused-ness' of theme is often regarded as a weakness by readers familiar with Western poetry, rather than a richness with profound qualities. In this case, the theme that virtually all the texts chosen for discussion have in common is a view of humanity – what being human means, what humane-ness is, and how it is being strengthened or threatened.

Analysis of poems in terms of rich points

Every poem selected here deserves a full paper to do justice to its aesthetic qualities, its layered content, its context and the history of the poet, the way it functions within a multilingual space, and especially how it has been translated. For the purposes of demonstrating the value of analysing Indigenous texts, I limit the discussion to one rich point per poem.

In a fragmented and globalized country such as South Africa, it has become a near insurmountable challenge 'to build a life of equity' as speakers of local languages and knowledges have been 'invisibilized, comprising to all intents and purposes an effective form of "epistemicide" (Santos, 2010) the erasure of a body of knowledge through epistemic violence' (Stroud, 2018: 34). It is with this awareness that one must approach the poems.

Text translated from the |Xam: *The Broken String* as told by Díä!kwãin

Díä!kwãin was a member of the |Xam, a subgroup of the San living as part of the last generation of hunter-gatherers in the nineteenth century in the arid Northern Cape. Like the San all over southern Africa, the land where they once roamed freely was invaded by settlers. Drinking from waterholes or hunting game then became 'crimes' that made them 'trespassers' and 'thieves'. Hedley Twidle suggests that the very names of those |Xam narrators 'embody a history of forced acculturation, genocidal violence and language death that resulted from colonial settlement meeting with hunter-gatherer economy in the arid regions south of the Orange River' (2012: 21).

As such, many of them found themselves inmates of the Breakwater Prison in Cape Town, which is where the Berlin linguist, Dr Wilhelm Bleek, and his sister-in-law, Lucy Lloyd, recorded their language, customs and stories. In 1911, a book of examples was published as *Specimens of Bushman folklore*. In August 1875, a man named Díä!kwãin was recorded as explaining a range of formidable transitions/transformations/metamorphosis:

> The wind does thus when we die, our [own] wind blows; for we, who are human beings, we possess wind; we make clouds, when we die. Therefore ... when () we die, the wind makes dust, because it intends to blow, taking away our footprints ...

and our gall, when we die, sits in the sky .... Mother spoke, she said: 'The moon is carrying people who are dead.' ... The hair of our head will resemble clouds when we die, when we in this manner make clouds.

(Bleek and Lloyd, 1911: 397)

He also said, 'The star does in this manner, at the time when our heart falls down, that is the time when the star also falls down; for the star feels that our heart () falls over' (1911: 380).

In a footnote to a song by Díä!kwāin, the following remark was made: 'The above is a lament, sung by !nu̱iṅlkúï-t after the death of his friend, the magician and rainmaker, Ẋăă-ttīṅ; who died from the effects of a shot he received, when going about, by night, in the form of a lion' (Bleek and Lloyd, 1911: 236).

|Han≠kassó – another one of the 'informants' as they have become known – also described an astonishing array of physical bodily transformations: 'The Wind (i.e. the Wind's son) was formerly a man. He became a bird. And he was flying, while he no longer walked as he used to do; for, he () was flying' (Bleek and Lloyd, 1911: 107).

|Xam shaman |Kabbo tried to explain how this self was functioning within a broader universe: 'The Bushmen's letters are in their bodies. They (the letters) speak, they move, they make their (the Bushmen's) bodies move ... The presentiment is that which speaks the truth; ... among the trees and green spruits you have seen the springbok with your body' (Bleek and Lloyd, 1911: 331, 333).

The century in which these texts were recorded saw the ascendancy of science, and these descriptions were obviously regarded as primitive superstition and animism. But, again thanks to science, we are being made aware nowadays that we are nothing but stardust, that nothing of our physical being disappears totally, but is used by the earth in an endless variety of ways.

So from these texts one can surmise at least three characteristics of a possible self: first, the radical physical capacity to transform the self from being a man into a bird, or a lion into a man, or to be a man now, but yesterday a bird and tomorrow the wind; second, the recognition of a particular kind of cord or link which binds us with vibrations from our body right through to a universe where our death influences the stars. Third, it is not a mere mental understanding of empathy, or close observation, but a daily bodily awareness, a physical intactness with a universe in which we talk lion and bird, make with our bodies wind, dust, clouds, and read the coming and going of animals, birds and stars in our bodies.

And this is what is new: the rich point of a self that is multiple – a self that co-exists with multiple forms of life, experiencing an interaction that is intimate. At the same time, this self is also underpinned by a kind of centring within multiplicity, a self-ness freely engaging with the universe and not (yet) experiencing loss or displacement when a person slips from one entity into another.

But another kind of theme was also produced by the |Xam in which the first cruel push into decentring was formulated. A song was recorded which became the most famous of all |Xam texts. Díä!kwãin describes how white people broke the connection of the |Xam with the land. In the context of their hunter-gatherer lifestyle destroyed by the incoming white settlers and dispossessed of their waterholes and access to game, Díä!kwãin narrates how this unravelled the rituals and belief systems of their lives as it destroyed their complex interwovenness with the universe.

Bleek's daughter, Dorothea, who visited the area where this narrator once lived, wrote in 1929: 'Fifty years ago every adult Bushman knew all his people's lore. A tale begun by a person from one place could be finished by someone from another place at a later date.' But at the beginning of the twentieth century, she discovered that 'not one of them knew a single story … the folklore was dead, killed by a life of service among strangers and the breaking up of families' (Bleek and Lloyd, 1911: 311; see also Twidle, 2012: 21).

In this poem the string, used to make music and to call the rain or used in a bow to hunt – therefore, a rich point – was no longer making a sound (ringing through the air), and this changed the community's whole relationship to the cosmos and the world, totally disrupting and displacing them.

> People were those who
> Broke for me the string.
> Therefore,
> The place ( ) became like this to me.
> On account of it.
> Because the string was that which broke for me
> (The ringing sound in the sky is no longer heard by the singer)
> Therefore,
> The place does not feel to me,
> As the place used to feel to me,
> On account of it.
> For
> The place feels as if it stood open before me,
> ( ) Because the string has broken for me,

> Therefore,
> The place does not feel pleasant to me,
> On account of it.
>
> (Bleek and Lloyd, 1911: 237)

Central to the lament is the fact that it was 'people' (as if to say, not animals, but people) who caused this destruction. The land, where the |Xam formerly could dive into various selves, was cut loose and became disjointed, gaping and strange. Also note the repetition of the phrase: on account of it, as if to pinpoint accurately the origin of the painful 'splitting'. Although the text is titled a 'song', as a rich point it evades that particular indexing by being more of a lament describing an epistemological devastation. In this way, the first texts by Southern Africa's First People present examples of a free engaging self as well as markings of the first signs of distress and displacement.

IsiXhosa text of *Ukufinyezwa nokubiywa komhlaba* (The Contraction and Enclosure of the Land) by St. J. Page Yako (1958)

Ngũgĩ wa Thiong'o defines colonialism as a cultural bomb. The 'effect of a cultural bomb is to annihilate a people's belief in their names, in their language, in their environment, in their heritage of struggle, in their unity, in their capacities and ultimately in themselves. It makes them see their past as one wasteland of non-achievement and it makes them want to distance themselves from that wasteland' (2005: 3). Ngũgĩ wa Thiong'o calls this process decentring:

> 'Nothing you see or hear or taste or experience can be approached from your own viewpoint. You live like a person drifting in space with no connection, no horizon, no knowledge or understanding of anything accept this body of which every limb and organ has lost its meaning for you. Imperialism is the rule of consolidated capital and since 1884 this monopolistic parasitic capital has affected and continues to affect the lives even of peasants in the remotest corners of our universe.'
>
> (2005: 2)

In his poem about land, St J Page Yako rivetingly describes this decentring. As with the history of the |Xam, it begins with the invasion of land which in the end destroys all sense-making customs, leaving people 'drifting in space with no connection'.

Ukufinyezwa nokubiywa komhlaba
(St. J. Page Yako)

Batsho bon' abantwana begazi,
Noxa lon' ilizwe lingaselilo lethu.
Lo mhlab' uza kusongwa ngokwengubo,
Ube ngangentende yesandla.
Inkabi yeleqe yogaxelek' ezingcingweni,
Ayisakuba naw' amandl' okuxhentsa,
Iya kub' iduketile yidyokhwe nayimpuluwa.
Sigilane ngezifuba njengezabonkol' emcepheni,
Iintombi zethu zolotyolwa ngamaqhosha;
Zintwe' ezi man' ukuqhawuka zihlangana.
Kuthiwa namhl' igazi malingaphalali,
Ukuhlanganis' amathile namathile;
Ukuze singakhothani njengemaz' ikhoth' ithole,
Iqhutywa luthando na bubushushu begazi.
Linako n' iqhosh' ukukhoth' elinye?
Ew' indod' igilane nomolokazana,
Unyan' angamhlonel' unizala,
Sisong' amadolo singabi nak' ukunaba,
Kub' unhlab' ufinyeziwe.

The Contraction and Enclosure of the Land
(*translated from isiXhosa by Koos Oosthuysen*)[1]

So say the children of the Royal House,
although the land is no longer ours.
This land will be folded like a blanket,
until it is the size of the palm of a hand.
The racing ox will become entangled in the fencing wire.
It no longer has the strength to dance free.
It will be worn out by the yoke and the plough.
We will bump breast to breast like tadpoles in a calabash ladle.
The bride price of our daughters will be paid in coins –
trivial things that come and go, constantly being exchanged.
Nowadays it is said that blood should not be spilled,
so that one nation can unite with another,
but now we no longer lick each other like a cow licks her calf,
driven by love and inborn instinct.
Can one coin lick another caringly?

A man may now have words with his son's wife,
and a son refrains from showing respect to his wife's mother.
We fold up our knees – unable to stretch out,
because the land has been shrunk.

The first stanza opens with reference to what centred amaXhosa: land and the ancestors – the ancestors speak from ancestral land, 'although the land may no longer (be) ours' – suggesting that even if the land has been taken away, the ancestors continue to validate the amaXhosa ownership. Whites fold the land of black people as if it is a mere blanket until it is as small as 'the palm of a hand'.

The ǀXam poet refers to the string binding him to the universe; the Xhosa poet uses cattle – an image which presents a rich point in the fullest sense of the word. 'The racing ox will become entangled in the wire, / worn out by the dance of the yoke and the plough' and 'Our girls have their lobola paid / with trivial things, coins that come and go' and no longer with cattle.

In Indigenous groups, cattle held (and still hold in the rural areas) the key to life and personhood. Cattle are not merely chattel but are known in Setswana as *Modimo o nkô e metsi* (God-with-the-wet-nose). Cattle are a personal extension of the self. A Setswana idiom says: 'A fool with an ox is no longer a fool.' One of the prescribed poems for schools by P. Leseyana (1938) says:

Malenkhu a marumo
they who produce warm milky milk
seapaa letoutou
they, the wet-nosed gods
modimo o nko e metsi
with their intense nourishing drink
mogodungwane o molelo
have cream that scorches the whiskers of men
more o fisang banna ditedu
the whiskers drip with cream that they did not plaster on themselves.

Cattle were the key to both 'wealth' and 'power'. They not only had the capacity 'to create and embody value but also the wherewithal to permit its transformation. In the context of exchange, sacrifice and ritual commensality they could construct or disentangle human identities and relations, and in rites of passage their slaughter marked the alteration of social status' (Comaroff and Comaroff, 1992: 145; see also Willoughby, 1928: 187, 196, 330; Shapera, 1959: 365–7).

The exchange and payment via cattle signifies much more than a negotiated deal. By paying cattle as lobola, or lending to the poor, or exchanging cattle with a chief, or taking cattle as a result of conquering others in war, one interweaves oneself in other social relations. As one's cattle become part of other herds, so one's reputation and spiritual interest grow. Cattle make you human. 'Cattle, in sum, were the pliable symbolic vehicles through which men formed and reformed their world of social and spiritual relations' (Comaroff and Comaroff, 1992: 145). 'Apart from their capacity to represent particular identities and bonds, cattle also validate the authority of a specific world view and the social order of which it was part' (Comaroff and Comaroff, 1992: 146; for another kind of discussion, see Andries du Toit, 2018).

In this poem, Page St Yako describes the loss of ancestral land followed by the entrapment of an ox by wire (used to fence off colonialists' farms) and heavy workloads. It can no longer 'dance' free. This halt in the free-flowing of cattle means a halt in the 'accretion of riches in family and social relations, in cattle and clients, in position and possessions; all of which was also held to contribute to the common good'. The creation of these forms of value through cattle was dubbed 'great work', the effect of which was 'to extend the self through ties of interdependence' (Comaroff and Comaroff, 2001: 274). Thus the significance of property, most notably cattle, was that it linked people.

First came the loss of land, then the loss of cattle which brings with it loss of space (crowded like tadpoles in a calabash ladle), loss of respecting the in-law family, because instead of cattle, money is used to pay the bride price. Money cannot grow. Money has no identity. It comes and goes – in this pocket and then in that one. No one knows where it comes from. It links you to no one. 'The defining feature of cattle-linkage was the fact that a brother became the recipient of his sister's bridewealth. These beasts, it was said, were to succour her in times of need' (Comaroff and Comaroff, 1992: 136).

All of this contributes to the greatest of all losses: a loss of caring (like a cow for her newborn calf). People are supposed to reconcile into a new nation (a plea relevant and interrogated until today), but with their livelihood and world view savaged, those severely displaced and split are unable to reconcile – they pull their knees in towards their bodies, the position of the dead in a grave.

The fact that cattle are replaced by money suggests that the mediation of money greatly aggravates the landless situation: it cuts one loose from embeddedness in the social fabric. It has no lasting value; it does not carry anything of the giver; it does not multiply, taking on vibrations of the new owner. Therefore, there is no respect for elders or for women. One may as well 'pull up one's knees' – one is as good as dead.

This poem is an excellent example of the hidden complicity between the rhetoric of modernity and the logic of coloniality that 'should become the target of epistemic de-colonization'. This can only happen if the rich points of the 'colonised culture' are allowed to reveal themselves.

Setswana text of *Sempe a Lešoboro* by M. O. M. Seboni and E. P. Lekhela (1970)

We see in the next poem evidence of a concerted effort to recentre the self by taking control of one's circumstances, attempting to undo some of the harm. This happens by various means: the poem is in an Indigenous language but is in itself shot through with dialogue and other languages (e.g. all the words in bold are 'Tswanafied' Afrikaans words; the word in upper case is *slang* Setswana). The poet no longer clings to outdated and conservative ideas of purity but is fully multilingual and pluriversal in its vocabulary, knowledge and strategies.

Sempe a Lešoboro
By M. O. M. Seboni and E. P. Lekhela

Legougou la lona **dimense**,
E rile go twe **gougou** *ka tshoga,*
Pelo ya tshoga ya ntika morago
Ke itlhoina lo raya nna ka nosi,
Ntekwane lo re raya, le lona lo itheye
Lo bo lo reye le banyana ba **dimense**.
Ramapotwana o potapota gaisi,
O tlhola a tikela mo gaising,
Lekobakoba la goora Lešoboro,
Sempe, e kete go bolawa noga,
E bile e kete go bolawa molelemedi,
Le mefinyana ya dilepe e a wa.
Go buile MmaSelemela a re,
'Nnaha Sempe wa ga ka, o bolawa eng?'
A re, 'Mma, ke bolawa ke ditšhentšha banna;
Nna ke bolawa ke kgomomoney ya PEREKO.
Mogolokwanez wa lela, wa lela phetelela,
Kwa lwapeng lwa ga Mma Selemela;
A bona Sempe a tla a e kgweetsa,
A re, 'Ngwanaka mme ntla o humile thata?'
A itumelela go tla a thibile moroba.

Ngwale boela yoo o mmokile,
O boka o sa itse ina la gagwe,
Ina la gagwe ke Matsodimatsoke.

Sempe of the Lešoboro clan
(translated by Stephen Masote and Tšepiso Mothibi)[1]

The Hurry-Up People said,
'Hurry up,' to me and I got a fright,
my heart jumped to stand right behind me
because I thought you people were talking only to me like that,
only to find you were also talking to your own like that
and even to your own daughters.
Ramapotwana, the boss, goes round and round his house --
he often disappears into it.
But running around always to do his work
is Sempe of the Lešoboro: as if he is killing a snake,
as if he is busy with a slitherer;
the handle of the axe breaks loose, so hard does he pretend.
MaSelemela speaks and asks,
'What's happening, Sempe, what's bothering you?'
He answers, 'Mme, I am being killed by this man-changing thing;
I am being killed by this ox called work.'
Ululation breaks loose and lasts a long time,
at the place of MaSelemela.
When people see Sempe driving a heifer,
 she asks, 'My child, did you work so hard today?'
because he is clearly delighted with the calf.
Young one, relax, you've achieved that,
you've glorified your name without knowing it,
your name is now interwoven like a rope.

The poem has some exquisite and playful imagery. Sempe is working for an Afrikaner boss who is not very industrious: despite him shouting 'Hurry up!' to everybody, even his daughters, he himself just strolls around, often disappearing into the house – to drink coffee or sleep, who knows? Sempe catches on. He also play-acts. The moment the boss appears, he jumps around as if he has seen a snake and chops wood so ferociously that the handle of the axe breaks. This should be an ideal situation. One has a job. One gets paid, but one only needs to work when the boss is watching. But suddenly Sempe's mother enters the poem asking: *'Nnaha Sempe wa ga ka, o bolawa eng?'* (Now Sempe, what is wrong?) and he answers: '*Mma, ke bolawa ke ditšhentšha banna; / Nna ke bolawa ke kgomo ya pereko.*' (Mme, I am being killed by this man-changing thing; / I am killed by this ox called work.)

Unless one realizes that the word for work, *pereko*, is a *rich point*, one could easily have concluded that Sempe was unwilling to work, and so working, even for an undemanding boss, is killing him.

In Setswana there are two words for work: *tiro* and *mmèrèkò*. *Tiro* means self-possessed labour, building the personhood by doing things from which everybody benefits. It covers a wide spectrum of activities, from cultivation, cooking and creating a family to pastoralism, politics and the performance of ritual. *Mmèrèkò* (*bereka* from the Afrikaans word *werk*) means wage work for others, usually whites. Bluntly put, *bereka* means to do as little work as possible for as much money as possible. According to Comaroff and Comaroff (2001: 13), the contrast between these two terms influenced the Southern Tswana thinking in the late colonial years: 'It underlay the way in which they imagined, and navigated, the South African economy and society under Apartheid.'

Building one's personhood was an irreducibly social process. 'The epistemic emphasis on self-construction was embodied, metonymically and meta-pragmatically, in the idea of *tiro*, labor.' *Tiro* was not an abstract quality, a commodity to be bought or sold. It could not exist as alienable labour power. 'Work, in short, was the positive, relational aspect of human social activity, of the making of self and others in the course of everyday life' (Comaroff and Comaroff, 2001: 13).

In the next stanza we see Sempe arriving among ululations, driving a heifer. It will only be in the light of cattle and money as two decisive rich points, discussed in the previous poem, that one would realize how Sempe is trying to minimize the effect of the 'ox called work' (*bereka/pereko*). He uses the feared 'money' – a rich point suggesting money belongs to no one, money does not enhance one's personhood – to buy a heifer. This animal will humanize him back into his community and dispel the destructive forces of white work. The God-with-a-wet-nose will 'interweave' him with others.

Conclusion

It is important to be aware that the incorporation of Indigenous texts as possible new knowledge systems is not without its challenges and could, of course, be just another form of conquest and abuse. This important point was made by Steiner (and later by Said) in his famous text, *After Babel. Aspects of Language and Translation* (Steiner, 1998). Steiner posed the question how knowledge that is non-dominative and non-coercive can be produced in a setting that is deeply inscribed with the politics, the considerations, the positions and the strategies of power (Steiner, 1998: 380). He raised awareness of the dangers of presenting 'an invented geography, an imaginary space built according to the ideology, cultural values and norms of the West' (Steiner, 1998: 381).

This is where the concept of Linguistic Citizenship is helpful. It moves away from the dichotomy of a pure dominant (colonial) culture destroying a pure weaker (colonized) one and suggests that in terms of South Africa, the majority of citizens find themselves constantly 'weaving' among or in and out of a variety of more than eleven languages, cultures and accents within an increasingly assertive cultural African-ness combined with English-ness. Heugh (2015) adds that the pervasiveness of globalization is forcing most citizens into a constantly interpreting and translating mode – whether ontological or epistemological. One has to linguistically navigate one's way as the 'usual rarefied hermetically sealed borders' no longer exist between or among languages (Heugh, 2015: 281–2). Stroud quotes Stuart Hall: 'The capacity to live with difference is, in my view, the coming question of the 21st century' (2015: 20).

Stroud (2018: 17) suggests that if 'we are to engage seriously with the lives of others', it is imperative to reconceptualize 'language in ways that can promote a diversity of voice and contribute to a mutuality and reciprocity of engagement across difference'. Studying poems written in Indigenous languages is an effective way of making the Indigenous languages audible in the lecture room and empowering its speakers. The use of Indigenous languages creates new relationships and makes and unmakes knowledges.

Indigenous literary texts are ideally placed to fracture hegemonic ideas. Exploring rich points can subvert a particular universality and produce epistemic shifts within traditional Western symbols around literature and more especially poetry. Normative systems of literature will be interrupted in ways that invigorate relationships among students and between students and teacher/lecturer. It will 'favour' the inputs of scholars who speak Indigenous languages, allowing them to delink from what are usually presented as the accepted matrixes of knowledge.

Furthermore, the poems themselves open up profoundly different ways of thinking about the world. Again, the transformative capacities of the rich points could restructure, change and transform sources; could empower mother-tongue speakers by affirming features of their own experience; and show new possibilities of how to identify and enter African literatures.

The poems discussed here all express an intense awareness and the explicit grief of being displaced, whether through the rich points of lexical items such as land, cattle and work or more fundamental notions of how the world works through a pluriversal interconnectedness. But to read them as simply expressing a desire to be *recentred* would be a superficial reading and a mere readaptation of the Western trope of centring. What the poetic voice regrets in these texts is how the interconnectedness-towards-a-wholeness, so superbly expressed in the Bushman poem, is being destroyed by whiteness. In this poem, centring means to be fully intact/placed within *a plurality*, with one another and the universum. It does not mean to return to a sealed-off centred individual in full control of one's destiny, but to live fully plural, even with that which is unknown, strange, to what is not one's own; it is to live in a way, even if in a limited sense, as if belonging to that which one does not fully know.

Finally, these poems in Indigenous languages move us away from what Mignolo describes as Western episteme through the use of literature that was specifically 'transmitted and developed in different contexts … through the operations of colonial expansion and the consequent global diaspora of millions of people' (Pym, [2010] 2014: 143). The texts allow students to delink from the colonial matrix of power, foregrounding 'other epistemologies, other principles of knowledge and understanding and, consequently, other economy, other politics, other ethics' (Mignolo, 2007: 453).

Poems written in South Africa's Indigenous languages open up the possibility of experiencing a multiversality.

Note

1   The English translations of the poems, *The Shrinking and Fencing in of the Land* and *Sempe of the Lešoboro Clan,* are reproduced by permission of Oxford University Press Southern Africa, from *Stitching a Whirlwind: An Anthology of Southern African Poems and Translations*, 2018, coordinated by Antjie Krog and edited by Megan Hall © Oxford University Press Southern Africa (Pty) Ltd.

References

Agar, M. (1991), 'The Biculture in Bilingual', *Language in Society*, 20: 167–81.
Baker, M. (2012), 'Decolonial Education: Meanings, Contexts, and Possibilities. Interpreting, Researching, & Transforming Colonial/Imperial Legacies in Education', American Educational Studies Association, Annual Conference Seattle, Washington, 31 October to 4 November 2012.

Bleek, W. H. I. and L. C. Lloyd (1911), *Specimens of Bushman Folklore*. London: George Allan. Available online: https://openlibrary.org/books/OL715233M/Specimens_of_Bushman_folklore (accessed 13 October 2019).

Casalis, E. ([1861] 1965), *The Basutos or Twenty Three Years in South Africa*. Cape Town: C. Struik.

Comaroff, J.L. and J. Comaroff. (1992), *Ethnography and the Historical Imagination*. Boulder, CO: Westview Press.

Comaroff, J. L. and J. Comaroff (2001), 'On Personhood: An Anthropological Perspective from Africa', *Social Identities*, 7 (2): 267–83.

Du Toit, A. (2018), 'Without the Blanket of the Land: Agrarian Change and Biopolitics in Post-Apartheid South Africa', *The Journal of Peasant Studies*, 45: 5–6. Available online: https://doi.org/10.1080/03066150.2018.1518320 (accessed 13 October 2019).

Du Toit, M. (2016), 'A Multilingual Approach to Teaching South African History', in R. Kaschula and E. Wolff (eds), *Multilingual Education for Africa: Concepts and Practices*, 132–48. Pretoria: Unisa Press.

Heugh, K. (2015), 'Epistemologies in Multilingual Education: Translanguaging and Genre Companions in Conversation with Policy and Practice', *Language and Education*, 29 (3): 280–5. Available online: http://dx.doi.org/10.1080/09500782.2014.994529 (accessed 13 October 2019).

King, D. W. (1998), *Deep Talk: Reading African American Literary Names*. Charlottesville: University Press of Virginia.

Lekhela, E. P. and M. O. M. Seboni (1970), 'Sempe A Lešoboro' from *iBoka Sentle*. Cape Town: Via Afrika.

Leseyane, P. (1938), *Buka ya go buisa*, Pretoria: Van Schaik Publishers. Available online: https://freeexampapers.com/exam-papers/IB/Setswana/Setswana-A/Standard/2004-Nov/Setswana-A1-SL-Paper-1.pdf (accessed 13 October 2019).

Mandela, N. (1994), *Long Walk to Freedom – The Autobiography of Nelson Mandela*. London: Abacus.

Mignolo, W. (2007), 'DELINKING', *Cultural Studies*, 21 (2–3): 449–514.

Pinchevski, A. (2005), 'The Ethics of Interruption: Towards a Levinasian Philosophy of Communication', *Social Semiotics*, 15 (2): 211–34.

Pym, A. ([2010] 2014), *Exploring Translation Theories*. New York: Routledge.

Santos, B. de S. 2010. Epistemologies of the South. Justice against Epistemicide. London: Taylor and Francis.

Shapera, I. (1959), *The Bantu-speaking Tribes of South Africa – An Ethnographical Survey*. Cape Town: Maskew Miller Limited. Available online: https://archive.org/stream/bantuspeakingtri032916mbp/bantuspeakingtri032916mbp_djvu.txt (accessed 13 October 2019).

Steiner, G. ([1976] 1998), *After Babel. Aspects of Language and Translation*. Oxford: Oxford University Press.

Stroud, C. (2018), 'Linguistic Citizenship', in L. Lim, C. Stroud and L. Wee (eds), *The Multilingual Citizen: Towards a Politics of Language for Agency and Change*, 17–39. Clevedon: Multilingual Matters.

Twidle, H. (2012), 'The Bushmen's Letters': |Xam Narratives of the Bleek and Lloyd Collection and Their Afterlives', in D. Attwell and D. Attridge (eds), *The Cambridge History of South African Literature*, 19–41, Cape Town: Cambridge University Press.

wa Thiong'o, Ngũgĩ ([1981] 2005), *Decolonising the Mind – the politics of language in African Literature*. Oxford: James Currey Nairoby: EAEP Portsmouth: Heinemann

Willoughby, W. (1928), *The Soul of the Bantu: A Sympathetic Study of the Magico-Religious Practices and Beliefs of the Bantu Tribes of Africa*. New York: Doubleday.

Yako, S. J. P. M. (1958), '*Ukufinyezwa nokubiywa komhlaba*' from *Umtha weLanga*. Alice: Lovedale Press.

4

Affect, Performance and Language: Implications for an Embodied and Interventionist Pedagogy

Miki Flockemann

Introduction

The productive effects of affective engagements in teaching contexts have been well documented (Allan, 2010; Hickey-Moodly and Page, 2015; Zembylas, 2009). My concern here is to explore how affective encounters can serve as an embodied and interventionist pedagogy by generating an 'immanently communicative event' (Murphie, 2018: v) which can be seen to resonate with notions of Linguistic Citizenship. I take my cue from Stroud (2018b) who claims that just as the notion of citizenship has become increasingly fluid, so too should the notion of 'linguistic' be rethought to include 'practices that can be known through a variety of discourses and modalities' (2018b: 23). To demonstrate potential synergies between affective communicative events and aspects of Linguistic Citizenship as outlined by Stroud, I will draw on responses by third-year English students at the University of the Western Cape (UWC) to a series of off-campus theatrical productions as part of a module which introduces students to diverse performance aesthetics – including the interplay between language, material objects, bodies in motion, sound and visual imagery.

In structuring this discussion, I will begin by identifying some of the reciprocities between features of Linguistic Citizenship described by Stroud (2018a) and student responses to live performance events. The aim here is to suggest that affective encounters can as it were 'fast track' or pre-empt situations conducive to engagement across difference. This is followed by a discussion of how affect is integral to the continuum between sensory, embodied and cognitive knowledge. Given the proliferation of affect studies (Gregg and Seigworth, 2010), and the wry observation that since affect manifests itself through the action of animate and inanimate bodies on one another, affect is 'only impossibly an object of study' (Murphie, 2018: 11), my approach to affect will be primarily practice-based (Wetherwell, 2015). In other words, affect will be understood in terms of a dynamic process when identifying how the effects of affective encounters have been registered viscerally and then communicated through language. However, I will also draw on a number of other perspectives, including the philosophically inflected approaches of Massumi (2002), as well as more pragmatic approaches such as those by Murphie (2018).

On the other hand, Mignolo's (2009) insistence on the primacy of embodiment and location as integral to the processes of decoloniality, as reflected in his claim, 'I am where i think' (2009: 235), provides the framework for the final section in which I will focus on the students' critically reflective evaluation of the affective experience. The aim here is to illustrate the decolonizing potential of such an interventionist pedagogy where the processes of decoloniality are experienced and enacted, rather than more abstractly theorized or discussed. In the concluding section, I return to the notion of Linguistic Citizenship and the post-identity 'politics of affinity'.

Reciprocities: Linguistic Citizenship and affective encounters as communicative events

Two interrelated features which emerged from student responses to affective encounters were the interleaving of sensorial and cognitive knowledge articulated through language, and a notion of community across difference. This sense of community, as I shall argue, has some resonances with what Stroud (2018: 18) describes as linguistically mediated and reciprocal 'engagement across difference', which he describes as one of the basic tenets of the notion of Linguistic Citizenship. Stroud (2018: 4) emphasizes the importance of participation and agency in the ways that languages can be employed, especially by marginalized people, 'to position themselves agentively' and to craft 'new, emergent subjectivities of political speakerhood', often outside institutional frameworks. He further notes that Linguistic Citizenship can be seen as 'an approach to a politics of language and multilingualism departing from a notion of *vulnerability*, understood here as the emergent and sensitive process of *disinhabiting* linguistically imposed and linguistically mediated subjectivities' (original italics, 2018a: 5). My approach to potential synergies between notions of Linguistic Citizenship and responses to affective encounters is, however, much more circumscribed than the field that Stroud outlines, which embraces political speakerhood and agency. I focus more narrowly on what Murphie (2018: v) refers to as 'the immanence of the communicative event' which is triggered by the affective encounter. Murphie describes this immanence as an awareness of 'the making of a moment' (vi), a moment that precedes but is inseparable from a cognitive understanding of it. Despite this more limited focus, there are a number of synergies between elements that have been identified as integral to an affective pedagogy and to Linguistic Citizenship 'as a blueprint for a conceptual space within which to think differently – and ethically – about language and ourselves' (Stroud, 2018b: 18).

It will become clear how students' written responses to the affective encounter with live performance events speak directly to Stroud's comments on how being placed in situations of linguistic vulnerability can be productive in rethinking conceptions of identity, as well as unsettling familiar processes of meaning-making. In addition, the experience of euphoric and utopian moments generated by 'acts' of Linguistic Citizenship produces a sense of foldedness within the humanity of others which results in empathetic connections (Stroud, 2018b: 17–18). In turn, the conceptual space of Linguistic Citizenship is envisioned as promoting reciprocal engagement through shifts and disruptions of linguistic hegemonies (Stroud, 2018a: 1–2). While I will return to these synergies between affectively experienced and linguistically structured encounters across difference referred to by Stroud, there are also some aspects of the 'immanence of the communicative event' generated by affective encounters that overlap with features of an affective pedagogy. These include the claim that affective encounters cause 'ideas to adhere' (Micciche, 2007) and that affect 'changes cognitive processes' and is indeed 'a mode of cognition' (Duncan and Barrett, 2007). Furthermore, epiphanic moments, where the everyday is suddenly experienced 'newly', have been described as provoking different ways of thinking (Allan, 2010).

In the next section I outline some of the basic attributes of affect as concept in relation to teaching and learning contexts and then explore how students' affective responses to live performance events reveal their awareness of the continuum between sensory and cognitive knowledge. This in turn shapes how engagements across difference are articulated.

Affect and cognition

Affect has commonly been viewed as virtually synonymous with feeling and emotion; however, following the 'turn to affect', distinctions have been drawn involving the operation of affect in terms of the limbic system of the brain, whereas cognition takes place in the neo-cortex. These distinctions have been explored in relation to a number of disciplines, including philosophy, psychology and pedagogy. As mentioned earlier, my focus is primarily on a practice-based approach to affect in relation to pedagogy with a focus on affect as a dynamic process which is attentive to relationality, negotiation and becoming (Blackman and Venn, 2010; Wetherwell, 2015). At the same time, it is also based on an understanding of affective responses as multisensory and prefiguring, but also integral to language (Pink, 2011: 266), which is in keeping with the notion of the immanence of the communicative event.

Massumi's (2002) explication of affect is useful here by way of providing a context for this approach. In broad summary, Massumi draws on Deleuze and Guattari via Spinoza to argue that affect is an unstructured, preconscious, non-signifying system, stressing that it is a separate system from emotion and cognition. Affect is experienced as a 'moment' or a 'flash'. Emotions result from the 'capture' of affect, but a capture that always includes an 'escape' (a capture-not-quite because the neo-cortical 'fixing' or linguistic naming of affect as emotion cannot quite 'capture' affect as it travels between bodies). Put another way, affect is that which is sensed (or resonates) as intensity, and at its most intense it is expressed as emotion (2002: 25). In fact, according to Massumi, affect shapes views, beliefs and thinking more than ideology does (2002: 39–41).

Susan Leys (2011) offers a comprehensive critique of what she sees as a binary between affect and cognition evident in the work of some affect theorists, and the focus has more recently shifted to the interrelatedness of affect and cognition. As noted by Duncan and Barrett (2007: 1184) there is no such thing as a 'non-affective thought', and affect and cognition should be seen as part of a 'synergic system, all the functions of which are exercised and linked together in the general action of being in the world' (Merleau Ponty, [1962] 2002 in Pink, 2011). The complex interaction between affect and cognition and how audiences make meaning is borne out by some of the responses I will explore in more detail in the next section.

Navigating sensorial and cognitive knowledge

A comment by acclaimed playwright and director, Lara Foot, provides a point of departure for my enquiry into affective encounters in a situated learning environment. Foot recalls how going to see Barney Simon's *Born in the RSA* as a teenager in the mid-1980s Apartheid South Africa triggered an embodied cognitive shift: 'Suddenly the curtains rose on my vision. I could see. I knew where I lived, I understood where I was from, I witnessed the truth, I was part of a community, which existed in that auditorium in that place at that time' (Foot, 2012: n.p.). At the same time, she experienced a type of epiphany about her situation as a privileged young white woman living in an unjust social order. To describe this, she uses the metaphor of 'curtains rising on her vision' so that she sees 'newly' as if seeing clearly for the first time. The repeated affirmations of 'I could see', 'I knew', 'I understood', and importantly, 'I witnessed' suggest a continuum between sensorial and cognitive knowledge (seeing and knowing), while witnessing the truth suggests an awareness of 'being there' in the body, but also part of a community of fellow witnesses. What is also significant about her comment is that it speaks directly to the interrelatedness of affect and cognition from the perspective of neuroscientific enquiry as described by Duncan and Barrett: 'Since all objects and events have somatovisceral consequences, cognitive and sensory experiences are necessarily affectively infused to some degree' (2007: 1184).

While it is clear that affective encounters stimulate student engagement and participation, what is less clear is how the crossover between sensorial and cognitive knowledge operates and why. Wenger (1998) describes a situated learning environment as one that offers students opportunities to navigate new meanings that are fundamentally experiential and social (in Hickey-Moody and Page, 2015: 13). As an historically black university, UWC has not had the same financial advantages as its historically privileged sister campuses in the same region (the Universities of Cape Town and Stellenbosch), and thus the third-year elective on theatre in the English department has over time included more immersive and practice-based components. Students usually attend five to six performances off-campus and then produce a conceptual frame for a comparative assessment of the performances, drawing on the theatre vocabulary which they have accumulated and become familiar with. Since they are also expected to present a showcase of their own short scenes before an audience at the end of the course, two professional theatre practitioners assisted with the script development and performance components.[1] Of interest is how student responses, both in their academic assignments and their course evaluations, describe a critically self-reflective, or perhaps better described as a 'diffractive' (Barad, 2007), perspective on the interleaving of affect and cognition in terms very similar to Lara Foot's account above. As pointed out by Bozalek and Zembylas (2016: 112, drawing on Haraway, 1997 and Barad, 2007), there is a concern that reflection has become associated with sameness or mirroring and 'the self as the locus of reflection' (Bozalek and Zembylas, 2016: 114), whereas the metaphor of diffraction (a term appropriated from the physical sciences) entails an incorporation or an accumulative assemblage of multiple perspectives. These diffractive perspectives are generated as a result of the effects (or the 'interference') of encounters with human and material objects, which operate as 'a means of becoming' and change (2016: 115).

'As I was sitting and watching': The effects of affective encounters

There are two possible reasons for the more inclusive and diffractive aspects of the 2018 cohort of student responses. The most obvious is the type of performances they chose to write about. It just so happened that in 2018 there were two powerfully political performances running back to back. The first was a hard-hitting piece called *Uloyiko: The Gukurahindi Genocide*,[2] performed at the Methodist Church Hall in Observatory, while *Ruth First: 117 Days*[3] was performed at the Arena Theatre at the Artscape Complex. Since they employed such divergent stage aesthetics, seeing these two works in quick succession in different venues turned out to be very productive. *Uloyiko* was 'in your face' agitprop kind of theatre with a large ensemble of performers who presented extremely graphic portrayals of the torture, rape and murder of Ndebele people of Zimbabwe by Zanu PF soldiers under Robert Mugabe's rule, and although presented by mainly amateur local performers it was undoubtedly a deeply disturbing, but compelling production. On the other hand, *Ruth First: 117 Days* was a more technically polished and theatrically conventional one-woman play.[4] The other reason for these more inclusive perspectives was that during the introductory lecture I introduced the notion of witnessing as opposed to spectating in relation to performance aesthetics, drawing on Brecht's distinction between witnessing an accident first-hand and listening to an account of the accident (Goldman, 2017). This notion of witnessing also ties in with the discussions on empathy in this chapter.

Because *Uloyiko* was an advocacy piece aimed at making the audience 'feel' the 'truth' of the untold story of the genocide, students were made very aware of their situatedness as witnesses, which was also emphasized in the post-production Q and A session in which the director and writer emphasized their commitment to tell it 'as it is', without mediating or 'aestheticizing' the events (though of course it was still a performative account). The kinds of productions on offer each year obviously shape the 'flavour' of student responses, which can be somewhat disconcerting but also deeply rewarding for the lecturer, who never knows what to expect. This keeps the teaching environment fresh as the additional unpredictability of how students might respond to the performances means that the lecturer is in a similar position of vulnerability to the students.

What follows is a selection of comments (in italics) made by students in their assignments which illustrate how they interweave notions of sensory and cognitive knowledge, which then leads to an often euphoric (and even utopian) sense of engagement across difference. This speaks to the claim that in theatre both the spectators and the theatre makers jointly participate in 'creating a space for critical reflection' (Breemen, 2017: 4). Theatre thus has political value, both as aesthetic act and as an everyday event, as borne out by Foot's comment about seeing herself as a 'witness to the truth' in a communal setting (though of course not all performances will have such an effect). At the same time, the understanding that 'the other is not me' and that 'the I who am watching am not the same as the actor that I am feeling empathy for' (Gruen in Bruun, 2018: 20) points to the communicative 'attunement' that is evident in the way student A (a mature returning student)[5] describes Ruth First's visceral action when, just after she had been released after 90 days' detention, she is rearrested for a further 90 days:

> *There was silence in the audience, and I felt so emotional and frustrated, I cried too. All the props engineered a tense and sad feeling in me. I became the same as her. In a nutshell the performance elicited an automatic empathy and I was no longer myself, I was Ruth First. There's no way that any human being can avoid that kind of feeling irrespective of gender, race, creed, it is a feeling that no one can control. You don't invite it, it just comes to you. Performances take us back to humanity.*

What is interesting about this response is the way it speaks to empathy as an almost 'automatic' or 'uninvited' response, which is in keeping with studies that show that empathy is triggered by neural mirroring, so that when you see someone else's pain, it is neutrally mirrored and transmitted (Bernhardt and Singer, 2012). At the same time she is aware of the fact that this is 'not me' – but the progression from *'I became the same as'*, to *'I was no longer myself'*, to *'I was Ruth First'* then evolves when she says: *'I completely forget that Ruth First was a white woman and I am a black woman from a poor background. It automatically dismantles the barriers or bridges. It touches your soul. It goes deeper. It goes to the unseen person in you.'* The present tense 'forget' could indicate that in writing about it she is back there in the immanence of the affective communicative 'moment' and yet also aware, as noted earlier, that the person she is identifying with is 'not me'. As Gruen notes, this is indicative of the kind of cognitive dissonance which is essential for an ethical empathy (in Bruun, 2018). Student A's shift from *'I'* to *'any human being'* is also in keeping with this, as well as the fact that she extrapolates her intensely personal experience to a universal one based on 'being human'. The repetition of *'It touches'*, *'It goes'*, etc., tracks her thought processes as she recalls her emotional responses, while the final statement *'it goes to the unseen person in you'* reads like a metaphoric description of her own folded-in humanness that she is grappling to describe and capture – almost as if it is a latent (unseen) potentiality within. *'Performances take us back to humanity'*.

In describing herself watching the play *Uloyiko,* student A recalls another memory which elicits similar emotions so that she is conscious of *'witnessing two events at the same time'* and connecting the Zimbabwean genocide with her memories of growing up in the township of Gugulethu during the height of the Apartheid oppression in the 1980s. This notion of being in two places at the same time speaks to the way memory is integral to the processes of learning. It has been noted that 'memories formed during a particular emotional state tend to be easily recalled during an emotional state later on' (Thayer, in Sylvester, 1994). Thus, situations that tie memories to emotional contexts enhance the learning process. A similar progression in which the affective encounter evolves into a cognitive understanding is evident in her final assessment of her own responses to another production, *Around the Fire,* which used a loosely structured collage of monologue, spoken-word poetry and live music as a framework for presenting the interlinked narrative of four women: *'It felt helpless. I became non-judging. I realized that we can't claim to be free while negating these issues especially with young kids because they are vulnerable'*. Here again we note the shift from emotion *'It felt'* to self-reflection, *'I became'*, to cognition, *'I realized'*.

On the other hand, in student B's response to *Around the Fire,* she states that she felt the performer was looking directly at her when delivering a satirical account of what being a woman in South Africa means, while also taking a side swipe at American youth exceptionalism. In her response to this encounter, we note a similar pattern in relation to student A, though from a differently situated perspective as a visiting international student. In addition, it is more directly expressed as an epiphany which is associated with shifts in cognitive thinking triggered by unsettling affective encounters.[6] Interestingly, student B connects her experience to that of Lara Foot to explain her experience and sums it up as follows:

> *For what might have been the first time, I acknowledged the inherent violence of my being here, for living my privileged Western life, and what others go without as a result of my luxuries. I could taste past the shame, guilt and denial somewhere into the truth.*

It is a searingly honest moment, for the reference to 'tasting' the truth refers back to a childhood memory of 'slurping oysters' at a young age with her father and the recollection of how often she had so easily trotted out the cliché, 'the world is your oyster', which now strikes her afresh as a 'shameful' assumption by being so unwittingly ignorant of how others live and for whom the world holds no such exotic potential. One has the sense that even if not articulated as such, the student is also experiencing herself as a witness to two different events at the same time, in the present of the performance, and formerly as a child. But in the sentence she works past the experience of 'shame' through 'guilt and denial' to an acknowledgement of 'the truth', which has a visceral dimension here as a taste. In stating '*I heard this line exactly when I needed to hear it*,' she acknowledges how an empathetic encounter triggered a newly discovered sense of herself as entangled in the lives of others.

Another aspect of the responses here is how students frequently note that the sensorial impact occurs as an effect of the theatre aesthetics and stage design employed. This is also in keeping with the claims of affect theorists (drawing on Spinoza), who explain that affect is not a 'thing' but the 'impingement' of one body (human or otherwise) acting upon or 'moving' another. In other words, affect is the effect of one body affecting another and being affected in turn (Massumi, 2002). This is also evident in the way students reacted to the materiality of the mise en scène of each production and how the inanimate objects, the props and stage design, created and carried meaning. These responses should be seen in terms of the 'polysemic character' and 'connotative breadth' of theatrical signs, since as Elam explains, 'an essential feature of the semiotic economy of the theatrical production is that it employs a limited repertory of sign-vehicles in order to generate a potentially unlimited range of cultural units' (Elam, [1980] 2003: 9). For instance, we recall student A saying of the Ruth First production: '*All the props engineered a tense and sad feeling in me*', while student C reflects:

> *The mise en scène is a fundamental aspect to theatre in bringing life to what the body or words cannot communicate. The placing of these items has a transcendent connection to the performance allowing the writer and director to manipulate these items to convey something powerful and symbolic.*

There are wider implications for the ethical dimension of empathy in relation to its potential role in interventionist pedagogy. As pointed out by theatre scholars working on spectatorship: 'When confronted with the other in the context of performance, spectators leave the theatre unsettled and inchoate, invited to reflect on their position in society and the implications of entanglement' (Grehan, 2009 in Micu, 2011: n.p.). For instance, in the responses to how the stage aesthetic and performance styles create meaning, there needs to be an implicit grasp of a critical distance, and an awareness that this is a performance, since it is this awareness that creates the cognitive dissonance that is associated with an ethical empathy. At the same time, it is also this very dissonance that paradoxically creates the intensity of the reaction; in other words, knowing that you are witnessing a performance establishes a kind of critical distance in the very act of intense engagement. As articulated by student C: '*Watching a performance is just observing what is happening and that's it, but to bear witness means to consciously take in what you are seeing and be moved by it, knowing that what you have seen cannot be unseen again, as if it has just scarred your memory.*' This brings us back to the point raised earlier about the emotional context of memory in the learning situation. Also significant is the continuum in her account between words indicating cognitive understanding and a 'scarred' memory, which suggests a kind of 'inchoate' impression, as in '*what was seen cannot be unseen*', while also looping back to student A's comment about performance reaching deep into '*the unseen person in you*'.

Ambivalence and a sense of unsettlement have also been seen as integral to an ethical response to performance, since they facilitate 'moments of self-recognition' (Grehan in Micu, 2010 n.p.), as well as scope for more diffractive responses as described earlier. This speaks to student A's observation: '*Theatre challenges and engages with oneself .... While you are sitting there you engage with yourself while watching and you get another perspective as it shapes your thinking about certain things*', while student E notes: '*Theatre is an experience which after leaving the venue has changed something in you, a perception, an emotion, an understanding.*' This formulation yet again repeats the pattern identified earlier in student A's comments in transitioning from 'felt' to 'became', to 'recognized'. Moreover, this links to Pink's description of how, although 'we tend to communicate linguistically about our embodied and sensory perception in terms of sensory categories', we nevertheless remain aware that 'one category is never enough to express exactly what we have actually experienced' (2011: 266). In this case we see how the sensory realm is expressed as 'felt' which then evolves into cognition ('recognized').

Discussion: *'I am where i think'* and the decolonizing potential of affective encounters

While the previous section illustrated how affective encounters are experienced and articulated, this discussion looks at how the students' final course evaluations speak to notions of decoloniality. For instance, Mignolo's revision of the Cartesian maxim, 'I think therefore I am', to 'I am where i think' foregrounds how thinking needs to be re-embodied and relocated in order to 'unmask the limited situation of modern knowledges and their links to coloniality' (Mignolo in Baker, 2012: 10). Although decoloniality per se was not the focus of the questions in the evaluation that they responded to, it is telling how their responses offer examples of what can be seen as decolonizing strategies such as those referred to by Mignolo (2002) and Baker (2012), but as it were, 'from below'. In other words, decoloniality is indirectly posited in terms of personal and communal experiences, rather than in terms of theoretical approaches to decolonizing the curriculum through the radical epistemic shifts which academic institutions have been urged to engage with in the wake of recent student protests across South African universities.

The questions posed in the evaluation form drew attention to different components of the course. Students were asked, for instance, if their participation changed their perceptions of themselves, their fellow students and university studies in general. They were also asked to reflect on the process of developing and performing the monologues and short scenes they had written for the showcase component, and there was also a question about how the excursions contributed to the course. Finally, they were asked, 'which section of the course helped you to learn the best', and the majority noted that it was the excursions component, which is perhaps not surprising since their major research assignments were based on the performances they attended.

What emerged from the course evaluations is structured here around four broadly intersecting issues which are briefly contextualized in relation to the implications for decoloniality. The first issue is 'voice', in the sense of being heard and listened to; the second focuses on the sense of a rhizomic rather than hierarchical learning process; the third refers to notions of embodiment and location, and the fourth points to epiphanies of empathy. The occasionally euphoric or even lyrical timbre of some of these observations (which can be contrasted to the conventional registers commonly associated with student feedback) could be seen as being in sync with the attempt to express affective and emotional experiences linguistically.

The first cluster of responses which refer to voice, not only in being able to speak, but also being heard and listened to, highlights how students often feel silenced and marginalized in the academic context. A primary reason for this is how they perceive critique of their writing as negative (and demoralizing), which instils anxiety and a sense of inadequacy. This is suggested in the comments below about feeling 'shunned' or 'afraid of giving the wrong answer'. On the other hand, the notion of being able to speak freely (expressed in terms of being able to 'breathe') points to a sense of seeing themselves as potentially autonomous epistemic subjects in the sense that what is learnt 'sticks' and is not simply 'forgotten'. This also loops back to comments about the role of affect in memory and the way what was seen cannot be unseen. While in some cases these remarks reveal epiphanies of the everyday referred to by Allan (2010), they also reveal 'the becoming nature of the self', as in 'I am what I am not yet' (Greene in Allan, 2010:13), and an awareness of the way postulated, relational and contingent identities are constructed through language as 'the stories we tell about ourselves':

> *Free to be you and not afraid of giving the wrong answer ... The course allows us to breathe and not feel like everything we learn is forgotten.*
>
> *This was the first place I felt comfortable (and valued, respected, liked, heard) at UWC (from an international student).*
>
> *We were writing without being shunned.*
>
> *I am grateful that everyone shared their beautiful works ... the focus on everyday struggles opened up what we wanted to tell.*
>
> *Through writing a monologue I could write my feelings in a way poetry and prose won't do.*
>
> *We got to know each other on new levels ... I also learnt that my fellow students each had a story to tell and theatre provided a platform.*
>
> *Faced one of my biggest fears; learned to be comfortable in my own skin – this course allows you to express yourself.*
>
> *Our identities are bound to the stories we tell about ourselves.*

Closely allied to the focus on voice is the role played by the 'democratic' exchange of ideas focused on in the second cluster of responses below. These refer to the post-performance tutorial discussions which were open-ended conversations, allowing a free-flowing exchange of ideas in a non-hierarchical setting (since everyone had first-hand access to the same work at the same time and place, including the lecturer). This created a climate where ideas could be experimented with, and one could change one's mind or acknowledge another person's point of view, even if one did not share the opinion given. The first comment about a 'horizontal' rather than 'vertical' (top down) teaching methodology resonates with discussion of learning contexts which are 'rhizomic'. In other words, there is the sense that 'discussions can go in unanticipated directions', thus 'provoking new beginnings' (Allan, 2010: 10), and in the process, the possibilities of alternative scenarios are not foreclosed (Allan, 2010: 10). The epiphanic aspect is again evident in the comment about tutorial discussions being 'full of creativity and wonder'. There was also the recognition of the relational aspect of knowledge itself, of 'new' ways of thinking, or 'thinking a little further than definitions in your course book', or being offered 'ways of thinking we hadn't thought about'. As noted in the previous section the polysemic character of performance semiotics encourages this kind of openness, which also accounts for the 'pleasure' experienced.

> *The teaching methodology is more horizontal than vertical, and ... the course allows for sensitive involvement ... the traditional hierarchy is not enacted.*
>
> *[It offered] room for creativity and different perspectives: It challenges you to think a little further than the definitions written in your course book.*
>
> *The excursions are an effective ways of learning, the tutorial discussions that followed where theory was applied to each performance, were full of creativity and wonder.*
>
> *The space of the classroom was full of positive energy ... in the theatre class we could have fun while learning and unpack our lives. We could share ideas and discuss issues. Each comment was of support and care. The class helped me deal with my traumatic experiences ....[it] gave each person a chance to speak.*
>
> *[It] enabled us to be aware of how the concepts and trends we study exist in the real world and this is what made the class very appealing. The conversations we had afterwards ... offered us ways of thinking we hadn't thought about.*

While, as noted earlier, students' responses are not consciously taking on the project of decoloniality as advocated by Mignolo (2002) and Baker (2012), there are nevertheless reciprocities in the way notions of re-embodiment and relocation are implicit in a number of responses (as in the reference to the 'real world'). As indicated in the next cluster of responses (which refer not only to the theatre excursions, but also to the drama improvisation 'showcase' classes), it is commonly a physical response to an affective encounter which triggers cognitive shifts. This is seen in the first comment where the student notes a transfer of affect between bodies, and parts of his own body-mind nexus, linking his 'mind' to his 'eyes' to his 'pen', while also being aware of the 'stories bound to his skin'. Similarly, the relocation of thought is suggestive here of the physical (off-campus) contexts in which learning occurs, as well as notions of the classroom as a non-hierarchical space of positive energy where everyone's voice is heard.

> *Delia [the showcase director] connected my mind to my pen to my eyes to my face to my arms and leg ... I felt a unity among my script, my body and my voice. I was a living story ... I harnessed the stories bound to my skin.*
>
> *Excursions and theatre 'bring you back to your body ... It brings back your human element. It reminds you that you are not a robot but a body with a faculty of reasoning ... These are the most crucial moments I experienced when seeing the plays and these moments are unavoidable and un-escapable.*
>
> *The plays hit home by showing us things we like to avoid, as it forced us to open up and feel the guilt of what is really happening in our era and how we can possibly take a stand on it.*
>
> *The ability to empathise with someone is crucial when stepping into another role.*
>
> *By feeling with and for our characters we were also learning how to be empathetic and conscious of our fellow students' struggles... Each piece was personal to the writer or held some kind of relevance to society ... Although I was not a performer I held my breath every time one of my fellow students performed; I felt nervous for them.*
>
> *In considering the perspectives of other students you realise that your perspective is totally different from that of other students.*

Embodiment is also linked here to feelings of empathy generated by a freshly discovered sense of community through engagement across difference. These feelings of empathy (as noted earlier) are often triggered by what Allan (2010: 13) describes as '[e]piphanies of the everyday', where there is a sense of seeing or recognizing aspects of daily life as if for the first time. These everyday epiphanies, as Allan notes, have ethical and political dimensions in binding one to the human being of another, again emphasizing relationality, entanglement and becoming, rather than difference (as in the reference to becoming conscious of fellow students' struggles). At the same time, as suggested earlier, these responses, in terms of references to voice, non-hierarchical learning contexts, embodiment as well as everyday epiphanies and empathy, can be seen as enactments of the processes of decoloniality, even if not framed as such.

Conclusion

Finally, in returning to the claim at the start of the chapter that communicative events generated through affective encounters can operate as interventionist pedagogy and resonate with aspects of notions of Linguistic Citizenship, it is necessary to revisit and elaborate on some of the synergies that were identified. For instance, it was noted that the conceptual space of Linguistic Citizenship as outlined by Stroud (2018a: 1–2) is envisioned as promoting reciprocal engagement through shifts and disruptions of linguistic hegemonies. At the same time, it was argued that being placed in situations of vulnerability can be productive in rethinking conceptions of identity as relational and situational, as an ongoing process of becoming, while also unsettling familiar and hegemonic processes of meaning-making. In addition to the experience of euphoric and utopian moments generated by 'acts' of Linguistic Citizenship, a sense of foldedness within the humanity of others, as Stroud points out (2018b: 17–18), results in empathetic connections across difference.

Two primary points of connection between the effects of affective encounters and features of Linguistic Citizenship noted above can be summed up as follows: namely the function of an 'immanent communicative event' (Murphie, 2018: v) and engagement across difference which, as in the case of the example I revisit here, speaks to a politics of affinity rather than the politics of identity (Phelan, 1995 in Stroud, 2018a: 4). For instance, student A's response to the howl of despair uttered by the actress playing Ruth First (when she is rearrested on her release from solitary confinement and sentenced to another 90 days' detention) discussed earlier is a good example of an immanent communicative event which seems all the more powerful precisely because of its non-verbalized, non-linguistic aspect. As Murphie explains, responding to the immanence of the communicative event involves attunement to the making of the moment (2018: vi). This attunement is evident when student A described her 'automatic' and 'uncontrollable' feelings during the silence following the scream: *'I became the same as her'* and *'I was no longer myself, I was Ruth First.'* Student A's comments are also telling. As noted earlier, she asserts the specificity and locatedness of her identity as a black woman from a poor background, in opposition to Ruth First as a white (and assumedly middle-class) woman, and yet the immanence of the communicative event enables an expression of affinity that (even if momentarily) suggests how affinity can transcend identity politics. This recalls the comment on how Linguistic Citizenship can be seen as departing from precisely such a position of vulnerability in 'disinhabiting' (Stroud, 2018a: 5) subjectivities that have been imposed and mediated through language.

As stated in the introductory section, the aim was also to show how affective encounters can as it were 'fast-track' or pre-empt situations conducive to engagement across difference. As indicated above, the communicative events referred to here result in (albeit transitory) euphoric and utopian and transformative revelations of 'being-together-in-difference', which Stroud suggests can operate as foreshadowing 'the potential to live otherwise' (Stroud, 2018b: 35).

Even though the students quoted here have not studied theories of affect as a form of cognition, nor were they deliberately responding to Mignolo's (2009) claim that 'I think where i am', it is nevertheless telling how their descriptions of affective encounters reveal a tacit awareness of the interleaving of sensorial and cognitive knowledge (as well as pointing to some of the processes of decoloniality). As seen in their responses to the excursions component and course evaluations, this sensory and cognitive continuum can prepare the ground for, or even catalyse, epiphanies of engagement across difference. Despite the fact that the epiphanies referred to often remain at the level of euphoric and foreshadowing 'moments', there is, nevertheless, value in envisioning such potential engagements as a strategy for negotiating a way through the challenges of the future.

Notes

1 Kim Euell (a visiting playwright from University of Massachusetts) ran introductory workshops on script development. Local theatre practitioner, Delia Meyer (who has a Master's in Applied Theatre from NYU), has directed the showcase component for the past five years. She has also worked with students to prepare their monologues and scenes for the showcase.
2 The Gukurahundi was a series of massacres of Ndebele civilians carried out by the Zimbabwe National Army from early 1983 to late 1987.
3 Ruth First was a South African anti-Apartheid activist. She was assassinated in Mozambique where she was working in exile, by a parcel bomb sent by South African police in 1983.
4 Additional performances we saw were *Around the Fire, Sainthood, Endgame* and *Othello: A Woman's Story*.
5 Students gave written permission for extracts from their assignments to be quoted anonymously as students A, B, etc.
6 As Julie Allan notes, an epiphany here refers to 'the sudden revelation of the whatness of a thing' (from Ellman, 1982), or as Taylor describes it, the notion of how a work of art is 'the manifestation which brings us into the presence of something which is otherwise inaccessible' (in Allan, 2010: 14).

References

Allan, J. (2010), 'The Inclusive Teacher Educator: Spaces for Civic Engagement', *Discourse: Studies in the Politics of Education*, 31 (4): 411–22. Available online: https://www.tandfonline.com/doi/full/10.1080/01596306.2010.504359?scroll=to&needAccess=true (accessed 20 July 2017).

Baker, M. (2012), 'Decolonial Education: Meanings, Contexts, and Possibilities', Unpublished Paper, Interpreting, Researching, & Transforming Colonial/Imperial Legacies in Education, American Educational Studies Association, Annual Conference, Seattle, Washington, 31 October to 4 November 2012.

Barad, K. (2007), *Meeting the Universe Halfway: Quantum physics and the entanglement of matter and meaning*. Durham, NC: Duke University Press.

Bernhardt, B. C. and T. Singer (2012), 'The Neural Basis of Empathy', *Annual Review of Neuroscience*, 35 (1): 1–23. Available online: https://www.google.com/search?client=firefoxb&q=Bernhardt+Boris+C.+and+Ta+nger%2C+%E2%80%9CThe+Neural+Basis+of+Empathy%E2%80%9D%2C (accessed 30 May 2018).

Blackman, L. and C. Venn (2010), 'Affect', *Body and Society*, 16 (1): 7–28.

Bozalek, V. and M. Zembylas (2016), 'Diffraction or Reflection? Sketching the Contours of Two Methodologies in Educational Research', *International Journal of Qualitative Studies in Education*, 30 (2): 111–27.

Breeman, A. (2017), 'Performance Philosophy: Audience Participation and Responsibility', *Performance Philosophy Journal*, 2 (2). Available online: http://www.performancephilosophy.org/journal/article/view/67/138 (accessed 2 May 2018).

Bruun, E. F. (2018), 'Teaching Empathy with Brecht as Prompter', *American International Journal of Social Science*, 7 (2): 20–8.

Duncan, S. and L. Barret (2007), 'Affect is a Form of Cognition: A Neurobiological Analysis', *Cognition in Emotion*, 21 (6): 1184–211.

Elam, K. ([1980] 2003), *The Semiotics of Theatre and Drama*. London: Routledge.

Ellman, R. (1982), *James Joyce*. New York: Oxford University Press.

Foot, L. (2012), 'Rewrite the Plot of Your Life', posted by Bernelle on 9 August 2012, extracts from TEDxCT@2012. Available online: https://www.youtube.com/watch?v=_6quThOKfWM (accessed 17 August 2016).

Gregg, M. and G. J. Seigworth, eds (2010), *The Affect Theory Reader*. Durham, NC: Duke University Press.

Grehan, Helena. (2009), *Performance, Ethics and Spectatorship in a Global Age*. London: Palgrave Macmillan.

Goldman, D. (2017), 'From Spectating to Witnessing: Performance in the Here and Now', *Art & International Affairs*, 12 (2). Available online: https://theartsjournal.net/2017/07/19/from-spectating-to-witnessing-performance-in-the-here-and-now/ (accessed 12 April 2018).

Haraway, D. (1997), Modest_Witness@SecondMillenium: FemaleMan_Meets_OncoMouse: Feminism and Technoscience. New York: Routledge.

Hickey-Moody, A. C. and T. Page, eds (2015), 'Making, Matter and Pedagogy', in *Arts, Pedagogies and Cultural Resistance: New Materialisms*, 1–20. London: Rowan and Littlefield.

Leys, R. (2011), 'The Turn to Affect: A Critique', *Critical Inquiry*, 37: 434–72.

Massumi, B. (2002), *Parables for the Virtual: Movement, Affect, Sensation*. Durham, NC: Duke University Press.

Merleau-Ponty, M. (2002 [1962]), *The Phenomenology of Perception*. London: Routledge.

Micciche, L. R. (2007), *Doing Emotion: Rhetoric, Writing Teaching*. Portsmouth: Boynton/Cook.

Micu, A. S. (2011), 'Book Review of *Performance, Ethics and Spectatorship in a Global Age* by Helena Grehan', *Liminalities*, 7 (1): 5. Available online: http://liminalities.net/7-1/grehan-rev.html (accessed 2 July 2018).

Mignolo, W. (2002), 'The Geopolitics of Knowledge and the Colonial Difference', *The South Atlantic Quarterly*, 101 (1): 57–96.

Mignolo, W. D. (2009), 'I Am Where I Think: Epistemology and the Colonial Difference', *Journal of Latin American Cultural Studies: Traversia*, 8 (2): 235–45.

Murphie, A. (2018), 'Fielding Affect: Some Propositions', *Capacious: Journal for Emerging Affect Inquiry*, 1 (3). Available online: http://capaciousjournal.com/cms/wp-content/uploads/2018/10/capacious-murphyfielding-affect.pdf (accessed 29 April 2019).

Phelan, S. (1995), 'The Space of Justice: Lesbians and Democratic Politics', in L. Nicholson and S. Seidman (eds), *Social Postmodernism*. Cambridge: Cambridge University Press.

Pink, S. (2011), 'Multimodality, Multisensoriality and Ethnographic Knowing: Social Semiotics and the Phenomenology of Perception', *Qualitative Research*, 11 (3): 261–76.

Stroud, C. (2018a), 'Introduction', in L. Lim, C. Stroud and L. Wee (eds), *The Multilingual Citizen: Towards a Politics of Language for Agency and Change*, 17–39. Clevedon: Multilingual Matters.

Stroud, C. (2018b), 'Linguistic Citizenship', in L. Lim, C. Stroud and L. Wee (eds), *The Multilingual Citizen: Towards a Politics of Language for Agency and Change*, 17–39. Clevedon: Multilingual Matters.

Sylvester, R. (1994), 'How Emotions Affect Learning', *Reporting What Students Are Learning*, 52 (2). Available online: http://www.ascd.org/publications/educational-leadership/oct94/vol52/num02/How-Emotions-Affect-Learning (accessed 29 April 2019).

Wenger, E. (1998), 'Communities of Practice: Learning as a Social System', *Systems Thinker*. Available online: https://psycnet.apa.org/record/1998-06054-000 (accessed 2 July 2018).

Wetherwell, M. (2015), 'Trends in a Turn to Affect: A Social Psychological Critique', *Body and Society*, 21 (2): 139–66.

Zembylas, M. (2009), 'Affect, 'Citizenship, Politics: Implications for Education', *Pedagogy, Culture & Society*, 17: 360–83.

5

Linguistic Citizenship as Decoloniality: Teaching Hip Hop Culture at an Historically Black University

Quentin Williams

Introduction

Universities in South Africa are experiencing an extended decolonial moment. Since the student protests in 2015, a complex matrix of power, resources, and politics of agency and voice has been exposed in a country in rapid transformation (Nyamnjoh, 2016; compare Jansen, 2017). Since the early 2000s, South Africa's higher education institutions have undergone significant transformation in shape and size, a recasting of old 'values, goals, and policies' (Kerfoot and Stroud, 2013: 396), incisive interrogation of curriculum content, a growth of the multilingual student demographic, and a renewed focus on the question of languages of teaching, learning and administration. However, not much attention has been paid to the bottom up, everyday contestations of what it means to perform and practise multilingual communication in a decolonial mode in such spaces. Not till recently, under pressure from student protests (Ndlovu, 2018) and other forces, have we seen an accelerated effort to decolonize university spaces in terms of 'what the University does in what it teaches, how it teaches and how it imagines learning might take place within it' (Soudien, 2011: 30).

This chapter contributes to the decolonial project by suggesting that purchase can be gained by framing instances, practices and performances of multilingualism, culture, agency and voice in decolonial spaces in terms of a revised notion of Linguistic Citizenship (Stroud, 2001, 2009; Williams and Stroud, 2015). Linguistic Citizenship, as a decolonial concept, is an approach to the study of multilingualism that highlights the manifold ways multilingual speakers mediate agency and voice. For the purpose of this chapter, Linguistic Citizenship refers to 'disruptive' linguistic engagements with the coloniality of language that involves the expansion or *retooling* of available linguistic resources and implicate language both as a *target* of 'change' and as a *medium*, for example, for social/epistemic transformation. Theorizing Linguistic Citizenship means understanding how new subjectivities and agencies are co-developed in synchrony with new registers and styles of speech. In this chapter, I bring current developments of the notion of Linguistic Citizenship into conversation with decolonial theorists, particularly with Veronelli's (2016) approach to *decolonial communication*. Veronelli makes the point that decoloniality theory has not sufficiently considered the 'communicational impasse' that has resulted from centuries of linguistic coloniality and that has crippled any attempt to establish 'decolonial dialogue' (that is, an honest attempt to cultivate a new register, a new way of talking and a new discourse of Being, in and through language and communication today).

The challenge of writing about language and communication in higher education from the perspective of decoloniality includes how we write about agency, communal voice, the body and new types of practices in decolonial communicative settings. In order for us to go beyond the coloniality of language, we need to bring into conversation the theoretical contribution that Linguistic Citizenship has made to sociolinguistics with that of decolonial theorists. By bringing Veronelli's concept of decolonial communication into close dialogue with Linguistic Citizenship, I argue, some of the lacunae in her notion find closure and that we have a language political tool well suited to further analyse transforming decolonial university spaces. I illustrate the argument with reference to a two-day course on teaching Hip Hop at a historically black university and how a notion of decolonial communication, as seen through the lens of Linguistic Citizenship, advances the rhetorical politics of decoloniality and critically highlights the relational dynamics of racialized and gendered agency and voice.

In what follows, I first lay the groundwork by presenting the key points of Veronelli's decolonial communication and provide a theoretical discussion on why Linguistic Citizenship as a notion is well suited to deal with decolonial communication in transformative contexts of decoloniality. I then move on to discuss the empirical subject of this chapter – teaching Hip Hop at university, analysed as a 'highly stylized' performance (Coupland, 2009), as, on the one hand, a decolonial communicative act and, on the other hand, an act of Linguistic Citizenship. By focusing on such an analysis, I attempt to answer the following question: What does it mean to teach and perform *with* and *through* Hip Hop[1] in order to further the decolonial project of a university space in South Africa? I attempt to answer this by suggesting that teaching Hip Hop culture foregrounds new forms of *relationality* and *interculturality* in decolonized spaces and a vision of new futures that make up the transformative forces necessary to shift the location of agency and voice away from the straightjacket of linguistic colonialities towards decoloniality (Williams and Stroud, 2014: 308). I conclude the chapter with a discussion of the implications of the analysis for designing pedagogies using Hip Hop that consider the multilingual and cultural experiences of multilingual students in decolonizing university spaces.

Linguistic Citizenship as decoloniality

In decolonial South Africa, it is not enough to recognize or affirm the difference and diversity of speakers and repertoires (particularly African mother tongue speakers). To do so simply disregards the problem eloquently noted by Veronelli of the impossibility of dialogue arising out of the coloniality of language that precludes all attempts to establish common ground. Veronelli's (2015, 2016) work is a fundamental critique of the Modernity/Coloniality Research Program and its assumption of transparency of communication. She grounds her argument in a revealing analysis of the violence of the colonial language project which has ramifications for the lack and distortion of dialogue and 'true' meaning exchange among the historically colonized. In Veronelli (2015), she explores the racialization of language and the differences and distinctions colonialism makes between those who have a language with a grammar (the colonizer) and those found difficult to be understood (the colonized), that is, those 'without language'. The colonizer sees the latter as 'simple communicators' using 'simple communication' (2015: 118), where 'simple communication' was equated with conveying 'infantile, primitive meaning expression' (2015: 118). The colonized, the argument went, did not possess the instruments of standardization (though see Meeuwis, 1999) or the intellectual resources to write grammars (for further illustration of this point, see Harries, 2007; Heller and McElhinny, 2017).

Veronelli's point is that simple communication advanced colonial fictions of language and racialized agency and voices as an integral part of the (successful) attempt to dehumanize the colonized. As such, from the inception of colonialism, the colonized existed as 'less than human communicatively' (2015: 118), because 'there are characteristics the colonizers thought colonized peoples had that made them communicatively inferior and their languages not fully languages' (2015: 118). Coloniality used language as a technology to imagine the 'colonized as having no language, that is no Eurocentrically valorized expressivity' (Veronelli, 2015: 119).

In decoloniality, not having a decolonial medium for sufficient dialogue sustains the closure of linguistic agency and voice and suspends the possibility of dialogue in a democratic society such as South Africa. And while coloniality presupposes that language is transparent, Veronelli's notion of decolonial communication suggests otherwise.

Veronelli (2016) comes to her idea of *decolonial communication* via the critical decolonial theory of feminist scholar Maria Lugones and her idea of *deep coalitions* and Edoaurd Glissant's notion of *intercultural relation*. Veronelli brings the two into conversation in an attempt to add to the erosion of discourses of coloniality of power (Quijano, 2000), by promoting a new framing of language and power 'that does not fit into a linear history of paradigms or epistemes' (Veronelli, 2015: 109). Veronelli's (2016) argument in this regard is that because the assumption of dialogue and relationality with the colonized, and in the mind of the colonizer, did not exist, the colonizers did not understand the complexity of communication with, and between, the colonized. The notion of decolonial communication begins the work of undoing and unlearning.

Decolonial communication aims to deconstruct the communicative practices of the colonizer and colonized in favour of a more relational notion of communication. For Veronelli, a relational form of communication is concerned with a feedback loop in communication practices that is not only about the recognition of difference, but about recognizing the variability in how speakers express themselves, but also hear others. Here Glissant's (1997) notion of *Relation* complements a decolonial notion of communication in Veronelli's sense, since it is 'an invitation to resituate ourselves in the sense of not just being differently connected in a complex world, but of being able to express and hear that complexity in terms of echoes' (Veronelli, 2016: 412). On the one hand, Glissant's *Relation* offers Veronelli the rhetorical means to argue for a departure from a monolingual, non-relational form of communication towards a relational idea of communication that recognizes the value of intercultural communication across contexts (Veronelli, 2016: 414–15; compare, for example, Fanon, 1952 and his thoughts on language[2]). Furthering the theorization and practice of decolonial communication requires us to rethink and retheorize language and human agency (or citizenship) as related to relational multilingualisms and egalitarian approaches to multilingual agency and voice (Stroud, 2009, 2018).

It is here that Linguistic Citizenship, built on a similar critique of the disastrous 'territorialisation' inherent in common views of languages as systems distinct from the complex multilingual engagements that have produced them (see Stroud, 2018), can articulate further the decoloniality of language.[3]

From a different beginning, Linguistic Citizenship has gradually evolved independently to encompass a similar understanding of decoloniality. Linguistic Citizenship as a decolonial concept highlights in like manner to Veronelli the way in which the colonial project delinked, abstracted and erased language from the colonized (see Stroud, 2007; compare also Stroud and Guissemo, 2015 for a parallel argument focusing on Mozambique). A hierarchy and discourse of 'racial inferiority' was introduced through colonial language practices, becoming naturalized and later politicized as a given, and further established (and somewhat sanitized) as an integral part of a system of capitalism that benefited largely white colonialists (Mafeje, 1991; Plaatje, 1982). Linguistic Citizenship offers an inroad to a 'process of engagement that opens doors for respectful and deconstructive negotiations around language forms and practices, (to) lay the groundwork for a mutuality and susceptibility to alternative forms of being-together-in-difference' (Stroud, 2018: 37).

In this chapter, I use an embodied and visual example to demonstrate the usefulness of Linguistic Citizenship as a decolonial concept to our endeavour to rethink the coloniality of being and becoming and to fashion new selves in a transformative context. Here the goal is to illustrate how acts of Linguistic Citizenship inform us about the formation of new socialities, not only their lifespan and futurity/utopic dimensions but also the embodied transmodality of new registers of hope, relationality and interculturality.

Recent work by Stroud (2018) and Williams and Stroud (2015) has argued for a transformative approach to language politics that can transcend the paradigm of Linguistic Human Rights (Stroud, 2001). According to Stroud (2018: 18), 'Linguistic Citizenship is fundamentally an invitation to rethink our understanding of language through the lens of citizenship and participatory democracy at the same time that we rethink understandings of citizenship through the lens of language' (compare Stroud and Heugh, 2004). As Stroud puts it: 'Linguistic Citizenship encourages us to critically rethink the notion of "linguistic" as practices that can be known through a variety of discourses and modalities' (2018: 23). The focus is always on acts of Linguistic Citizenship that bring to the fore what 'citizens' do with linguistic and non-linguistic resources as they chart a transformative understanding of their citizenship, ultimately shifting 'the location of agency and voice'. In what way, then, does Linguistic

Citizenship provide purchase for a decolonial project of the rehabilitation of multilingual speakers?

For Stroud, Linguistic Citizenship is already providing the rhetorical means to think language (including multilingualism, agency and voice) differently from 'the colonial construct we continue to struggle with' (Stroud, 2018: 33). As he succinctly puts it:

> Rethinking 'multilingualism' through the lens of Linguistic Citizenship would offer some traction in thinking about new, future, orderings of speakers and languages that go beyond or side step the more familiar affirmative politics of recognition with its dangers of colonial replication. Linguistic Citizenship seeks to interrupt such colonial regimes of language by building an inclusiveness of voice in ways that repair and rejuvenate relationships to self and others. Such rethinking would be cognizant of the historical particularities and context dependencies of different *multilingualisms*.
>
> (2018: 36)

Thus, in ways similar to Veronelli, Stroud sees the disruption and interrogation of linguistic colonial inheritance as a prerequisite for a decoloniality of language. However, unlike Veronelli, the emphasis in Linguistic Citizenship is equally on the emergent *alternative socialities*, the collectivities, or 'citizenships' in the sense of agencies and participatory frameworks, which disruptive linguistic practices give rise to. Linguistic Citizenship in a decolonial communicative mode is about semiotic conditions in which acts of citizenship emerge (Williams and Stroud, 2013), and perhaps importantly it is about the ways in which multilingual speakers define participatory spaces (see Kerfoot, 2011) to realize their acts of Linguistic Citizenship. Importantly, it recognizes that 'semiotic forms other than language contribute to the emergence of agency and voice at local points of production'[4] (Williams and Stroud, 2013: 308). Neither does Linguistic Citizenship see decoloniality as an event or process necessarily taking place in the present moment, but capitalizes on the 'utopian' value in the notion of citizenship itself – utopian in the sense of the philosopher Ernst Bloch as the 'not-yet' but nevertheless 'present' in utterances and actions (cf. Stroud and Williams, 2017). Thus, Linguistic Citizenship seen through a decolonial lens helps us to focus not only on the relationality, multimodality and transmodality of acts of citizenship (and of course multilingualism) – the variety of disruptive and alternative registers (Veronelli, 2015, 2016) – but also on how this simultaneously implicates the distribution of new (and utopian) relations of agency and voice in a way that requires us to think where diversity resides in the linguistic of everyday encounters (cf. Williams and Stroud, 2017: 107).

In what follows, I illustrate a specific instantiation of acts of Linguistic Citizenship as decolonial communication, namely the teaching of Hip Hop culture (what it is and what it comprises of) in higher education contexts (Cervantes and Saldana, 2015). Teaching Hip Hop is about relationality, about love,[5] about chaos in practice and linguistic diversity both in and outside the classroom (Alim and Haupt, 2017: 171; Love, 2016). In other words, teaching Hip Hop is about a comprehensive and inclusive humanism, agency and voice (see KRS-One, *The Gospel of Hip Hop*) and is one instance of how an act of Linguistic Citizenship (as performance) comprising both linguistic and non-linguistic resources contributes to the decolonial project.

Hip Hop education and its benefits for decoloniality

There are four teaching and learning course topics that are taught typically by Hip Hop artists: DJing, rapping, graffiti writing and breakdancing. The fifth course, Knowledge of Self, has theoretical and philosophical teaching and learning aims. Its learning outcomes are tied to a practice of ethics, empathy and sociocultural respect, originating (unsurprisingly) from a critique of colonialism and the pursuit of decolonial forms of communication.

Knowledge of Self was formulated by pioneering Hip Hop artist and creator of the Universal Zulu Nation, Afrika Bambaata, with the vision that such a course could be taught by various Hip Hop communities across former settler colonies around the world (see Haupt, Williams, Alim and Jansen, 2019; KRS-One, 2009). The course began as a Hip Hop event that combined Hip Hop music entertainment and education, known as edutainment (Gosa, 2015: 64). For the Universal Zulu Nation, Knowledge of Self is 'derived from the critical and self-reflective study of anything in the universe, as long as knowledge is deployed towards peace, unity, love and having fun' (Gosa, 2015: 64–5). This definition gave rise to supplementary teaching and learning material outlined in what came to be known as 'The Infinity Lessons'. These lessons allowed Hip Hop artists to teach Hip Hop as a new 'truth' with values tied to the promotion of the anti-racism movement.

Knowledge of Self is about 'the study of Hip Hop culture, music, and elements, alongside an examination of issues within one's surroundings to create positive change in one's community' (Love, 2013: 8, 2016). It is concerned with learning about physical, emotional and psychological self-discipline in Hip Hop and in the real world. It is about enhancing self-knowledge and how personal care unites Hip Hop artists and us all in the face of adversity, violence, poverty, discrimination and power abuse. As Gosa puts it, 'Knowledge of Self' refers 'to the Afro-diasporic mix of spiritual and political consciousness designed to empower members of oppressed groups' (2015: 57). Thus, Knowledge of Self has transformative and relational potential and offers the directions for 'spaces of healing for youth' (Love, 2016: 414), bringing to the centre what it means to possess 'complex personhood' (compare Pardue, 2007: 682–3).

Several current courses on how to teach with and through Hip Hop in the classroom have been pioneered by sociolinguists (including this author), cultural theorists, educationalists and Hip Hop artists (Alim, 2004; Hull and Schultz, 2002; Pennycook, 2007). However, a number of studies to date indicate that most teachers often find Hip Hop culture to be either too marginal and/or transgressive, or not suitable for engaging in or fostering the dialogue and relationality they envisage for their classrooms, despite the fact that their multilingual speakers, born after 1965, have been fully exposed to Hip Hop music and culture (see Yasin, 2009, and most recently, Paris and Alim, 2017; Hill, 2009; Alim, 2004). But many other studies recognize the 'lived curriculum' potential of Hip Hop and the impact it makes on the most vulnerable of young citizens (Dimitriadis, 2009). And they all point out that Hip Hop cultures are well suited for uptake because they are useful to reflect on other types of cultural practices and struggles for agency, voice and citizenship (Low, 2011; Pennycook, 2007: 150, 2005; Petchauer, 2012).

But the very fact that Hip Hop is critical of coloniality, of language and hegemonic forms of self, aside from its inherent pedagogical design, makes it well suited to demonstrate how Linguistic Citizenship appears in its practice and performance. Hip Hop artists' approach to recuperating lost agencies and voices in former settler colonies, the search for truth and empathy and the greater empowerment of the 'less thans' (see Williams, 2018) are indicative of how oppressive societies transform and create new socialities. The manifold transmodal ways in which Hip Hop creates 'empathies' among actors, broader constituencies ('publics') and convivial new socialities with transformative agendas that create new selves suggest that it is a prime site for studying the unfolding of Linguistic Citizenship as a decolonial communicative act.

Teaching Hip Hop culture at a historically black university

In this section of the chapter, I describe and analyse two examples of Linguistic Citizenship as decolonial communication. The data for the analyses forms part of the staging and teaching of Hip Hop at the first Heal the Hood Hip Hop Lecture Series (see Figure 5.1) held at the University of the Western Cape (UWC).

The lecture series was planned and delivered by the author in collaboration with Emile YX? (Heal the Hood), Adam Haupt (Staticphlow) and the Centre for Multilingualism and Diversities Research (CMDR). The teaching of the lectures was performed in conjunction with the Annual Hip Hop Indaba hosted at the Good Hope Centre and the Iconic Lounge. The list of teachers at the lecture series included DJ Ready D, Sipho Sithole, Hemelbesem, Sindiwe Magona, the cast of the Afrikaaps play and academics like H Samy Alim, Adam Haupt and Quentin Williams. The first day of the lecture series was titled 'Knowledge(ing) Your Creative Self: How to Succeed with Hip Hop for the University', and the second day was titled 'A Career in Hip Hop? Why an Education in the Humanities Matters'.

Suffice it to say, UWC is becoming a decolonizing space in the sense of Mignolo (2000): it is a place where knowledge is being produced, and where 'global designs meet local histories, the space in which global designs have to be adapted, adopted rejected, integrated, or ignored' (Mignolo, 2000: ix).

Teaching Hip Hop is to enact a performance comprising 'critical sites for the play of linguistic ideologies about types of people, the varieties they are

Figure 5.1 Poster for Hip Hop lecture series, AHHI.

supposed to speak and the indexical values associated with these varieties' (Lo and Kim, 2012: 258). An additional aspect to such performances is that they are 'highly stylized' (Coupland, 2009); that is, they 'tend to be among the most memorable, repeatable, reflexively accessible forms of discourse' (Bauman, 2005: 149). According to Williams and Stroud, 'performances are key sites for local enactments and depictions of "citizenship" in that they involve "audiences" and thus serve to bridge the private and the parochial to the public' (2013: 294). Importantly, Hip Hop performances often convey voices that are scripted to provide a critical view on the stereotypes, stances and identities formulated in colonialism. In this vein, performances of Hip Hop, as well as the teaching of Hip Hop as (a) performance, 'provide the frameworks of interpretation which people orient to in their everyday lives' (Lo and Kim, 2012: 258). In what follows, I analyse two examples of performance as acts of Linguistic Citizenship and subsequently also as decolonial communication, namely the teaching of breakdancing and graffiti writing.

Teaching knowledge in the body: Breakdancing

The first lecture I analyse here is the teaching performance of breakdancing convened by Emile YX?. After greeting the audience and welcoming everybody to the Hip Hop Lecture Series, Adam Haupt described the learning aims and outcomes of the lectures, providing a broad historical perspective on the themes to be covered. Next, Emile YX?, Cape Hip Hop's most respected breakdancer, began his lecture on the history, art, somatics and performance of breakdancing. The aim of Emile's session was to introduce the audience to (1) what breakdancing is, (2) the art of breakdancing as performed and (3) the philosophical tenets of what it means to live and do breakdancing as a living (see Figure 5.2).[6]

Emile YX? framed his teaching performance by reflecting on his own introduction to the Hip Hop culture, his interest in breakdancing and how he received his breakdance name, Warlock, and the importance of how he was apprenticed into the culture. He also offered a meta-discussion of his long-term engagement as a teacher of Black Consciousness and anti-Apartheid activism. His teaching performance stylized how the body can be pushed to do creative dance moves. By way of example, he illustrated the first breakdance choreographed move he was introduced to, popping and locking his arms. He went on to demonstrate how the body is able to generate new cultural knowledge, new embodied styles in the local Hip Hop culture, for example, in the remixing

Figure 5.2 Emile YX? performing his lecture.

of choreographed Khoi San (indigenous) dance moves with the backslide (or moonwalk), illustrating the corporeal formation of novel and disruptive (dance) registers.

In order to further showcase for the audience exactly how breakdancing is performed, the second part of Emile's lecture involved two breakdancers (otherwise known as break-boys or b-boys to those familiar with the metalinguistic vocabulary of Hip Hop), Malis and Muis (or mouse), core members of Mixed Mense (Mixed People). Before the demonstration, Emile explained how breakdance performers must first introduce themselves on the dance floor, by performing a dance move, and then freezing, 'as you would in gymnastics … you put your hand up and then you gooi (move)'.

For those audience members who were novices and outsiders to the Hip Hop culture and to breakdancing in particular, Emile first described how one performs breakdancing on the dance floor. As he puts it, 'you ride the beat (instrumental)' and become part of it, 'like you go into trance neh', and as a result 'your body becomes the instrument played by the music, neh (ok)?'.

After describing what goes on when listening to the beat, Emile began to co-construct his teaching performance with the two breakdancers on stage, stating:

When you get started that's (pointing to b-boy stance) *top rock*, *six step*, *a move* and *a freeze*, neh. So this is how you introduce yourself into the circle and the idea is that you try to create a ... once you learn the basics you create your own identity, you know. You create something that ... comes from your name or how you behave, you know.

It is at this point that Emile turned to the DJ on stage and asked him to play an instrumental with a beat so that b-boys Malis and Muis could demonstrate the first few basic breakdance moves that lead to a more complex, stylized (individualized) version of Hip Hop breakdancing. As the instrumental plays, Emile directed the students to clap hands and become involved in the performance, showing them how they too can synchronize with the breakdancers and to the timing of the instrumental, exclaiming 'Klap julle hande man! Is ja.' (Man, clap your hands! Oh yeah). In Figure 5.3, we see an illustration of Emile performing his teaching of breakdancing, as well as the two breakdancers performing Khoi San-inspired breakdance choreographed moves.

In Figure 5.3, we see Khoi San dance moves that are remixed into the breakdance choreography of b-boys Malis and Muis. Both performers transform into an indigenous animal as they incorporate traditional dance moves from the Khoi San culture. Figure 5.3 shows how b-boy Malis has overturned b-boy

Figure 5.3 B-boys Malis and Muis performing a Khoi San dance.

Muis to transform into a praying mantis. In this merger of different dance choreographies, the breakdancers enregister (Agha, 2007) characterologically indigenous personae – into capoeira-like signifying characters, such as an animal that rolls around (see Figure 5.3) – to revive an affective cultural praxis lost in the structural noise of settler colonialism. The reason for this is that convergence comes through a process of learning about indigenous Khoi San dance styles and unlearning the rigid dance styles of breakdancing to merge the former style and produce a new form of breakdancing that is firmly in a decolonial context of indigeneity. In so doing, they present to the students a decolonial aesthetics of dance that 'gestures towards creative, desirous futures' and expresses 'an active ongoing refusal of dispossession and erasure' (Recollet, 2016: 93).

Secondly, the breakdancers in these performances bring forward 'what is traditional into futurity' (Recollet, 2016: 94) and in so doing activate 'multiple indigenous scales' (Recollet, 2016: 94) as each gesture, move, and position reaches back into history and into the future to present a new discourse of hope (Recollet, 2016: 100), a hope that helps us make sense of the present. Thus, in this example, the students are taught a form of embodied decolonial communication that feeds potentially into acts of Linguistic Citizenship and that ultimately gestures towards, on the one hand, the *indigenous future* (following Recollet, 2016) of Khoi San rituals through the remixing of breakdance, but also, on the other hand, a rethinking and re-enunciation of how indigenous bodies have previously been minimized through misunderstanding of ritualized forms of dance.

In other words, in the remixing of 'registers' of Hip Hop breakdancing and the linking with indigenous knowledge and practice, Emile and the breakdancers 'intervene in settler colonialism's disappearances and erasures' (Recollet, 2016: 91), through the transformational and relational potential of teaching that enables a critique of the colonial corporeal regime. Here Hip Hop's appropriation of indigenous signs sows the potential for new acts of Linguistic Citizenship and decolonial communication. The hope and intention are that indigenous acts of Linguistic Citizenship become a defining feature of decoloniality, and not just a critical stance against colonialism.

Linguistic Citizenship comes even clearer to the fore when Emile lectures on what the students are able to learn from Knowledge of Self. For Emile, teaching Hip Hop is about wrestling with how a subjective sense of self, as racialized and marginalized historically through the colonial knowledge of being, can push individuals to not only the 'internalization of Knowledge of Self' but towards a collective understanding of Hip Hop community and solidarity (Gaztambide-Fernandez, 2012).

Emile argues that teaching Hip Hop as a breakdancer persuaded him to become as 'organized as the government', and when, on one occasion, he received the opportunity to bring the course content of the culture into the classroom, he 'started teaching the *laaities* (children) some of the raps' which in turn inspired him to write a song for them entitled 'A Day After', a song about global warming. This form of teaching and reflexivity through Hip Hop is what Cervantes and Saldana (2015) define as a 'decolonial pedagogical praxis' – in other words, to 'critique and expose domination and consciously aim to dismantle neo-colonial designs, create lyrical and musical spaces for epistemological resistance and decolonial praxis' (2015: 89). In this sense, Emile and his fellow co-creators of embodied breakdance moves stylize the body socioculturally (coming into contact with Khoi San cultural dance and rituals) to present new and alternative ways to reimagine dance and resist highly racialized colonial constructs of embodiment. Of course, this is the design of Hip Hop culture: to resist with the body but to celebrate with the body and to highlight bodily movements and dance which have been invisibilized by racialization since colonialism.

Towards the end of his lecture Emile informed the students that if they also take the philosophical side of Hip Hop seriously, that is Knowledge of Self, then they would be successful at the 'internalization' of content (knowledge). The central point of Emile's argument here is that teaching Hip Hop is just not about knowing *about* the culture alone, but to be knowledgeable *in/with* the culture, because 'it's one thing to have the knowledge it's another thing to make it a part of your life, neh'. He illustrated this point with the following example: the breakdancer, he says, 'contributes bloody shoulders and actual physical pain' and this should be 'proof (of) your dedication'. Here we see a clear link to Linguistic Citizenship as what Emile says about the body ties into an alter-ontology where the emphasis is on new socialities, new selves and new epistemes.

Throughout his lecture, Emile went beyond merely teaching breakdancing in order to wrestle with a subjective sense of self that sought to move beyond colonial communicative orders and towards an emancipatory idea of agency and voice. The emphasis on sociocultural embodiment is crucial. In other words, the cross-cultural relations in interactions are crucial to the everyday performance of decolonial communication as an act of Linguistic Citizenship. Emile's teachings link to an alternative notion of knowledge, that is, 'diversity of thought' (Stroud, 2015: 34), which suggests a renewed effort is possible when we seek to cultivate participatory spaces in decolonial universities. To that end, he (and others during the course) advocated for a participatory space where the audience could act equally and truly engage diversity of thought, recognizing that spaces are never 'neither neutral nor separable from other spaces of association, whether domestic, spiritual or occupational' (see Kerfoot, 2011). In other words, what you learn in one place, you transfer to another. Significantly in this case, participatory spaces also provide for the conditions for decolonial communication and as such for acts of Linguistic Citizenship to be realized. The co-authoring of such a space, if only temporary, points to the decolonial potential of teaching in decolonial university classrooms and rethinking of pedagogy to sustain an intersectional practice of bodies and cultures in welcoming Linguistic Citizenship spaces.

Thus, Emile's stylization of his teaching of breakdancing is ultimately an attempt to urge the students in the audience and his fellow Hip Hop artists to consider teaching Hip Hop as a medium to manage 'linguistically mediated diversity' and as a mode of relational engagement that connects with 'the ways in which the humanity of each of us depends on respectful recognition of, and engagement with, the linguistically mediated humanity of others' (Stroud, 2015: 35). Emile's performance suggests a type of Linguistic Citizenship as decolonial communication that urges the internalization of knowledge so that the audience can think critically of ways to shift the location of agency and voice through the enactment/embodiment of the value of intercultural relations. His emphasis on Knowledge of Self in this case is designed not only to acknowledge the early structure of edutainment advocated by Afrika Bambaata, but to adhere to the early cultural principals of Hip Hop culture more strictly. As such, he enunciates Knowledge of Self as a prescription not to realize decolonial linguistic agency and voice, but to highlight acts of Linguistic Citizenship as relationally tied to decolonial diversity ethics and virtues and values of humanism. Hip Hop is about performing decoloniality and reopening the closures on agency and voice brought about by colonialism, and bringing about awareness of exclusions. In this regard, Emile's focus is a form of decolonial communication as an embodied act of Linguistic Citizenship.

Teaching graffiti writing: A decolonial gesture

Returning to the points made by Veronelli on how decolonial communication is only possible once the speaker removes himself or herself from the strictures of language (as we know it) and Stroud's observation that much of agency finds articulation through a variety of multi/transmodal semiotics, it is reasonable to claim that a decolonial *locus of enunciation* is best seen as transmodal. Decoloniality, and by extension decolonial communication, is about recognizing that it is the coming together of knowledges and genres in affiliative co-constitution that makes for meaningful decolonial events. Graffiti is one of the constitutive genres of a transmodal expression of decoloniality. Graffiti is generally writing with invisible authors. Graffiti artists are the unseen authors whose representational choices in visualizing Hip Hop and other cultural communities are framed by a graffiti writing register that is only learned when Hip Hop artists are apprenticed into the culture. Again, the decoloniality of graffiti communication resides in going beyond 'conventional' languages with their historical baggage of coloniality and within a new affiliative sociality across which meaning unfolds through resemiotizing acts of Linguistic Citizenship (Stroud, 2001, 2018; Veronelli, 2015/16). In the context of this chapter, graffiti writing constitutes a decolonial gesture (Mignolo, 2014).

Mignolo (2014) recently analysed several graffiti art types that he defines as 'gestures of protest' which arose, on the one hand, out of a social transforming context of radical contestation and, on the other hand, out of a community where the meaning of graffiti is attached to a representational politics that is not necessarily radical or direct. He compares graffiti in Cairo and Tunisia to San Antonio (California) and surmises that the graffiti painted in Cairo and Tunisia, as protest art, form part of a larger social phenomena and reflect (1) 'implied body gestures (the movements of the hands) and the sensations of the entire body, the anger and the anguish, the indignation and the humor needed to deal with the absurdity of the situation'; and (2) the 'non-fictional as they are fictional gestures and visual outcomes'. Comparatively, in San Antonio, the graffiti 'celebrates the deeds and memories of the Chicano and Chicana community' and is 'gestures of community building'. Mignolo goes on to say that they 'make visible the sensibility and the inegalitarian conditions of the Chicano/a nation within a state controlled by the imaginary of an Anglo/a nation'.

Mignolo's (2014) analysis of graffiti in Cairo, Tunisia and San Antonio leads to the question of whether protest graffiti and celebratory-memorializing graffiti are '*decolonial* gestures?' He argues that a first consideration is whether they fit the definition of decolonial in terms of the situated location from where those who argue for decolonization define the locus of enunciation. As he points out:

> This is a general rule of interpretation. To talk about 'cubist painting' will depend on the meaning the interpreter assigns to 'cubism' in relation to the painting. Reversing the direction, if an artist is aware that 'cubism' provides a conceptual structure for a tendency in the world of art, the artist herself could shape her work in conversation with such frame. The same reasoning is valid, in my view, for the expression 'decolonial gestures'.

Decolonial gestures index the path of transformation towards a future where spaces in transformation transcend differences for commonality and where (in this case graffiti) the visual world more accurately and perhaps more honestly reflects our lived reality free from injurious discourses. This form of gesture is also critical of identity exceptionalism in a world where dignity in diversity supersedes the neocolonial fractures and attenuates such discontents today.

This brings us to the performance of the third lecture taught and stylized by pioneering graffiti artist, Mak1One, with the assistance of graffiti artist, Sergio. Mak1One began the teaching of graffiti by first reflecting on his own apprenticeship in the culture. He stylized his teaching performance in this way to locate himself in the history of graffiti in South Africa since he is one of the pioneering figures. He thereby carefully prepared his location of enunciation. From that location, he began to co-perform a highly stylized interaction between himself and Sergio by teaching the audience that, besides knowing how to write (to be literate), the graffiti artist needs the following tools: spray can, a colour scheme in the mind and a developed, 'idiosyncratic' style. And before Sergio began painting the canvas with a graffiti piece, Mak1One informed the student audience that his co-performer would paint the theme in his lecture.

A clear picture emerges from the trace in the collage in Figure 5.4: here the graffiti piece is a celebration of Hip Hop (the words not in the shot) and the head of Mak1One as one of the Hip Hop heads (long-term members, pioneering in his case) of the culture. What is striking about the stylization of his teaching performance is that his lecture is based on a type of multimodal and creative interaction that does not directly involve the student audience in the production

Figure 5.4 Graffiti artist Sergio (seated on the floor) starts to draw.

Figure 5.5 Mak1One (standing) narrates over drawing.

Figure 5.6 Finished Graffiti drawing by artist Sergio and Mak1One.

of the piece but allows them to share in the possible interpretations that could be assigned – as the piece was developing. Halfway through the lecture (see Figures 5.5 and 5.6), it becomes clear that something new is emerging. While most audience members thought the graffiti was only a piece about Mak1One, yet as he narrated his apprenticeship in Hip Hop, he connects this to the art of writing (as he elaborates in the below extract). It was also apparent that his co-constructed performance provided the pedagogical tools, and indeed the conceptual structure, to engage in a type of decolonial communication that centred the focus on the agency and voice of the artist. This much Mak1One makes clear when he explains how he paints, why he paints and the resources he draws on to paint graffiti pieces:

> I'm really good at doing this lettering and doing what nots and learning about information. It's not copied information and it's not out of a book. I'm not saying this is what I wanna do or learn because I respect learning about Knowledge of Self … so all this stuff is learnt, that's going on paintings trials and errors cause everyone says paint your name (makes painting gestures) and everyone says my name I can spell what else can I do

In a decolonial context, such narratives of art offer insight into graffiti as a literacy form and what goes into the authenticity and maintenance of Hip Hop culture (see also MacDonald, 2001). For the individual Hip Hop artist, graffiti writing is about conveying, through various developed styles, the history, biography and repertoires of the Hip Hop community while also conveying her/his individual cognitive and social experiences of that community. The goal of graffiti writing as such is not only to simply write on a wall to convey artistic flair, but it is about the transmission of how to do graffiti writing and to engage in graffiti writing as a literacy event and practice and to preserve the aesthetics and authenticity of what is after all graffiti literacy. In the local Hip Hop community, to engage in graffiti literacy events and practise is to continuously introduce new styles of graffiti writing practices and as such sustain what is best in Hip Hop culture.

The themes of the lecture are linked to an understanding of decolonial communication as a visual semiotic act of Linguistic Citizenship, designed as a visual dialogue between Sergio and Mak1One, and the audience. The graffiti writing Sergio performed and the verbal content conveyed by Mak1One constitute a performance of decoloniality that brings into view what it takes to act out Linguistic Citizenship visually. Firstly, the graffiti gesture can be seen as a visual semiotics of Linguistic Citizenship that gives due consideration not only to cultural and linguistic biography (in the sense of how Mak1One and Sergio performed it), but also to optically establish agency and voice in the interpersonal and the multivocality it draws from multiple publics. Secondly, graffiti seen as the visual dimension of Hip Hop shows the transmodal and resemiotized kernel of acts of Linguistic Citizenship as decolonial communication. In the analysis above, Mak1One and Sergio demonstrate how the potential of narrative and the multimodal painting of a graffiti piece combine to create transmodality and as a result may help us understand how the speaker visually represents acts of Linguistic Citizenship as decolonial communication. Thirdly, the decolonial gesture by Mak1One and Sergio challenges our perceptions of Hip Hop culture in general and the participants' creative, multimodal practices specifically. In other words, to focus on multimodal painting limits visual possibilities, and as a result a fusing of narrative and other embodied practices is necessary for a movement towards transmodality. In the stylization of their performance of graffiti, they opened up a space of decolonial possibility for understanding the agency and voice of subjects historically concealed by colonialism. This space of possibility makes linguistic, social and cultural interruptions possible, a not-yet future where new forms of emancipatory agencies and voices have yet to be realized. In this regard, Mak1One and Sergio's teaching takes a critical stance against monolithic and monolingual discourses that seek new forms of language-ing crucial for decolonial communication.

An approach to decolonial communication as a visual semiotic act of Linguistic Citizenship additionally breaks down visual dichotomies to the extent that it helps us with how to read the cultural and linguistic trajectories of communities in various places and spaces across the world. In particular, graffiti as decolonial gesture indexes how individuals and communities may tend to feel in and out of place and provide key indicators 'to any sense of belonging, agency and participation' (Stroud and Jegels, 2014). This is another core feature of Linguistic Citizenship as a decolonial concept.

Conclusions

In this chapter, I have explored what it means to teach with and through Hip Hop at a university currently undergoing decolonization. The main premise of the chapter was to demonstrate the decolonial, analytical utility of the notion Linguistic Citizenship and how it is well suited to analyse decoloniality in South Africa, and how it could enter into conversation with decoloniality theorists, in particular with Veronelli (2016). In this regard, Linguistic Citizenship functioned as a decolonial lens to look at 'highly stylized' teaching performances as forms of decolonial communication.

I have argued that Linguistic Citizenship is a useful notion to frame a decolonial perspective on language and multilingualism in ways that address some of the concerns, together with Veronelli's perspective on decolonial communication.

Linguistic Citizenship is about how multilingual speakers' agency is constituted through non-institutional means where language negotiations are transgressive and central to the creation of a (new) normative order of (local) voices. Linguistic Citizenship helps us to ask questions about the scale, mobility and resourcing of alternative and new forms of agency and voice in decolonial contexts; about the semiotics of space; about new types of interactions tied to new aspirations and lifestyles. For example, I have demonstrated how Emile and his co-breakdancers bring into action diversity through the incorporation of a multitude of dance moves. By doing so, they show the decolonial 'productivity' in the sense of voices and senses that emerge out of such participatory spaces and produce new knowledge of 'Self' and 'Other' – an indication of what a decolonial higher education might look like. In the case of Mak1One and Sergio and their graffiti painting, the potential of acts of Linguistic Citizenship are evident in the choices they make in creating the painting and what it suggests of a future of diversity and relationality; that is in itself is a decolonial gesture.

Furthermore, the analysis of teaching Hip Hop provides us with useful indicators as to how to further conduct research on decolonial communication as acts of Linguistic Citizenship. It suggests that there is pedagogical potential in furthering research on Linguistic Citizenship as decoloniality in the university context. In this respect, the data analysed suggests that Hip Hop is good for advancing not only the decolonial agenda of indigeneity, local knowledge, but also alternative futures of languages and language-ing – important aspects for multilingual participants in decolonial spaces. A decolonial university space and classroom, that seriously considers decolonial communication, challenges the dominant narrative and framework and also challenges colonial privileging (see Milu, 2018). Here Linguistic Citizenship could be a useful armour against remains of colonialism and Apartheid in present-day South Africa. On the other hand, Linguistic Citizenship also seeks to sustain cultural pedagogy (following Alim and Haupt, 2017) and an ethics of care (Stroud, 2018). The analysis of teaching Hip Hop in this respect – whether it is about bringing corporeal regimes into contact, about more gender participation in a patriarchal system or about painting decoloniality – suggests that what Linguistic Citizenship as decoloniality seeks to sustain is the continued 'retrieval of voice' (Nascimento, 2018: 229).

Notes

1   Hip Hop is defined as a cultural way of life and is defined by five elements: rapping, graffiti writing, deejaying, b-boying and b-girling with Knowledge of Self as the most important one.

2   Fanon's perspective on the coloniality of language is a familiar one to sociolinguists. In his seminal book, *Black Skin, White Masks*, his chapter on the black man's language concerns the problem of assimilation into a colonial language. But it is also about the existential and psychological issues that underline how uncouth, uncivilized speakers – so portrayed by the colonizers – take a stance against civilizing, hegemonic languages such as French (following his description). For Fanon, the consequence of language contact and mobility and having a healthy contempt for speaking dialect are indicators not only of a relational idea of communication, but also of what is ultimately an ontological shift in a multilingual self of the colonized.

3   In the South African context, a precondition for a settler colony was a racist colony of slaves, later to transform into a racialized capitalism on the abolition of slavery, much to the benefit of the colonizers and 'Apartheid racial technicians' (Willoughby-Herard, 2015). Willoughby-Herard's insightful study on the Carnegie *Poor White Study* in South Africa reinforces the point I am trying to make: the linguistic violence of colonialism has been so immense in former settler colonies such as South Africa that today whatever remains of what we perceive to be multilingual dialogue in the everyday life of institutions is under incessant pressure by discourses of colonialism and Apartheid. Rather vexingly, true dialogue is often suspended.

4   A similar point is raised by Veronelli who emphasizes that 'emotionalities' have more or the same effect in much the same way as non-propositional language use.

5   This is an implicit reference point in Linguistic Citizenship study where an emphasis on conditionality of empathy and love is a communal feature of the design of encounters of conviviality and the establishing of friendship (see Stroud, 2018).

6   Acknowledgements to the artist, Julia Davies, for the line drawings in this chapter.

References

Agha, A. (2007), *Language and Social Relations*. Cambridge: Cambridge University Press.

Alim, H. S. (2004), *You know My Steez: An Ethnographic and Sociolinguistic Study of Styleshifting in a Black American Speech Community*, Book 89, Durham, NC, and London: Duke University Press.

Alim, H. S. and A. Haupt (2017), 'Reviving Soul(s) with Afrikaaps: Hip Hop as Culturally Sustaining Pedagogy in Cape Town, South Africa', in D. Paris, H. S. (ed.), *Cultural Sustaining Pedagogies: Teaching and Learning for Justice in a Changing World*, 157–74. New York and London: Teachers College Press.

Bauman, R. (2005), 'Commentary: Indirect Indexicality, Identity, Performance, Dialogic Observations', *Journal of Linguistic Anthropology*, 15 (1): 145–50.

Cervantes, M. A. and L. P. Saldana (2015), 'Hip Hop and *neuva concion* as Decolonial Pedagogies of Epistemic Justice', *Decolonization: Indigeneity, Education & Society*, 4 (1): 84–108.
Coupland, M. (2009), *Style: Language Variation and Identity*. Cambridge: Cambridge University Press.
Dimitriadis, G. (2009), *Performing Identity/Performing Culture: Hip Hop as Text Pedagogy, and Lived Practice*, revised edn. New York: Peter Lang.
Fanon, F. (1952), *Black Skin, White Masks*. New York: Grove Press.
Gaztambide-Fernandez, R.A. (2012), 'Decolonization and the Pedagogy of Solidarity', *Decolonization: Indigeneity, Education & Society*, 1 (1): 41–67.
Glissant, E. (1997), *Poetics of Relation*. Ann Arbor, MI: University of Michigan Press.
Gosa, T. L. (2015), 'The Fifth Element: Knowledge', in J. Williams (ed.), *The Cambridge Companion to Hip Hop*, 56–70. Cambridge: Cambridge University Press.
Harries, P. (2007), *Butterflies & Barbarians: Swiss Missionaries & Systems of Knowledge in Southern Africa*. Ohio: Ohio University Press.
Haupt, A. Q. Williams, H. Samy Alim and Emile Jansen, eds (2019), *Neva Again: Hip Hop Art, Activism and Education in post-Apartheid South Africa*. Cape Town: HSRC Press.
Heller, M. and B. McElhinny 2017. *Language, Capitalism and Colonialism: Toward a Critical History*. Toronto: University of Toronto Press.
Hill, M. L. (2009), *Beats, Rhymes, and Classroom Life: Hip Hop Pedagogies and the Politics of Identity*. New York: Teachers College Press.
Hull, G. and K. Schultz, eds (2002), *School's Out! Bridging Out-of-School Literacies with Classroom Practice*. New York, NY: Teachers College Press.
Jansen, J. (2017), *As by Fire: The End of the South African University*. Cape Town: Tafelberg.
Kerfoot, C. (2011), 'Making and Shaping Participatory Spaces: Resemiotization and Citizenship Agency in South Africa', *International Multilingual Research Journal*, 5 (2): 87–102.
Kerfoot, C. and C. Stroud (2013), 'Towards Rethinking Multilingualism and Language Policy for Academic Literacies', *Linguistics and Education*, 24 (4): 396–405.
KRS-One (2009), *The Gospel of Hip Hop: First Instrument*. New York: Power House Books.
Lo, A. and J. C. Kim (2012), 'Linguistic Competency and Citizenship: Contrasting Portraits of Multilingualism in the South Korean Public Media', *Journal of Sociolinguistics*, 16: 255–76.
Love, B. L. (2013), '"Oh, they're sending a bad message": Black Males Resisting and Challenging Eurocentric Notions of Blackness within Hip Hop and the Mass Media through Critical Pedagogy', *International Journal of Critical Pedagogy*, 4 (3): 24–39.
Love, B. L. (2016), 'Complex Personhood of Hip Hop and the Sensibilities of the Culture That Fosters Knowledge of Self and Self-Determination', *Equity & Excellence in Education*, 49 (4): 414–27.

Low, B. E. (2011), *Slam School: Learning through Conflict in the Hip Hop and Spoken Word Classroom*. Stanford, CA: Stanford University Press.

Macdonald, N. (2001), *The Graffiti Subculture: Youth, Masculinity, and identity in London and New York*. London: Palgrave Macmillan.

Mafeje, A. (1991), *The Theory and Ethnography of African Social Formations: The Case of the Interlacustrine Kingdoms*. London: CODESA.

Meeuwis, M. (1999), 'The White Fathers of Luganda. To the Origins of French Missionary Linguistics in Lake Victoria Region', *Annales Aequatoria*, 20: 413–43.

Mignolo, W. (2000), *Local Histories/Global Designs: Coloniality, Subaltern Knowledges, and Border Thinking*. Princeton, NJ: Princeton University Press.

Mignolo, W. (2014), 'Graffiti as a Decolonial Gesture', Special issue on decolonia gesture e-misferica, 11: 1. Available online: https://hemisphericinstitute.org/en/emisferica-11-1-decolonial-gesture/11-1-essays/looking-for-the-meaning-of-decolonial-gesture.html (accessed 31 December 2019).

Milu, E. (2018), 'Translingualism, Kenyan Hip Hop and Emergent Ethnicities: Implications for Language Theory and Pedagogy', *International Multilingualism Research Journal*, 12 (2): 96–108.

Nascimento, A. M. D. (2018), 'Counter-Hegemonic Linguistic Ideologies and Practices in Brazilian Indigenous Rap', in A. S. Ross and D. J. Rivers (eds), *The Sociolinguistics of Hip Hop as Critical Conscience: Dissatisfaction and Dissent*, 213–36. London: Palgrave Macmillan.

Ndlovu, M. W. (2018), *#FeesMustFall and Youth Mobilisation in South Africa: Reform or Resolution?* London: Routledge.

Nyamnjoh, F. (2016), *#RhodesMustFall: Nibbling at Resilient Colonialism in South Africa*. Oxford: African Books Collective.

Pardue, D. (2007), 'Hip Hop as Pedagogy: A Look into "Heaven" and "Soul" São Paulo, Brazil', *Anthropological Quarterly*, 80 (3): 673–709.

Paris, D. and H. S. Alim, eds (2017), *Culturally Sustaining Pedagogies: Teaching and Learning for Justice in a Changing World*. New York and London: Teachers College Press.

Pennycook, A. (2005), 'Teaching the Flow: Fixity and Fluidity in Education', *Asia Pacific Journal of Education*, 25 (1): 29–43.

Pennycook, A. (2007), *Global Englishes and Transcultural Flows*. London: Routledge.

Petchauer, E. (2012), *Hip Hop Culture in College Students' Lives: Elements, Embodiment, and Higher Edutainment*. London: Routledge.

Plaatje, S. (1982), *Native Life in South Africa: Before and since the European War and the Boer Rebellion*. Johannesburg: Raven Press.

Quijano, A. (2000), 'Coloniality of Power, Eurocentrism, and Latin America', *Neplanta*, 1 (3): 533–80.

Recollet, K. (2016), 'Gesturing Indigenous Futurities through the Remix', *Dance Research Journal*, 48 (1): 91–105.

Soudien, C. (2011), 'The Arhythmic Pulse of Transformation in South African Higher Education', *Alternation*, 18 (2): 15–34.

Stroud, C. (2001), 'African Mother Tongue Programs and the Politics of Language: Linguistic Citizenship versus Linguistic Human Rights', *Journal of Multilingual and Multicultural Development*, 22 (4): 339–55.

Stroud, C. (2007), 'Bilingualism: Colonialism and Postcolonialism', in M. Heller (ed.), *Bilingualism: A Social Approach*, 25–49. Basingstoke: Palgrave Macmillan.

Stroud, C. (2009), 'A Postliberal Critique of Language Rights: Toward a Politics of Language for a Linguistics of Contact', in John E. Petrovic (ed.), *International Perspectives on Bilingual Education: Policy, Practice and Controversy*, 191–218. Charlotte: Information Age Publishing.

Stroud, C. (2009), 'Towards a Postliberal Theory of Citizenship', in J. E. Petrovic (ed.), *International Perspectives on Bilingual Education: Policy, Practice and Controversy*, 191–218, New York: Information Age Publishing.

Stroud, C. (2015), 'Dignity in Diversity: Turbulent Approaches to Linguistic Citizenship', keynote address delivered at the Sociolinguistics of Globalization: (De)Centering and (Re)Standardization, Hong-Kong.

Stroud, C. (2018), 'Linguistic Citizenship', in L. Lim, C. Stroud and L. Wee (eds), *The Multilingual Citizen. Towards a Politics of Language for Agency and Change*, 17–39. Clevedon: Multilingual Matters.

Stroud, C. and K. Heugh (2004), 'Linguistic Human Rights and Linguistic Citizenship', in D. Patrick and J. Freeland (eds), *Language Rights and Language Survival: A Sociolinguistic Exploration*, 191–218. Manchester: St Jerome.

Stroud, C. and M. Guissemo (2015), 'Linguistic Messianism', *Multilingual Margins*, 2 (2): 6–19.

Stroud, C. and D. Jegels. (2014), 'Semiotic Landscapes and Mobile Narrations of Place: Performing the Local', *International Journal of the Sociology of Language*, 2014 (228): 179–99.

Veronelli, G. (2015), 'The Coloniality of Language: Race, Expressivity, Power, and the Darker Side of Modernity', *Waguda*, 13: 108–34.

Veronelli, G. (2016), 'A Coalitional Approach to Theorizing Decolonial Communication', *Hypatia*, 31 (2): 401–520.

Williams, Q. (2018), 'Multilingual Activism in South African Hip Hop', *Journal of World Popular Music*, 5 (1): 31–49.

Williams, Q. and C. Stroud (2013), 'Multilingualism in Transformative Spaces: Contact and Conviviality', *Language Policy*, 12: 289–311.

Williams, Q. and C. Stroud. (2015), 'Linguistic Citizenship: Language and Politics in Postnational Modernities', *Journal of Language and Politics*, 14 (3): 406–430.

Williams, Q. and C. Stroud (2017), 'Linguistic Citizenship: Language and Politics in Postnational Modernities', in T. Milani (ed.), *Language and Citizenship: Broadening the Agenda*, 89–112. Amsterdam: Johns Benjamins Publishing Company.

Willoughby-Herard, T. (2015), *Waste of a White Skin: The Carnegie Corporation and the Racial Logic of White Vulnerability*. Los Angeles: University of California Press.

Yasin, J. A. (2009), 'Rockin' the Classroom: Using Hip Hop as an Educational Tool', in J.-A. Kleifjen and G. Bond (eds), *The Languages of African and Diaspora: Eliciting for Language Awareness*, 270–86. Clevedon: Multilingual Matters.

6

Teaching Modern South African History in the Aftermath of the Marikana Massacre: A Multimodal Pedagogy for Critical Citizenship

Marijke du Toit

Introduction

What are the possibilities of teaching modern South African history to the country's 'born free' generation during the ongoing crisis of our constitutional democracy? How could my students be prompted to explore South African history as if it mattered to them, personally? These were questions that emerged while I was teaching a semester-long course to third years at the University of KwaZulu-Natal (UKZN) in Durban, South Africa's largest east-coast city. My classes typically had a number of black students, most of whom were from isiZulu-speaking backgrounds, others from KwaZulu-Natal's diasporic Indian community. There were also a few white students with English or, like me, Afrikaans settler ancestries. How could I draw them into inquisitive engagement with contemporary political events and social dynamics, while also learning how to engage critically with narratives of South African history? From 2011 to 2014, tumultuous years of post-Apartheid history, I grappled with these questions.

In this chapter, I discuss key elements of the teaching experiment that resulted. I discuss a multimodal pedagogy designed to place questions of critical and multilingual citizenship at the centre of a course in modern South African history. How did this effort cohere with ideas of 'decolonial' pedagogy? The course moved beyond the conventional approach of introducing students to a canon of scholarly texts. Much of what we read were, arguably, typical of many long-established courses in modern South African history: students were introduced to radical (historical materialist and feminist) arguments about the making of modern South Africa that explored white racism, capitalist exploitation, the politics of an emerging black proletariat and the 'ambiguities of dependence' that characterized early black nationalist leadership. Crucially, however, students were not only expected to engage with historians' writings about segregation and Apartheid. This was a course that sought to present questions about 'who, when, where, why and for whom knowledge' is 'generated' (Mignolo, 2009: 2) while it invited students to grapple with the complex roots and 'unsettled histories' of contemporary injustices (Witz, Minkley and Rassool, 2017). The experiments in multimodal, multilingual and interlingual reading that I discuss here suggest some of the ways in which teaching history can involve interruption of a linguistic status quo, thus also opening up new possibilities of 'Linguistic Citizenship' (Stroud, 2018: 18). This was an approach that drew students into collaborative analysis of various modalities of archival texts, even when they were being asked to engage with an argument between academic historians. A key element of the course's transformative potential was its juxtaposition of archival texts of settler photography and the canon of (white-dominated) scholarly publications with examples of African self-representation through various means. The introduction of texts from multilingual and African, indigenous language newspapers, assertive of the creation of a black public sphere in the early years of segregationist rule proved particularly important. Students were invited to consider their own relationships with available pasts through inquisitive engagement with various modalities of text and imaginative participation in acts of analysis. At the same time, relationships of power in the traditionally English-dominant classroom began to be questioned. As Stroud has argued, experimenting with ideas of Linguistic Citizenship may help open up a space 'where senses of self may be juxtaposed and refashioned as part of the deconstruction of dominant voices and more equitable linguistic engagement with others' (Stroud, 2018: 18).

    The cracks in the dream of freedom after Apartheid opened up with particular starkness some three weeks after the start of class in 2012. On the morning of 16 August, I presented a lecture about the white mineworkers' revolt that took place in the Witwatersrand region in 1922 – the miners fought in defence of racially discriminatory job reservation on Johannesburg's gold mines. I discussed not only the work of historians who emphasized how 'militantly racist workers' had assaulted 'African working-class peers', but also (to the disbelief of some students) showed photographs of the planes used by the government to bomb white working-class suburbs in order to subdue the strike (Breckenridge, 2007; Callinicos, 1987; Krikler, 2005). As we discovered afterwards, this was exactly the same time of day (on 16 August 2012) that thirty-four striking mineworkers were gunned down by a South African police tactical response unit at the Lonmin platinum mine at Marikana in the country's North-West Province.[1] The following week, my effort to make sense of current events (I did this by incorporating explicit discussion of the events at Marikana into my lecture on the history of black trade unions from early to late Apartheid) took place in the context of violent conflict at my university. Student demonstrations, usually focused on financial and academic exclusions, had become almost a regular occurrence over several years. More recently, police response had become harsher and protests more volatile. My students had chosen to continue the class behind locked doors (because a minority of students sometimes forcibly disrupted the class). On this particular afternoon, our discussion paused whenever demonstrating students hammered loudly on the door. We stopped when police shot teargas and chased students past our second-floor windows from where we had a bird's eye view. As we waited for a quiet moment so that students could slip away safely, I discussed essay topics.

Indeed, even as I had sought to draw students into various, multimodal and multilingual activities of critical reading, the status quo of academic authorship and author-ity had largely been maintained. The first version of the class incorporated much of what is discussed in this chapter, particularly the discussion of photographic, personal and artistic portraiture and multilingual, textual analysis. At the same time, however, written assignments focused on these activities were followed by a major class assignment in the form of a conventional essay on scholarly writing. Students wrote sit-down examinations at the end of the course. Political events also now prompted me to confront the shortcomings of assessment that still foregrounded students' grasp of relevant historiography. The contemporary moment of post-Apartheid South African politics was forcing us to reconsider the relationship between past and present and was literally intruding into our classroom. It was only by involving students in explicit efforts to grapple with contemporary politics and the relationship between past and present that the structural contradictions inherent in this approach to assessing South African history in the post-Apartheid could be resolved. In the following year, students were no longer given conventional essay topics or examinations. Instead, each student worked on a research project, which was presented as a website. The focus was on contemporary controversies about constitutional rights, placed in historical perspective. Critical citizenship was thus placed at the centre of an approach that invited students to consider their own relationships with available pasts and to draw on a range of resources to do research-directed writing and analysis.

Course design and structure

From the outset, students were alerted to the focus of the course: on current controversies about constitutional rights. The course started with a focus on the political contestation involved in the making of South Africa's current constitution, particularly through showing the documentary film *The Deadline*. An explicit, interrogative interrelationship between past and present structured course activities. In the first six weeks, students completed several written tutorial assignments. Every two weeks or so, historiographic debate on a particular theme in South African history, more or less chronologically arranged, was introduced. Thus the first discussions about 'history and memory' were followed by a focus on land and segregation, the politics of early twentieth-century African elites, worker struggles, and gender and racial segregation. For each thematic focus students completed a 'guided reading assignment' that required close reading of relevant historiography. In the first term a few of these were also paired with assignments that required analysis of a selection of archival extracts (photographs and newspaper articles).

The approach to working with internet-based resources and the choice to have students create portfolio-style research projects, published in the form of websites, drew strongly on several years of teaching courses as part of a degree in Internet Studies, offered by the History Department at UKZN. These had been undergraduate, strongly research-focused courses that combined interrogation of the history and politics of digital with online technologies.[2] Students participated in practicals that assisted them with presenting their projects as websites. The version of the course that I taught from 2014 drew on an approach that I had developed in that context (Du Toit, 2016a). It aimed at involving students in systematic analysis of internet-based texts and integrated a scaffolded approach towards research and writing with the creation of websites. From the start, online resources suggested wide-ranging possible topics to students. These reflected the way black farmworkers and landless tenants, workers on the mines, women living in former Bantustans or homelands or residents of townships built during Apartheid, for example, struggled for resources and to have control over their own lives. Hands-on tutorial activities also introduced the building blocks of working towards a research proposal, involving students in the creation of several annotated bibliographies. The final project required the presentation of three distinct bibliographies – academic publications, material from the 'open internet', and a selection of newspaper articles from an online archive. Students first worked with their selection of sources to construct a research proposal and then wrote an analysis and argument. Central to the completed projects were two complementary sections of critical discussion, variously focused on current debate and relevant history.

Most of my students, who were third-year undergraduates, had no previous research experience. I could not assume their enthusiasm for the details of modern South African history. I had first taught this course for a year or two, five years after South Africa's transition to constitutional democracy. In hindsight, my approach had relied heavily on students' own experience of Apartheid. For history lecturers of my generation, a subtle and yet profound transition was taking place. Almost without exception, students no longer had personal experience of the Apartheid-era racial discrimination and violent state repression seared into the collective remembrance of older generations. I could also not assume that students were avid followers of current news and politics. My challenge was how to draw them into participating in a labour-intensive course that sought to reposition them as researchers, to think about questions about human rights in contemporary South Africa and to publicly present their arguments online. Below, I argue that the multimodal approach, particularly my use of a variety of visual texts, integrated with a shift towards multilingual presentation and interaction played a crucial role in drawing students into inquisitive engagement, acts of analysis and author-ity.

Visual history for participatory analysis

My approach was shaped by the shift in southern African historical studies (already from the 1990s) towards researching the visual economies of colonialism. In order to introduce major themes and arguments to students in the classroom, I also drew on a visual methodology that I had developed as part of a local history project, of 'conversation through photography' (Du Toit, 2016b). This had involved looking at a photograph (often a portrait taken as part of the project) together with others and asking open-ended questions to elicit a range of responses. Examples of questions are: What do you see when you look at this photograph? What comes into your mind? What feelings do you experience when you look at this picture? Does it bring back memories? I adopted this approach as part of my conversations with my third year students to draw them into an exploration of the complex meanings that could be made from photographs and film, as powerful technologies of the twentieth century.

As part of the overall design, particularly in lecture-type presentations, I introduced each course theme via diverse visual texts so I could immediately draw students into discussion. This meant working with a range of photographic genres: for example, the visual economy of the early twentieth century included not only the product of professional studios, but also snapshots made with hand-held Kodak-type cameras. Photographs that circulated in South Africa from the early to late twentieth century had variously been produced as family snapshots, as entries for amateur Kodak photo competitions, as formal studio portraits or as part of social documentary projects. The section on history of migrant labour on the Rand and the exploitation of black miners by white mining magnates was introduced via William Kentridge's animated stop-motion film, *Mine* (1991). This section of the course also included archival images from early twentieth-century strikes in South Africa, as well as Sergei Eisenstein's Battleship Potemkin (1925), as an example of montage-style propaganda about mutiny and massacre in Tsarist Russia. The juxtaposition of various modalities of image-text and an early emphasis on artistic representation was a crucial means of sparking students' imaginations to encourage students to respond personally and also to validate emotional responses to received histories of exploitation and resistance, even while we analysed the layered meanings of images.

To clarify how this was part of a multimodal pedagogy for working with a particular generation of South African students, I need to provide more detail about how I introduced particular photographs for discussion from the very outset of the course. These introduced the course theme of 'History, Memory and Identity' and set the scene for the first written assignment. The photographs also formed part of my strategy for working with students from the born-free generation through inviting exploration of family histories and autobiographies. For their first course assignment, students were asked: 'Reflect on the place that "history" or a (shared?) sense of the past has for you as an individual. Is your sense of who you are as a person informed by a particular understanding of, or particular narrative about the past?' More detailed prompts for their writing included questions about whether 'knowledge of family history or ancestry' was part of 'memory-making in your family'; whether they grew up with 'a sense of participating in/being part of shared history', inclusive of narratives about the South African past. More questions followed: students were asked to find and discuss 'public, political examples of how … shared ideas of the past have been mobilized … for a particular purpose in the recent past'. They could also discuss 'examples of how South African intellectuals/artists have drawn on aspects of South African history in order to comment on an aspect of contemporary society'.

To open up the initial conversations, I chose an image of artwork by Mary Sibande, involving performative, photographic art, together with personal photographs from my own family archive. This was designed to invite students to begin investigating how their own sense of self involved ideas about the past. The photographs of Sibande's flamboyant and strongly autobiographical series of sculptures, 'Long live the Dead Queen', proved ideal for introducing students to new possibilities for critical and creative exploration of South African and personal pasts. The photographs were in themselves careful artistic productions that complemented exhibitions of her actual sculptures in various art galleries.[3] The work was Sibande's complex exploration of self, identity and family history through creating an alter-ego, 'Sophie', that made this a powerful focus for initial discussion. In her own words: 'I started her as a celebration of the women in my family, who were all maids – from my great-grandmother up to my mother.' Born in the 1980s, she says of herself: '[I] had a different upbringing and a very different life compared to generations of South African women before me: I'm the first woman in my family who attended university'[4] (Wellererhaus, 2013). Sophie's work comprised life-size sculptures, usually clothed in magnificent and intricate dresses that 'hybridize(d) a different identity by forging the blue fabric that usually makes workers overalls with the suggested form of a Victorian dress'. The 'alternative maid's uniform thus created attempted to 'symbolically transcend beyond the dichotomy set up by the racial ideology of the colonial and Apartheid gaze'. Sibande argued that instead of responding to this oppressive context by 'describing themselves as inferior', they presented to her 'the possibility of multiplicity' (Kosi, 2016). For Sibande, 'Sophie's most powerful gift is her ability to dream. She goes to work wearing her maid's uniform. But then she closes her eyes and starts to imagine things.'[5] Sibande's artistic creations proved a powerful starting point for the opening theme of 'History, Memory and Identity', not only because I was able to foreground questions of gender, race and colonialism through powerful and complex images but also in order to assert that personal storytelling and imaginative engagement with the past was an important part of the class.[6]

Usually, only a few students had begun to read some of the material about Mary Sibande and her creations that were available on the course website before this section began. In class, I first asked students to make sense of the image itself before offering information about the title of an artwork and details about the artist and her own interpretation of the work. Inviting students to collaboratively explore the range of possible meanings of these visual images helped to communicate to class participants that they could draw on personal knowledge to build relevant critical analysis. We analysed a photograph of 'The Reign', in which Sibande's alter ego Sophie, dressed in a voluminous and deep blue Victorian dress, sits astride a powerful, rearing black horse and another of Sophie, similarly dressed and holding a dainty white umbrella, titled 'I am a lady'.

As photographs of works of art, Sibande's images were exuberant performances of post-colonial critique, carefully staged, every element deliberately crafted. The archival images that students went on to consider in subsequent course sections, as part of our study of white, settler rule and black political struggle in early twentieth-century South Africa, could be thought of as 'revenants' or ghostly apparitions from the past. As photographs, they also often had an inclusivity of detail that lent itself to interpretation beyond the intended meaning. It was 'precisely photography's inability to discriminate, its inability to exclude, that makes it so textured and so fertile' (Pinney, 2003: 6). Elizabeth Edwards characterizes photographs as 'raw histories in both senses of the word – the unprocessed and the painful' (2001: 6). She argues that 'inherent to the medium itself' is an 'unprocessed quality', a 'randomness' and 'minute indexicality'. Yet it is 'precisely this quality of "inclusive randomness of photographs as inscriptions" and "the heightening theatricality of their nature" that contain their own future, because of the near-infinite possibilities of new meanings to be absorbed' (ibid.). The photographic products of colonial visual economies had all been 'intended to present some closure within a specific body of practice'. The very rawness of such images also 'present, instead, points of fracture, an opening out' (Edwards, 2001: 6). These were powerful ideas to draw on in order to 'think aloud with' photographs from within post-colonial localities, together with my students. Doing so also brought registers of emotive response to the surface. The conversations through photography in which we engaged, therefore, involved confronting and working with the rawness of sometimes painful photographic images. As students with diverse subject positions articulated their responses and ideas, we explored possibilities for imaginative engagement with aspects of colonial and Apartheid history, through visual analysis and complex dynamic of memory and emotion. I was also specifically working with ideas of portraiture, visual authority and subjectivity in colonial-era photography, often through contrasting portraits taken with 'honorific' intent, with others that could be read as exemplifying a colonizing gaze.

Figure 6.1 Marijke at three years old. Personal property.

At the same time, I was experimenting with a pedagogy of foregrounding my own inheritance of complicity with colonialism, through sharing personal and family history and by deliberately placing representations of (my)self within a narrative colonial and Apartheid history (see Figure 6.1). The invitation to discuss Sibande's imaginative exploration of self and identity was thus accompanied by a presentation of snapshots from my own family album. As one example, I showed students an image in which a little girl was in focus, with the blurry figure of a woman in the background. Only after they had experimented with what was represented in the image, did I explain that this was me when I was three years old and that the black woman was likely a nanny or domestic worker. As part of my strategy of conversation through photography, I therefore invited students to first articulate their own responses to the photographs, without giving any hint of my own interpretations and the personal meanings that such photographs might hold.

As another example of this approach of placing myself within the history of racism and white settler rule, I used contrasting images in an introductory lecture on the theme 'Segregation and the Politics of land and Labour'. I first presented a snapshot from the 1930s of my maternal grandparents, pictured on the smallholding that they farmed, as part of the Dutch Reformed Church's rehabilitation scheme for landless whites (see Figure 6.2). Students were only

Figure 6.2 My great grandparents, c 1930s. Personal property.

told the approximate year when the image had been taken before being asked open ended questions: What was this photograph about? Why are these people posing like this in this space? More specifically, does this photograph lend them dignity? How or how not? What relationships of power were implied by the photograph or could be read into the photograph?[7]

Students were then asked to answer the same questions in relation to a second photograph, which was first published in 1917 in *Die Huisgenoot* (*The Home Companion*), as part of an effort to create a popular, white Afrikaner nationalist culture. This was another portrait-like image with a man and woman seated in what seemed to be a rural landscape, holding two small children on their laps (see Figure 6.3). Students were usually intrigued by the uneasy resemblance that this image had to family and studio photography. They identified what had probably interested the photographer – the deliberately symmetrical arrangement of black and white drew attention to the contrasting dark and light skin colour of the two children. It was only after students had tried to make sense of the image that I would reveal the racist caption: 'Een albinokafferkind' (an Albino-kaffir-child). I explained that this descriptive, probably invented for this specific photograph, belonged to a long-practised tradition in Afrikaans, of highly

Figure 6.3 Photograph by Miss Buyske, *Die Huisgenoot*, 1917.

derogatory, racist compound nouns. This was a photograph produced in the context of white, settler domination, and published (as part of a Kodak camera competition) in a magazine central to the creation of a racially circumscribed 'imagined community' of Afrikaners.

As I also explained, the text accompanying the photograph informed readers that it was the winning picture of regular Kodak camera competition, taken by a Miss S. Buyske on a farm belonging to friends. Students sometimes noticed, or I pointed out, that the man in this photograph was neatly dressed in what seemed to be his best suit, but that his feet were bare, suggestive of this family's status as farm labourers or tenants. Taken together, I suggested, the two photographs could be read as communicating histories of conquest and also specifically, of legislated assertions of white land ownership. My great grandparents had been granted land in the 1930s because they were regarded as white, as part of an ethnic nationalist initiative (a church scheme for landless whites). By contrast, the second photograph was published in 1917, four years after the passing of the 1913 Natives Land Act, which prohibited Africans from buying land or entering into rental arrangements in 93 per cent of South Africa.

Introducing students to the practice of analysing the force-field of a photograph was an important strategy for prompting students to think about questions of power, authority and the creation of dominant historical narratives. Evidently, these were also visual texts saturated with racism and, so one might argue, burdened with histories of privilege and dispossession. The strategy of presenting a series of interrelated images for collaborative analysis partly mitigated the weight of this history. Students were also introduced to reproductions of portraits that photographer Santu Mofokeng found in the homes of black South African families. For Mofokeng, these images 'tell us a little about how these people imagined themselves. We see these images in the terms determined by the subject themselves, for they have made them their own' (1996: 54).

These were powerful ideas to draw on in order to 'think aloud with' photographs from within post-colonial localities, together with my students. Doing so also brought registers of emotive response to the surface. The rawness of sometimes painful photographic images presented possibilities of imaginative engagement with aspects of colonial and Apartheid history, through visual analysis and the complex dynamic of memory and emotion.

Print culture as a source for multilingual teaching

As a group, my students were linguistically diverse. Many spoke one or more indigenous languages at home: mostly isiZulu but also isiXhosa and seSesotho or Setswana. A small minority of students had Afrikaans as their first language. Those with English as their first language included not only white South Africans but also young women and men from Durban's diasporic Indian community – sometimes older family members still spoke Hindi, Tamil, Gujarati or another south-east Asian language. Even though students were being drawn into analysis of photographs as major sources and performances of history, they did so in a context in which articulation of visual perception was conventionally mediated through English as the dominant language of academic discourse. My own linguistic identity was hybrid: I regard English as my academic language but grew up speaking Afrikaans at home. I had intermediate knowledge of isiZulu and isiXhosa, languages that I understood fairly well, read with some confidence and spoke haltingly.

Historical studies in South Africa – in line with the humanities and social sciences generally – is firmly established with English as the dominant language. UKZN had adopted a new language policy in 2006. Officially, the university was now committed to developing 'an awareness of multilingualism through acknowledgement of all official languages of KwaZulu-Natal, namely isiZulu, English and Afrikaans' (Language Policy of the University, 2006). In practice a bilingual policy of teaching and learning that was envisaged to incrementally increase isiZulu's institutional and academic status was favoured. From 2013 it was also compulsory for students who had no proficiency in isiZulu to take introductory classes.[8] Indigenous African languages were still, however, largely relegated to informal use, outside of classroom doors. The vast majority of reading lists contained English texts and students were also conventionally expected to write in English.

I was teaching in a context of overt institutional commitment towards the 'intellectualisation' of African languages and of bolstering 'indigenous knowledge systems' in higher education (Mkhize and Hlongwa, 2014). My own approach, however, differed significantly from official plans for incremental movement towards 'dual medium teaching' in English and isiZulu and offering modules 'in the bilingual mode' (Mkhize and Hlongwa, 2014: 28). In my own understanding, translation of selected course 'content' into isiZulu and presentation of this alongside English (as was officially envisaged) could easily be associated with the regional history of ethnic mobilization and Zulu nationalism. My challenge was to introduce elements of multilingualism that would enable students to 'engage ethically with others across difference', particularly since 'the idea of "multilingualism" itself' comes with a 'colonial pedigree and continues to engage and contain diversity in ways that reproduce essential features of colonial social logics in contemporary "postcolonial" societies' (Stroud, 2018: 17). In the binary of 'metropolitan' versus 'non-metropolitan' (in this case African) languages, the latter are often positioned as 'languages in the "becoming" (in need of intellectualization) or languages of times past (in need of revitalization)'. This 'temporal displacement of speakers of these languages produces a subaltern who is only able to engage linguistically in the present through the words of the metropolitan language' (Stroud, 2018: 17). UKZN's language policy envisaged a future of bilingual language equality. Meanwhile, in the majority of courses, mother tongue speakers of indigenous languages could not use these (at least formally and explicitly) to engage in academic, intellectual activities. Any assumptions that students might want to study 'in' an African language would also have to consider the long shadow of Apartheid-era policies of forcible ethnic categorization and enforced 'mother-tongue' education. How, then, could my course in South African history prompt critical engagement with the politics of language and enable academic work to happen within, between or across indigenous languages and English? How could I invite my students to engage in 'acts of Linguistic Citizenship' so as to begin reconfiguring how to think, 'politically and ethically about language and ourselves' (Stroud, 2018: 18)?

My strategy for beginning to move away from the dominant monolingual teaching practices included three distinct and interrelated aspects that sought to open up questions about the politics of language and to create opportunities for students to engage with colonial history through indigenous language archival texts. At the start of the course, students were first asked to consider the politics of language in relation to how they themselves had acquired a sense of history – this was also how I began learning about the range of relationships with languages and linguistic identities as articulated by class participants. As part of their first assignment, I asked them whether people in contemporary South Africa 'share memories or share a sense of history, or another aspect of the past in the same way, regardless of the language that they are speaking or writing?'[9] Secondly, lecture presentations intermittently included archival excerpts of isiZulu text, presented together with translation. Reproductions – usually of a page, presented only in the original isiZulu (sometimes isiXhosa) – were also occasionally distributed for reading and discussion in class. Thirdly, two guided reading assignments that aimed to build students' comprehension of academic texts, complemented by written exercises in documentary analysis, focused on newspaper extracts written by black South Africans in isiZulu and also, to a lesser extent, in English and Afrikaans.

The exercise of asking questions about language as part of the invitation to explore the factors that had influenced and shaped one's own sense of a shared past resulted in a range of responses by students – personal, reflective narratives in which they explored interrelationships of political, familial, cultural and linguistic identity. Black students, in particular, answered my question about language and power in a variety of ways. One student, for example, discussed intergenerational tensions and how an older relative commented pejoratively on his nieces' fluency in English. Others discussed the variants of isiZulu or isiXhosa spoken within their families and communities or discussed the politics involved in the changing status of indigenous languages, relative to each other. Overall, a complex terrain of linguistic politics and possible relationships between languages and identities was suggested through students' own writings. Over the three years in which I taught the course, a selection of submissions also became part of what cohorts of students read in preparation for their own answers, thus also contributing to an implicit understanding of identity as dynamic and complex. Subsequent cohorts of students thus encountered discussions by fellow students about questions of relative power and tension between various indigenous languages or regional varieties of an official 'language'. Student writing also sometimes engaged critically with complex linguistic identities that encompassed various indigenous languages alongside English.[10]

While English remained the dominant language for reading and critical analysis, a few teaching sessions were planned to experiment explicitly with possibilities of multilingual interaction. The earliest introduction of a newspaper extract from *Ilanga lase Natal* was expressly intended to temporarily upend the dominance of English in the classroom. At the start of one lecture and discussion style session about the Natives Land Act of 1913, students were given an extract in the original isiZulu and asked to work in groups in order to make sense of it. The exercise was planned as a dramatic encounter with an archival document that communicated information about a momentous event in South African history and that could only be made sense of by persons with good isiZulu-language skills. As a form of 'disruptive pedagogy', however, this activity also involved presentation of a text that was reproduced in the original typeface and orthography (see also Mkhize, 2015). Collaborative sense-making was necessary as students proceeded with reading and tried to place the text in historical context, before my lecture presentation gave more detail. This was an advertisement for freehold land, published for the last time before the act would largely outlaw such transactions. It was evident that students experienced this exercise as unusual. Having students work together helped to contain any discomfort that students who understood no isiZulu experienced. Moreover, initial discomfort by some fluent speakers of African languages about possible assumptions that they could or should read 'their' language was mitigated by group work that placed them with confident and enthusiastic readers. For at least some students, this was an activity that integrated knowledge of (in the words of one student) 'our ethnic languages' as part of shared intellectual activity: '(i)t just adds more substance to our academic work'.[11]

I was drawing on specifically local possibilities of teaching African political and intellectual history multilingually. Arguably, this was also one starting point for working against post/colonial discursive practices that position African languages as academically inadequate in the present and as moving towards a future of becoming fully intellectualized. In Durban, the sight of posters emblazoned with the latest news serves as a daily reminder of a vigorous regional, isiZulu language print culture. Compared to other South African provinces, KwaZulu-Natal has an exceptional record of sustaining a variety of indigenous language newspapers.[12] The oldest surviving newspaper, *Ilanga*, has been in existence for more than a century. Course material and lectures introduced students to research about the emergence of a 'public sphere ... amongst the African population in South Africa' (Breckenridge, 1998: 73) of the early twentieth century and of how the first generation of mission-educated Africans created a network of writers and readers, writing in isiZulu to share 'similar thoughts and dreams' (Khumalo, 2006: 115). Our list of academic readings included historical accounts of South Africa's 'black' press in which African language newspapers were written into a chronology of African nationalist protest and resistance – often with little attention to the detail of discussion and debate on the indigenous language pages of these publications. Our discussion about early African nationalist thought, however, also drew on Hlonipha Mokoena's (2009b) intellectual history of Magema Fuze, popular historian and 'tin-trunk literate' who (writing in isiZulu) engaged readers of his columns in *Ilanga lase Natal* in debates about the meaning of reading and writing. Mokoena (2009a: 596) built on Khumalo's observation that the term 'ibandla', as used by the letter writers of the Ekukhanyeni mission station, referred to 'sphere' or 'public'.[13] She demonstrated how Magema Fuze 'borrowed, constructed and attempted to publicise a vocabulary for defining the ibandla' in debating the role of the newspaper's reader (ibid.).

The exercise of sense-making focused on the isiZulu language advertisement for free-hold land was followed by the lecture-style presentation on the history and extant scholarship about the Natives Land Act. I started by showing several photographs as discussed earlier in this chapter. Debates between scholars about the history of the Natives Land Act were then introduced, interspersed with discussions about bilingually presented extracts (in isiZulu and with English translation) from letters and editorials published in *Ilanga lase Natal*.

Throughout, students were thus invited to pay attention to questions of authorship, subjectivity, the construction of competing versions of history and the range of possible interpretations of documentary 'evidence'. It was this approach to introducing historiography together with diverse modalities of text that drew attention to the politics of language while opening up possibilities of speaking, writing and analysing history beyond possible assumptions of hegemonic scholarly expertise.

My approach was also to deliberately juxtapose texts drawn from early twentieth-century print culture, variously produced for white and black readerships. After class participants offered their interpretations of the photograph from *Die Huisgenoot,* I pointed out the likelihood that this was a family affected by the Natives Land Act. This was followed by my question as to what effect the Natives Land Act had had. I then presented excerpts from editorials and letters written to *Ilanga lase Natal* – political critique and narratives of personal experience of evictions of sharecropping families from white-owned farms, written in isiZulu and with accompanying translation (see Figure 6.4). Volunteers were quick to respond to my request that someone read it aloud. The act of voicing an indigenous language text – a document written as witness in opposition to colonial injustice – at a university that was otherwise dominated by acts of reading in English had evident emotive power. The presence of a racist image-text in our classroom was thus followed by performative reading of the newspaper excerpt in isiZulu. As part of the discussion, students were also invited to critique the translations presented in class. These letters, expressive as they were of black experience and of a terrain of public politics embedded in African languages, also powerfully suggested that settler politics and culture had not been hegemonic. Even when students were being introduced to public, political writings authored by disenfranchised black South Africans from the early twentieth century, they were participating in the reconfiguration of the economy of knowledge within our classroom in which fluency in and understanding of Nguni languages became valuable.[14]

The third component of this multilingual approach to teaching history was to set assignments specifically focused on the analysis of selected extracts from the early twentieth-century vernacular press. Students first participated in workshop-style small group sessions and then completed individual written assignments. They were also asked to provide critical feedback about their experience of this exercise. The result was two sets of newspaper extracts, presented with brief introductions and questions for analysis – African language texts were flanked with translations into English. The first thematic focus was

> **Bupi Ubuhle Kulomteto?**
>
> Wonke umuntu uyazi ukuti seloku kwaba nini umuntu omnyama azange enzelelwe luto pluhle. Nalokú esikuzwayo lapa amanxusa eti afuna ukuhlamba aye pesheya, sizwe kutiwa oGenene Bota qabo siyanilungisela. Bayati abelungu bamaplazi bedhlala ngabantu bobasusa emuzweni nabo kube kutule kute cwaka. Yiniku elungiswayo lokubnyasho bona futi kona pakati ukuti asinakngonla okwenziwe. uMpakati wetu. Poku uma kungenakuguquhwa sekwenziwe, usizo soze silutolepi? Futi ukuti ake kubnyo iKomisheni kusizani loku naku iti ingakafezi umselenzi wayo noko umteto woma senyaqutshwn. Asizwa kahle sizwa kashazishazi. Kodwa nempela kuhle kwabauihlope kona loku okwenziwa kubauntu, bedingiswa ngoba kade babehlupeku abelungu indaba yabantu. Bekuluma nge "Native Question." "Black Peril" njalo. Namhla sehenza loku nje kade behlezi Olulusheni lokucabanga ngetshe abanga letwesa umuntu omnyama, useletwele abasamlamleli kwa bakubo.

Every person knows that nothing good has ever been done for black people. Even the current attempts of the representatives who say they want to go overseas will not help much...

They say that the white farmers play with the people, they evict people from their lands, and all is quiet. There is nothing that can be done to remedy the situation, what is being done to our community. But if we cannot do change what has been done, where will we find help?

... The Commission... what will that help us sinceit refuses to reveal its work, even as the law isimplemented...

In truth, it suits the whites to do these things and not inform black people. **They talk about the 'Native Question" and likewise "Black Peril". Today we sit in a place of poverty, while the whites devise ways of putting a rock on top of black people and no one tries to intervene."**

Figure 6.4 Lecture slide with quote from letter to *Ilanga lase Natal* in isiZulu and English translation. Courtesy *Ilanga lase Natal*.

on the dispossession of land by means of the Natives Land Act of 1913 and featured editorials and letters to *Ilanga lase Natal* soon after it was passed. With the exception of one English language letter, all the texts were written in isiZulu. The second thematic focus was explicitly about an aspect of colonial history and the politics of language. Students read letters in which black South Africans debated whether the medium of instruction in segregation-era black primary schools should be English or mother tongue. While two letters were variously written in English and Afrikaans, most were written in isiZulu. All African language texts were presented in the original with English translation in an adjacent column. As first-time translations and because they were intended to complement the original as accurately as possible, these were often quite literal and provided direct renderings of metaphors. Accompanying questions and inserted comments drew attention to argument, tone of voice, intended audiences and issues of political representation (see Figure 6.5).

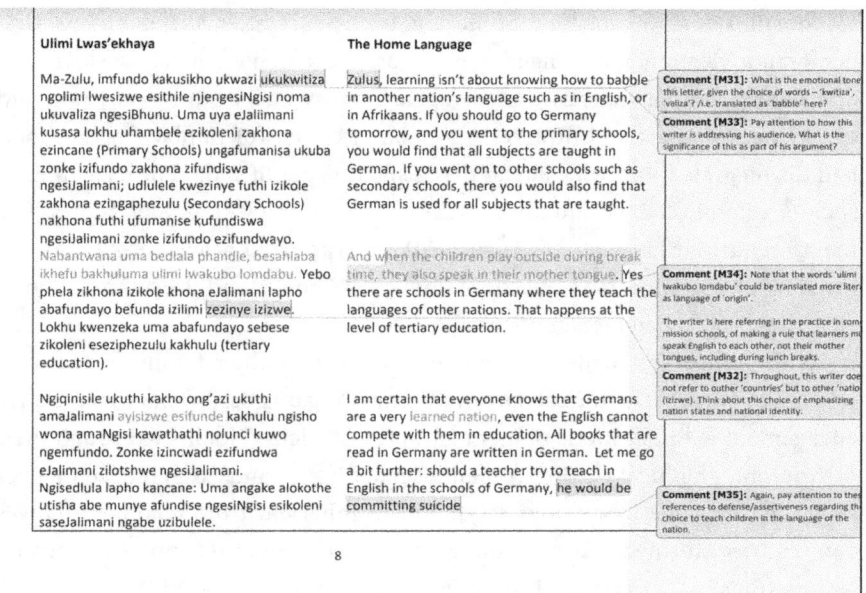

Figure 6.5 Example of annotated text from assignment on language and power.

Student evaluations of this exercise hinted at its potential for opening up a sense of the possibility of challenging dominant academic narrative. As one student wrote, the extracts were 'informative, they gave a new perspective … written by Africans, in an African language, for other Africans'. This was 'debate by Africans amongst themselves', a 'refreshing' change from having to read 'the African history' written by 'white academics'. As another student wrote, the texts brought 'about better understanding in terms of experiencing first-hand, so to speak, of how and why the "Black" people of that time responded in the manner that they did'. If the act of reading aloud in our classroom been powerfully emotive, many students also commented on the experience of reading letters written in their home languages that were strongly expressive of emotions, by writers who argued, sometimes bitterly, angrily and passionately, about how to survive after colonial conquest and in a situation of white settler dominance.

Conclusion

This chapter discusses strategies for teaching South African history to a generation of students born in the early years of South Africa's transition to constitutional democracy. Some eighteen years after the country's first democratic election, it no longer seemed possible to invite critical consideration of a widely familiar narrative of 'struggle' history and to draw on first-hand experiences of Apartheid. Moreover, popular discourses of 'rainbow' nationhood had disintegrated into widespread dissatisfaction about stalled programmes of socio-economic change and the persistence of race and gender hierarchies. The massacre at Marikana on 16 August 2012, perpetrated a few weeks into our teaching programme, gave questions about state power and the nature of post-Apartheid rule a heightened urgency.

At the outset, students were invited to consider their family histories in relation to available historical narratives – opening up possibilities for reflective engagement with questions of memory and historicized identity through their own autobiographical writings. Sibande's magnificent and exuberant sculptures suggested how the imagery and symbolism inherited from colonial archives could be transformed and knitted together into new hybrid forms, overturning assumptions of power and privilege and creating possibilities for self-expression. Classroom discussions of photographs to encourage collaborative exploration of possible meanings and to nudge participants into thinking about the interrelationship between individual located-ness and sense-making was important as part of communicating to students that they were not expected to act as consumers of dominant and fixed historical narratives. As revenants from the colonial past, ambiguous and often painful, photographs can draw a range of students into complex interpretative discussion and explicit consideration of questions about power, authority and how dominant historical narratives may be challenged. This was also a deeply personal approach in that I invited students to interpret my family photographs from my own childhood that placed me into a settler history of dispossession. This was partly to stimulate interest in complex arguments about the origins of raced and gendered selves and identities and in arguments about the historical roots of flashpoints of struggle in post-Apartheid.

It was also via documentary analysis of indigenous language texts from the archives of African print culture that students were able to engage explicitly with questions about the authority of historical argument and interpretation. Official university policy to promote English/isiZulu bilingualism celebrated the introduction of compulsory basic isiZulu for mother tongue speakers of European languages. However, African language skills were still largely irrelevant to courses in the Humanities. Presentation of indigenous language texts, in the original, together with translation, created new opportunities for multilingual students to read and interpret texts that in themselves complicated any assumptions about isiZulu or isiXhosa as languages 'in the becoming' or 'of times past' (in need of revitalization'). While students were grappling with images produced by colonizing cameras, the public debate amongst African newspaper editors and readers about how to survive and oppose settler rule was suggestive of rich African intellectual history. The difficulties of reading and interpreting early orthographies also opened up notions of an unstable past, open to diverse interpretations and personal responses.

The visceral shock of events at Marikana also resulted in a crucial reorganization of the course, away from a more strictly chronological approach. Students were thus positioned as researchers, tasked to explore explicitly the interlinkages between colonial/Apartheid pasts and contemporary contestations around constitutional rights. Moreover, as writers and authors of online projects, they were no longer merely readers of scholarly texts. Discussions now pivoted around questions about the relationship between past and present. Students were invited to consider a fundamental tension of social justice in our constitutional democracy. South Africa's constitution explicitly rejected the injustices of the past (De Vos, 2011). Figuring out the dynamics of contemporary alliances of power and privileges, of discrimination and exploitation or struggles for inclusive citizenship also involved understanding how the past was itself contested terrain. Historiographies about the rise of nationalisms, labour and gender in modern South Africa were then explored to find out how these helped one make sense of twenty-first-century contestations about state policies and power.

Notes

1 The state-orchestrated deaths of impoverished black mineworkers at the Lonmin Mine on 16 August 2012 soon became known as the Marikana Massacre and was widely seen as a seismic betrayal of South Africa's post-Apartheid social contract.
2 I had taught a second-year module called Electronic Images (2005–9) and the Internet and a third year module, Applied Internet Publishing, for several years (2006–10) as part of a BA in Internet Studies that was offered by the Department of History, in addition to the BA in History.
3 For examples of art works by Mary Sibande that were available online in 2012, see 'The Work of South African Artist Mary Sibande – in Pictures', https://www.theguardian.com/artanddesign/gallery/2012/aug/26/south-african-artist-mary-sibande (accessed 19 May 2018).

4 A conversation with the artist Mary Sibande, http://www.contemporaryand.com/magazines/sophieis-not-the-only-strong-woman-populating-our-art-scene-at-the-moment/
5 A conversation with the artist Mary Sibande, see endnote 4.
6 See also *The Guardian*, https://www.theguardian.com/world/2014/jan/07/marysibande-south-africa-art (accessed 19 October 2017).
7 Course Notes, History 302, August 2012.
8 https://www.iol.co.za/dailynews/opinion/evolution-of-language-at-ukzn-1724028, 23 July 2014 (accessed 16 March 2018).
9 For more detailed discussion of student interaction as part of this exercise and subsequent evaluations, see M. du Toit (2016a).
10 Student writings and evaluations of this exercise are discussed in more detail in M. du Toit (2016a).
11 Du Toit (2016a)
12 Newspapers published in isiZulu include *Ilanga* which was acquired by the Inkatha Freedom Party in 1987. For an analysis of recent political discourse in *Ilanga*, see Ngwane (2018). *Ilanga* and *Isolezwe*, launched in 2002, have increased their circulation figures while English-language papers nationally have declining sales (see Gilwald, 1988; Tolsi, 2007; Wasserman and Ndlovo, 2015).
13 Magema Fuze went to school at the Ekukhanyeni mission station (which had been established by John William Collenso) from age twelve. Hlonipha Mokoena's (2009b) book is presented as a biographical study of a kholwa intellectual, 'structured around a set of dialogues and contestations that Fuze conducted with his readers and critics' (19), especially through the letter pages of *Ilanga lase Natal*. Khumalo (2006) explored the private 'epistolary networks' in which Fuze participated together with others of the 'Class of 1856', first generation converts to Christianity who studied together at *Ekukhanyeni*.
14 The 'Nguni language cluster' are the mutually intelligible Bantu languages of southern Africa to which isiZulu belongs. Other languages within this cluster include isiXhosa, isiNdebele and Siswati.

References

Breckenridge, K. (1998), '"We Must Speak for Ourselves": The Rise and Fall of a Public Sphere on the South African Gold Mines, 1920–1931.

Breckenridge, K. (2007), 'Fighting for a White South Africa: White Working-Class Racism and the 1922 Rand Revolt', *South African Historical Journal*, 57 (1): 228–43.

Callinicos, L. (1987), *Working Life, 1886–1940: Factories, Townships, and Popular Culture on the Rand, People's History of South Africa vol. 2*. Johannesburg: Ravan Press.

Comparative Studies in Society and History 40(1), 71–108

'A Conversation with the Artist Mary Sibande' (n.d.). Available online: http://www.contemporaryand.com/magazines/sophieis-not-the-only-strong-woman-populating-our-art-scene-at-the-moment/ (accessed 3 November 2019).

De Vos, P. (2011), 'Why Historical Context Still Matters in South Africa'. Constitutionally Speaking (Blog), 16 November. Available online: https://constitutionallyspeaking.co.za/why-historical-context-still-matters-in-south-africa/ (accessed 3 November 2019).

Du Toit, M. (2001), 'Blank Verbeeld, or the Incredible Whiteness of Being: Amateur Photography and Afrikaner Nationalist Historical Narrative', *Kronos*, 27: 77–113.

Du Toit, M. (2016a), 'A Multilingual Approach to Teaching History', in R. H. Kaschula and H. E. Wolff (eds), *Multilingual Education for Africa: Concepts and Practices*, Pretoria: Unisa Press.

Du Toit, M. (2016b), 'Photography through Conversation, Conversation through Photography', in M. Du Toit and J. Gordon (eds), *Breathing Spaces: Environmental Portraits of South Durban*, Durban: UKZN Press.

Du Toit, M. and J. Gordon (2009), 'Photographic Portraiture, Neighbourhood Activism and Apartheid's Industrial Legacy: Reflections on the Breathing Spaces Exhibition', *Kronos*, 35 (1): 175–93.

Edwards, E. (2001), *Raw Histories: Photographs, Anthropology and Museums*. London: Berg Publishers.

Gilwald, A. (1988), 'A Black Coup' – Inkatha and the Sale of Ilanga', *Transformation*, 7: 27–37.

Hayes, P., and A. Bank (2001), 'Introduction', *Kronos*, 27: 1–14.

The Deadline (1997), film, dir. David Jammy, Icarus Films.

Khosi, M. (2016), 'Taking Back Control Over the Black Imagination: In Conversation with Mary Sibande', 10 August. Available online: https://bubblegumclub.co.za/features/taking-back-control-over-the-black-imagination-in-conversation-with-mary-sibande/ (accessed 3 November 2019).

Khumalo, L. (2015), 'Advances in Developing Corpora in African Languages', *Kuwala*, (2): 21–30.

Khumalo, V. (2006), 'Ekukhanyeni Letter-Writers: A Historical Inquiry into Epistolary Network(s) and Political Imagination in KwaZulu-Natal, South Africa', in K. Barber (ed.), *Africa's Hidden Histories: Everyday Literacies and Making the Self*, Bloomington: Indianna University Press.

Krikler, J. (2005), *White Rising: The 1922 Insurrection and Racial Killing in South Africa*. Manchester: Manchester University Press.

Language Policy of the University of KwaZulu-Natal, approved by Council 1 September 2006. Available online: http://registrar.ukzn.ac.za/Libraries/policies/Language_Policy_-_CO02010906.sflb.ashx (accessed 18 June 2018).

Mignolo, W. (2009), 'Epistemic Disobedience, Independent Thought and Decolonial Freedom', *Theory, Culture and Society*, 26 (7–8): 1–23.

Mkhize, N. (2015), 'On Language and Disruptive Pedagogy', The Con., 4 March. Available online: http://www.theconmag.co.za/2015/03/04/on-language-disruptive-pedagogy/ (accessed 3 November 2019).

Mkhize, N. and N. Ndimande-Hlongwa (2014), 'African Languages, Indigenous Knowledge Systems (IKS) and the Transformation of the Humanities and Social Sciences in Higher Education', *Alternation*, 21 (2): 10–37.

Mofokeng, S. (1996), 'The Black Photo Album/Look at Me 1890–1900s', *Nka: Journal of Contemporary African Art*, 4: 54–7.

Mokoena, H. (2009a), 'An Assembly of Readers: Magema Fuze and his *Ilanga lase Natal* Readers', *Journal of Southern African Studies*, 35 (3): 595–607.

Mokoena, H. (2009b), *Magema Fuze: The Making of a Kholwa Intellectual*. Durban: University of KwaZulu-Natal Press.

Ngwane, S. (2018). 'ILanga Nodlame Lokucwaswa Ngokubuzwe: The May 2008 Xenophobic Riots Mediated in isiZulu', *African Journalism Studies*, 38 (3–4): 118–39.

Opland, J. (2007), *The Nation's Bounty: The Xhosa Poetry of Nontsizi Mgqwetho*. Johannesburg: Wits University Press.

Pinney, C. (2003), 'Introduction: How the Other Half … ', in C. Pinney and N. Peterson (eds), *Photography's Other Histories*, 1–16, Durham, NC: Duke University Press.

Stoler, A. (2002), 'Colonial Archives and the Arts of Governance: On the Content in the Form', in C. Pickover, R. Saleh and J. Taylor (eds), *Refiguring the Archive*, 83–102, Berlin: Springer.

Stroud, C. (2018), 'Linguistic Citizenship', in L. Lim, C. Stroud and L. Wee (eds), *The Multilingual Citizen: Towards a Politics of Language for Agency and Change*, 17–39, Clevedon: Multilingual Matters.

Tolsi, N. (2007), 'The All New Zulu', *Mail & Guardian*, 28 May. Available online: https://mg.co.za/article/2007-05-28-the-all-new-zulu (accessed 3 November 2019).

Wasserman, H. and M. Ndlovu (2015), 'Reading Tabloids in IsiZulu', *Communitas*, 20: 140–58.

Wellerershaus, E. (2013), '"Sophie is Not the Only Strong Woman Populating Our Art Scene at the Moment." A Conversation with the Artist Mary Sibande', 24 June. Available online: https://www.contemporaryand.com/magazines/sophieis-not-the-only-strong-woman-populating-our-art-scene-at-the-moment/ (accessed 3 November 2019).

Witz, L., G. Minkley and C. Rassool (2017), *Unsettled History: Making South African Public Pasts*. Ann Arbor, MI: University of Michigan Press.

'The Work of South African Artist Mary Sibande – in Pictures' (2012). Available online: https://www.theguardian.com/artanddesign/gallery/2012/aug/26/south-african-artist-mary-sibande (accessed 19 May 2018).

7

Delinking from Colonial Language Ideologies: Creating Third Spaces in Teacher Education

Soraya Abdulatief, Xolisa Guzula and Carolyn McKinney

Introduction

In postcolonial contexts, it is commonplace for colonial languages to dominate the education system and for proficiency in a European language and script to be seen as the sole marker of being educated. It is also the Western episteme that is largely responsible for monoglossic myths that construct monolingualism as the norm in formal education, including schooling and universities. In South Africa, it is proficiency and literate practices in particular forms of 'standard' English that are often perceived as the exclusive marker of being educated. Recent student movements such as #RMF (#RhodesMustFall) and #FMF (#FeesMustFall) calling for 'Free Decolonized Education' have put the spotlight on the continuing coloniality of university spaces such as our own location, the University of Cape Town (UCT). Drawing on decolonial theory, the notion of language ideologies and third spaces, in this chapter we present two case studies of interventions in a teacher education programme at an elite university. Both interventions are framed as attempts to *delink* (Mignolo, 2007) from coloniality in an elite university context with a multilingual student body, and aimed to challenge monoglossic and Anglonormative ideologies of language.

The first case study in our current intervention focuses on student teachers of primary school children (years 1–3) in a course on multilingualism and multiliteracies. Our goal here is to show how in changing the normative language practices of the classroom, power relations are shifted and previously marginalized multilingual students are given opportunities to move to centre stage. We analyse the embodied responses of a group of students from different language, cultural and social class backgrounds as they present to their peers the product of their collaborative work. The second case focuses on high school science student teachers in an academic literacy workshop and considers how translanguaging for learning can be modelled in this space. The cases are drawn from two distinct research projects. The first is from a collaborative project between Guzula and McKinney which explores 'translanguaging as pedagogy' in a module of the postgraduate certificate in education for early primary (PGCE), while the second is drawn from Abdulatief's doctoral research on extending academic literacy practices with a small group of students from non-dominant backgrounds in the PGCE for high school science and mathematics teachers. Both of these case studies proceed from our acknowledgement that decolonizing the curriculum entails a shift institutionally and pedagogically from prioritizing English as monolingual language of learning and teaching (LoLT) to viewing multilingualism as a resource for teaching and learning (Heugh, Plüddemann and Siegruhn, 1995; Kapp, 1998; Stroud and Kerfoot, 2013). We begin by elaborating on the theoretical concepts that have informed our research and practice.

Coloniality and language ideologies

Maldonado-Torres (2007) describes coloniality as that which 'survives colonialism'. In contrast to colonialism, coloniality refers to 'long-standing patterns of power that have emerged as a result of colonialism, but that define culture, labor, intersubjective relations, and knowledge production well beyond the strict limits of colonial administrations' (Maldonado-Torres, 2007: 243). The multiple and entangled power relations of superiority and inferiority established under colonialism – the colonial matrix of power – thus continue to produce unequal relations of power globally and locally. Hierarchies of language and culture are crucial aspects of the colonial matrix of power (wa Thiong'o, 1986) such that alternatives to the dominance of European languages in education have become almost unthinkable for policymakers, government departments, and thus in the schooling system. Language ideologies, that is, the sets of beliefs, values and cultural frames that continually circulate in society, informing the ways in which language is conceptualized and represented, as well as how it is used, and how its users are positioned (Makoe and McKinney, 2014) are profoundly shaped by the colonial matrix of power.

Coloniality shapes language ideologies in at least three ways that are significant for our work. Firstly in the construction of named languages as autonomous, bounded objects: In southern Africa, scholars such as Makoni

(1998) and Makalela (2015) draw attention to the colonial invention of indigenous languages as a product of missionary interventions. Secondly, in the continuing exclusive valuing of a European language and script in post-Apartheid South Africa where English is the home language of less than 10 per cent of South Africans while the vast majority of the population are multilingual in African languages. It is also the reason for the power of the Dutch-derived-creole Afrikaans, relative to other indigenous languages. The construction of Afrikaans as the language of white settlers of Dutch descent ('The Afrikaners') was a distinct project of Afrikaner nationalism during Apartheid. Afrikaans-medium universities were established, bilingualism in Afrikaans and English was enforced for white school learners and notoriously, the attempt in 1976 to enforce Afrikaans medium for the teaching of 50 per cent of secondary school subjects, particularly mathematics to African language–speaking learners, resulted in a student revolt in June of that year the labelling of Afrikaans as the 'language of the oppressor'.[1,2] Thirdly, Eurocentric language ideologies privilege monolingualism in European languages over multilingualism in 'other[ed]' languages that are often characterized as inadequate (Stroud, 2007) and position monolingualism in a European language as normative. Recognizing the power of coloniality in shaping what counts as legitimate language practices in South African education is central to our goal of valuing multilingual repertoires and disrupting monoglossic norms in teacher education.

In South Africa, proficiency and literate practices in particular forms of 'standard' English are often equated with being educated and even with intelligence (Makoe and McKinney, 2014). The dominant language ideology can be described with the term 'Anglonormativity': 'The expectation that people will be and should be proficient in English and are deficient, even deviant, if they are not' (McKinney, 2017: 80).[3] Yet, education in a foreign language or through a language in which a student is not sufficiently proficient effectively removes the most valuable resource that he or she brings to the classroom: their linguistic repertoire. While the perception is that the earlier children begin learning in and through English, the better their English proficiency will be, the reality in South African schools is that this practice leads to limited proficiency in English and lack of understanding of curriculum content (Heugh, 2013; McKinney, 2017). This problem of the exclusive valuing of English language and literacy resources continues through schooling into higher education and is, as many have argued, one of the reasons for the persistently poor performance of South Africa's education system (Heugh, 2013; McKinney, 2017; Plüddemann, 2015). Through the coloniality of language in South Africa, the education system continually fails its students and positions educators as linguistically incompetent, while policy-makers and educators often view the problem as residing in the learner, referencing learners' poor proficiency in standard English.

Delinking and transforming – constructing third spaces

Following Mignolo, working against coloniality in language and literacy education would involve *delinking* (Mignolo, 2007) from the dominant monolingual approach and transforming pedagogies as well as language in education policies. It also means recognizing that rather than discrete objects, operating autonomously from one another, named languages are social constructs. However, in an education system where the use of indigenous language resources has become so marginalized, we advocate the kind of action that takes power relations at macro and micro levels within a particular context into account when deciding how to work productively with students' language resources (see also Stroud, 2018). In some moments, it is key to deconstruct the myth of 'pure' standard languages in order to legitimize the hybrid or mixed language use that is most familiar to urban students, while in other moments we might require students to work with a range of named language resources in order to surface and legitimize resources other than monolingual English. Thus at times, we recognize the importance of naming language resources in order to make them visible, thus arguing for a form of strategic essentialism (Fuss, 1989; Spivak, 1988). We propose that disrupting Anglonormativity can happen explicitly, through critical language awareness work that counters hegemonic language ideologies. And it can also take place implicitly through making visible, embracing and enabling the use of students' full linguistic repertoires as well as their meaning-making across a range of modes as legitimate resources for learning.

The notion of third spaces (Anzaldua, 1987; Bhabha, 1994; Gutiérrez, 2008) is useful to us in characterizing the kinds of learning spaces which delink from monolingual, autonomous notions of language use and which embrace multiple modes for meaning-making. Gutiérrez (2008: 152) defines the third space as 'a transformative space where the potential for an expanded form of learning and the development of new knowledge are heightened'. She argues for the importance of collaborative or collective *third space* as 'interactionally constituted' and characterized by hybrid language and literacy practices, leading us to what Flores and García (2013) term linguistic third spaces. Soja (1996: 5) describes third space 'as a space of extra-ordinary openness, a place of critical exchange where geographical imagination can be expanded to encompass multiplicity of perspectives that have heretofore been considered by epistemological referees to be incompatible, uncombinable'. In the case studies below, we show how the *third spaces* concept helps us to work with the notions of both named languages and translanguaging to disrupt Anglonormativity and monolingualism in the classroom space. Given Gutiérrez 's proposal of third spaces as 'interactionally constituted', an expanded notion of translanguaging which proceeds from multilingual languaging as the norm helps us to describe and plan for dynamic languaging beyond the constraints of monolingual ideologies. The concept of translanguaging (García, 2009; García and Li Wei, 2014; Makalela, 2015) has been defined in a number of ways that emphasize the description of communicative practices involving a wide range of linguistic and semiotic resources, as well as on the ideological dimension of disrupting a monoglossic and monomodal understanding of language. Blackledge and Creese (2017: 253) also foreground the ways in which people 'bring into contact different biographies, histories and linguistic backgrounds' as they translanguage, thus emphasizing the ways in which our histories and biographies shape our linguistic resources and practices. Translanguaging as a progressive educational practice – especially when it brings previously marginalized languages into the classroom in symbolically significant ways – can be aligned with Stroud's (2018) notion of 'Linguistic Citizenship' which emphasizes the agentic and transformative use of language in order that speakers may be heard.

Case study 1: Surfacing and legitimizing 'non-English' resources in the lecture room

The first case study is drawn from the small-scale exploratory research conducted in a module on multilingualism and multiliteracies education which took place over four workshops (three and a half hours each) with a class of twenty-five students studying a Foundation Phase (grade 1–3) Postgraduate Certificate in Education. Xolisa taught this module, modelling for these future teachers of young children how to embody active learning using the full linguistic repertoires of children in the classroom. For the first time in their teacher education programme, a third space was established to expose students to multilingual and hybrid communicative practices and pedagogy. As a lecturer with a multilingual repertoire, Xolisa realized the importance of surfacing students' linguistic repertoires and engaging with language ideologies, before she could model multilingual pedagogy. The initial lecture on monolingual ideologies challenged students steeped in English dominant ideology and presented them with concepts such as heteroglossia that allowed them to consider their own language ideology and what counts as legitimate language use in society and in schools. The language backgrounds of students ranged from those who identified as isiXhosa speaking (and thus were bilingual in isiXhosa/English), those identifying as English/Afrikaans bilingual (mostly coloured students)[4] to those who identified as monolingual English speakers (mostly white students), despite the fact that they had studied and passed Afrikaans at school for twelve years. There are a number of possible reasons for white English dominant speakers' denial of competence in Afrikaans. A history of hostility, conflict and geographical segregation means that Afrikaans can be identified as 'language of the enemy', and specifically 'language of the oppressor' during Apartheid; this history also means that English speakers will have had limited exposure to Afrikaans outside of school, with students' exposure being limited to formal teaching, learning and assessments at school.

In the third workshop, Xolisa designed a class around an oral performance of a story about a beautiful bird that brings rain. In order to decentre English, Xolisa first asked for equivalent terms for 'bird' in isiXhosa and Afrikaans and then elicited from the class their knowledge about different birds, recording the names in English, isiXhosa and Afrikaans before eliciting relevant songs and rhymes. She did this to build on students' prior knowledge as well as to legitimize the multiple languages in the classroom. Xolisa's use of named languages even though she works with a heteroglossic notion of language shows her concern to make visible marginalized language resources. Pietikäinen and Pitkänen-Huhta (2014: 140) draw attention to the contradictions between acknowledging named languages as constructs at the same time as making marginalized resources visible: 'These language conceptualizations and practices and their consequences include questions about how one defines their identity and brings into a learning space marginalized languages in the crossfire of dominant ideologies that either emphasize the fixed and bounded nature of languages or advocate for fluid ways.'

Through these activities, the students shared their knowledge as well as experimented with unfamiliar songs and language resources using isiXhosa, Afrikaans and English. Xolisa told the story of the rain bird in English, inserting songs in isiXhosa to make the performance more interactive and bilingual. She then divided the class into four groups. Group 2, our focus here, was asked to come up with action songs and rhymes based on the story, thus demonstrating practically what working multilingually and multimodally might look and feel like in practice.

Here we focus our analysis on Group 2 students' working together and on the presentation of their work to the class. In the context of marginalized language resources in the university space such as isiXhosa and Afrikaans,[5] the students made particular linguistic choices both in the poster they created and their presentation of their poster. These choices include surfacing of isiXhosa and Afrikaans resources. We argue that speakers positioned themselves as knowers, enacting their knowledge with confidence or discomfort depending on their language histories. Just as language practices are embodied, so too are our language histories and language ideologies. We focus on the embodied language practices of two students[6]: Lisa, whose home language is isiXhosa, a language usually excluded from the formal university classroom, and Tracey who presents in Afrikaans, knowledge of which she had disavowed when initially describing her linguistic repertoire.

Group 2 began working with three English-dominant students who had all studied Afrikaans at school and who were currently taking a course in isiXhosa communication as part of their PGCE. They were later joined by a fourth isiXhosa/English bilingual student, Lisa. At the start of the group work, Nicky introduced and explained her idea for a non-verbal activity which involved stomping of feet, slapping hands on the thighs and clicking of fingers to make the sounds of a rain storm (as performed in Extract 7.1). While Nicky's activity was being written up on newsprint, Lisa arrived for class and joined the group. One student explained the story Xolisa had told and the group task. Lisa

Figure 7.1 Nicky (second from right) uses body percussion to make the sound of rain by clapping her hands on her thighs.

immediately began singing an isiXhosa song, *'Imvula imvula chapha chapha chapha imanz' ilokhwe yam'* [It's raining, it's raining, drop drop drop, my dress is wet] and Nicky responded enthusiastically with 'beautiful!'. Lisa said 'Yessss!' showing how excited she was that the group appreciated her contribution. Nicky then asked her to explain the song. However, Lisa began by translating the parts that the others were able to understand because of the accompanying gestures – '*chapha chapha*' sound of rain and '*gqum gqum liyaduduma*' [boom boom, it's thundering], and not *imanz ilokhwe yam* [my dress is wet] which they didn't understand. It took some time for the others to identify the words they didn't understand. This translation highlighted a moment where the English dominant students were totally dependent on Lisa's linguistic repertoire.

The group created a multilingual and multimodal poster using three distinct named languages isiXhosa, Afrikaans and English as can be seen in Figure 7.2 below. They chose not to include written translations of the songs/activities described. While some activities/songs were well known to individuals in the group, others were original compositions.[7]

In analysing Lisa's and Tracey's presentations to the class, we draw on Busch's (2015) notion of embodied language ideologies and linguistic repertoires as lived experience as well as Blackledge and Creese's (2017) notion of embodied communicative practice. We demonstrate that Lisa's isiXhosa/English bilingual repertoire has positioned her as being knowledgeable, and a valued, active participant in class, while Tracey's repertoire has positioned her as less comfortable with the Afrikaans language resources that she uses. The multilingual nature of their activity requires students in the group to recognize and acknowledge their own linguistic resources. This is a novel and potentially uncomfortable idea for many English-speaking students who resist their English/Afrikaans bilingualism.

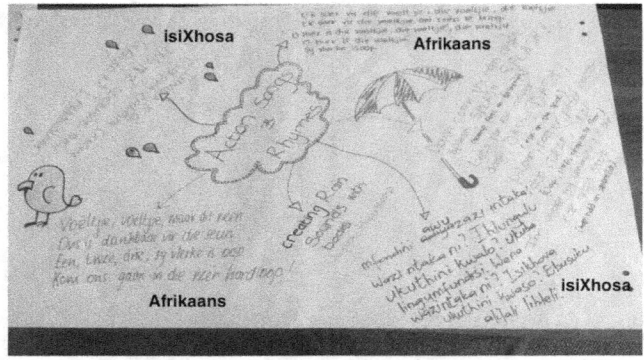

Figure 7.2 Multilingual and multimodal newsprint poster created by Group 2.

Delinking from Colonial Language Ideologies

Below we provide a transcription of the first part of Group 2's presentation to the class.

Extract 7.1. First part of Group 2's presentation

Verbal text	**Body movement and Gaze**
Nicky: Ok. We focused on action songs and rhyme. Um and the first one we looked at was where you get children to create the … ja, the rain while you're in a story so that you start with: [Snaps fingers] Slowly and then you go like that [Claps, slaps thighs, and stomps feet] and they make rain together. I think it might be fun.	Nicky Faces the class See Figure 7.1.
And then we've got a really lovely song over here that uh Lisa could sing for us. [Laughs]	Nicky looks over to Lisa and moves to take poster from her so that she and Tracey are holding it and Lisa can face the audience.
Lisa: This song is about *imvula neh*? That's rain, where they have to sing the song like: [singing] *Imvula, imvula, chapha chapha chapha, imanz' ilokhwe yam, chapha chapha chapha, imanz' ilokhwe yam, gqum gqum kuyaduduma gqum gqum kuyadudma imanz' ilokhwe yam, imanz' ilokhwe yam*[end singing] There we also show you also the rhyme like that: *gqum* That's a sound of a thunderstorm when it's raining. That's what we were trying to (do)	See Figure 7.3. L raises arms up and down at chapha chapha; Xolisa joins in with singing and actions. Cindy stands with arms folded across chest and Tracey with arms at side. Both are mouthing the words – lips moving though inaudible.
Tracey: We wrote a little Afrikaans poem. It goes: *Voeltjie, voeltjie maak dit reen, ons is dankbaar vir die seun, een twee drie, sy vlerke is oop, kom ons gaan in die reen hardloop.*	See Figure 7.4 Tracey turns away from the class and reads off the poster. All three other members look at the poster as she does this.
Tracey: So that means: Bird, bird, make it rain, we are thankful for the boy, one two three his wings are open, let's go and run in the rain. Carolyn: Did you make that up? Tracey: Ja. Carolyn: Oh, wow!	

Figure 7.3 Lisa (second from right) performing and the lecturer (far right) joining in here.

Figure 7.4 Tracey (second from left) reading the Afrikaans poem off the left-hand bottom corner of the poster.

Acts of recognition and legitimation of Lisa's embodied knowledge

Group 2's presentation takes a multimodal form where gestural, visual, oral and written communications are intertwined. Nicky's rain-making through body percussion foregrounds embodied communication using an inclusive semiotic repertoire. Nicky then introduces the 'lovely song' to be sung by Lisa with a nervous laugh, suggesting her discomfort with the group's dependence on Lisa as the only one who knows the song in isiXhosa. Nicky relieves Lisa from holding the poster so Lisa can take the stage while she and others move to the background. Lisa establishes her presence by looking at the class and maintaining eye contact. She stands with both feet apart, firmly planted on the ground signalling her confidence. Then she moves her hands up and down as she sings to show the drop, drop, dropping of the raindrops. The positioning of Lisa as a knowledgeable and competent contributor to the group despite her having joined the class late builds her confidence which we see in her performance. In including an isiXhosa song, the white English-speaking students have relied on Lisa to overcome their own linguistic gap. Lisa's body constitutes and gives meaning to the language and the song.

Xolisa's immediate joining in with Lisa's singing and actions shows how the students' knowledge and the lecturer's coalesce. It also creates a context which legitimizes and lends authority to Lisa's contribution. The moment of singing and doing actions together signals the lecturer's identification with the students' embodied language history, and constitutes a powerful moment of recognition for the student. Sharing experiences and common narratives, in this case, songs and actions by Lisa and Xolisa help to establish communal commitment to learning as well as to raise the status of isiXhosa language resources in an English-dominant class.

Tracey's self-positioning as a reluctant bilingual

After Lisa has explained the meaning of the onomatopoeic sound 'gqum' for thunder, Nicky hands over the next activity to Tracey. Tracey begins by saying, 'We wrote a little Afrikaans poem' and pausing before she starts reading from the poster. She turns her back on the audience to read the words written in Afrikaans on the poster, suggesting a less comfortable embodied history in relation to this linguistic resource. While Lisa has drawn on highly familiar resources from her linguistic and cultural repertoire in performing a well-known isiXhosa song, Tracey doesn't seem to have this cultural repertoire in Afrikaans. Her schooled competence, however, enables her to compose an appropriate rhyme, and to translate it into English for the class without any difficulty. Tracey's communicative practice resembles that of a language learner who has learnt the grammar of the language without having experienced it personally. It is striking to us that Tracey has the linguistic resources to create an original rhyme in Afrikaans and translate it into English with ease, despite her self-positioning as a monolingual English speaker at the beginning of the course. The Apartheid history of standard Afrikaans as language of the oppressor and of enforced bilingualism in English/Afrikaans for white South African students during Apartheid schooling as well as the nature of her language learning provide possible reasons for Tracey's embodied language ideology positioning her as a reluctant bilingual.

The contrast between Lisa's and Tracey's embodied language histories as seen in the group performance is striking. Tracey seems to demonstrate a particular schooled language and literacy history rather than a cultural repertoire. Unlike Tracey who focuses more on the written word than the audience, Lisa's embodied history means she can face the audience and perform from the heart. For Tracey, reading from the text makes her feel more comfortable, even if it means not facing the audience. Lisa's isiXhosa multimodal song requires the use of the body and oral language simultaneously to assist with meaning-making. Because there is no translation of the song, the non-isiXhosa-speaking students in the audience are forced to read Lisa's hand and body movements. Not translating also disrupts the English students' comfortability. It moves them to the background, foregrounding Lisa and giving her voice. This is embodied by Cindy who stands with arms folded protectively across her chest (far left, Figure 7.3) during Lisa's performance.

Case Study 2: Using multilingualism as a resource in preservice science teacher training

In our second case study, delinking from Anglonormative and monolingual language ideologies involved creating a translingual third space in which the facilitator, Soraya, an English/Afrikaans bilingual modelled using language as a resource for African language-speaking preservice science teachers.[8] In order to support and expand the student teachers' implementation and practice of multilingual and bilingual pedagogy in the science classroom, Soraya drew on Gutiérrez's (2008) conception of the third space, as a space where 'students begin to reconceive who they are and what they may be able to accomplish academically and beyond' (p. 148). Soraya created a series of workshops aimed at socializing preservice science teachers into particular literacy practices so that they could put the theory they had learned in their course on using language as a resource into practice. Like the previous case study, Soraya introduced multilingual participatory practices by enabling her students to explore how they could use African language translation activities to support high school science learning. The workshops took place in the last week of the winter holiday and involved five African language-speaking students. Four of them were training to be grades

8 to 12 science teachers and one to be a mathematics teacher. There were three females Xara (F), Lera (F), Zinzi (F) and two males, Kagiso (M) and Thebo (M). The data discussed in this section is from the second of the day-long workshops where the facilitator took the students through an extended literacy cycle starting with a brain teaser, followed by a practical experiment. Next, they did an exercise on creating a multilingual glossary and this was followed by writing a scientific report on the experiment using a writing frame. The workshop ended with a visit to a science centre in the afternoon.

Two transcripts are used as data, the first transcript is an extract from the section of the workshop where the facilitator is modelling building a multilingual glossary of terms using the linguistic repertoires of the students in the classroom. The second transcript is an extract from an interview with one of the participants, Lera, on her own language practices during university study.

Building a glossary of terms in the science class

Soraya, the facilitator started the segment on using multilingualism as a resource and building a multilingual glossary of scientific terms by discussing Gibbons's (2009) idea of amplifying the curriculum for English Second Language (ESL) learners. Unlike the traditional approach to teaching multilingual learners that involves simplifying the curriculum, Gibbons argues that multilingual learners be offered a high level of support on curriculum content by creating a glossary using the learners' home language and multiple modes (illustrations, videos, photos etc.). After the students completed an activity in which they created an electromagnet, Soraya put this question to the students, 'If you had to use your mother tongue, which words [in the written instructions] would you translate?' Lera, a Setswana speaker, answered by saying that she would not translate a text without being aware of the languages spoken by the learners. Next Zinzi, an isiZulu speaker, suggested that the translations be done in isiXhosa since it was the language of three of the five students in the workshop. As both Lera and Zinzi's responses suggest, the decision on which language to use as a resource that supports learning in classrooms where learners speak multiple languages is often a difficult one for teachers, especially student teachers or newly qualified teachers. If the teacher does not speak any of the multiple languages in her class, English becomes the de facto lingua franca. Soraya, an English/Afrikaans bilingual who does not speak an African language, modelled how to use the language resources of the class in contexts where the teacher does not speak the learners' languages. She suggested that the participants build a multilingual glossary using all the language varieties present in the group, isiXhosa, isiZulu and Setswana. The suggestion to build a multilingual glossary was met with silence which could be interpreted as students' not knowing how to proceed or a reluctance to use African languages in the science classroom. The transcript below starts after the facilitator asked the participants a second time which aspects of the text on how to create an electromagnet they would translate for their learners:

Transcript 1

Zinzi: I would translate difficult terms.
Soraya: Like what for example? Ok let's use, let's use the experiment that worked which was the magnetic one right. Ok, so look at that experiment and then what would you translate? (Giving the book on science experiments to Zinzi and Xara)
Zinzi: I would translate 'stripped ends'. (Looking at the experiment in the book)
Soraya: Stripped ends? Stripped ends, ok.
Zinzi: Especially 'stripped'. What does stripped mean?
Soraya: Ok, then what would you, then what would be the isiXhosa equivalent of that?
Zinzi: Stripped means *'ichuthiwe'* (*it's plucked*), *ukuchutha* (*to pluck*), like this (hand movements) *ewe chutha* (*yes pluck*)
(yes, pluck), *yisuse* (*remove it*).
Xara: So you just said, *yisuse* (*remove it*)
Kagiso: Chipped off, stripped is like chipped. *Ukucola* (*grind*).
Soraya: Ok, spell that for me ...
Thebo: *Hayi!* (*No!*)
Soraya: No, you disagree? (Turning to Thebo)
Xara: No, *ukucola* (*grind*) is (hand movements), you like ... grinding.
Thebo: *Ukucola* is to grind.
Zinzi: *Ukuchutha ngesZulu* (*to pluck in isiZulu*), you understand Zulu? (pointing at Thebo)
Thebo: *Xhwitha*, isiXhosa (*pluck*).
Xara: Cause *ngasusa* the feathers (*I removed the feathers*) (hand movements mimic plucking).
Zinzi: Exactly! And in isiZulu, *ukuchutha* (*to pluck*).
Soraya: Ok, spell that for me.
Kagiso: A.u.No, u ... k (attempting to spell the word '*ukuxhwitha*').

Xara: Kagiso is using the BEE spelling.
Kagiso: I think I'm the wrong guy ... *Ukuxhw* ... (to pluc ...) yth (say) no, with with ... a
Soraya: Ok, what does this mean? And what does this mean?
Zinzi: Stripped.
Kagiso: Stripped ends.
Soraya: And this is the isiXhosa.
Chorus: Yes.
Soraya: Now what is the isiZulu word?
Zinzi: *U ... uku* (to).
Soraya: *uku* (to).
Zinzi: *Ukuchutha (to pluck)*.

At first the facilitator is surprised at Zinzi's choice of 'stripped ends' as an example of difficult words, as evidenced by her questioning tone and repetition of the phrase 'Stripped ends? Stripped ends, ok'. Unlike the common assumption made in most textbook glossaries that only the scientific concepts need translation, Zinzi surfaces the challenge of the metalanguage of science experiments. She identifies the action verb 'stripped' as a 'difficult' word when she says 'Especially stripped. What does stripped mean?' Lemke (1998: 2) points out that 'scientists use specialized languages and use common language in specialized ways'. In this case 'stripped' can be both common language and part of the 'actional-operational "languages" of science' or scientific register that forms part of the instructions and actions in the book on how to create an electromagnet (Lemke, 1998: 5). When the facilitator responds to Zinzi's answer with the question, 'What would be the isiXhosa equivalent of that?' Zinzi, the only isiZulu speaker in the group, answers by saying, 'Stripped means *'ichuthiwe'* (it's plucked), *'ukuchutha'* (to pluck), like this (hand movements) *'ewe ukuchutha'* (yes, pluck), *'yisuse'''* (remove it). The facilitator accepts Zinzi's response as accurate and it is not contested by the other students. However, three isiXhosa speakers in the group of five students, Zara, Kagiso and Thebo, continue to discuss and negotiate the translation of the word 'stripped' into isiXhosa. Kagiso says 'Chipped off, stripped is like chipped. Ukucola (to grind)' and while the facilitator accepts his translation (not being able to speak isiXhosa herself) by saying 'Ok, spell that for me', both Xara and Thebo object. Thebo says *'Hayi'* (No) while Xara says 'No, *ukucola* (to grind) is (making hand movements), you like ... grinding'. Thebo offers *'Xhwitha'* (pluck) in isiXhosa instead. Xara concurs, saying, 'Cause *ngasu sa the feathers*' (I removed the feathers) (hand movements mimic plucking). Zinzi's translation into isiZulu remains uncontested but she points at Thebo and asks him '*Ukuthini ngesiZulu*, you understand Zulu?' It is possible that her question offers information and a challenge: Thebo objected to Kagiso's answer, and she wants to determine whether he will also challenge her isiZulu example. The students eventually provided these translations for stripped:

isiXhosa: *ukuxhwitha* (to pluck – isiXhosa)
isiZulu: *ukuchutha* (to pluck – isiZulu)
Setswana: *go tlhoba* (to pluck – Setswana)

At this stage, the facilitator is unaware that literally translated, the words (*ukuxhwitha, ukuchutha and go tlhoba*) mean 'to pluck', most often used in 'to pluck feathers'. Xara in fact enacts the plucking movement when she translanguages saying, '*Ngasu sae* the feathers' (I removed the feathers).

There are several points to consider here: firstly, students may have as much difficulty with 'common words used in specialized ways' as with the metalanguage of science in English. Secondly, when the metalanguage is translated without understanding the meaning of the word in English, the translation may refer to a synonym that is the translator's best understanding of the word and may not be appropriate to the context of the science lesson. Thirdly, while the use of student languages may be considered a good practice, how does the teacher ensure that the answers are correct if the teacher does not speak the home languages of the students? This concern is addressed in one of the examples in Dong's (2011) study demonstrating how a biology teacher teaching English language learners from multiple language backgrounds in the United States uses an English dictionary, while her students use their own bilingual dictionaries to support learning and understanding an English science textbook and lesson. During task analysis, the teacher firstly asked a student to look up the English word and read its meaning aloud to the rest of the class; secondly, she asked students to look up the word and meaning in their bilingual dictionaries; thirdly, she asked the students to write the word in their home language next to the English word in the textbook. Fourthly, she clarified the meaning of the word in the context of the task or lesson. Dong writes that the teacher 'not only told but modelled for her students how to approach a new word in the reading and how to highlight key concepts for reading comprehension and review' (2011: 263).

While dictionary use may be considered an outdated practice and is often associated with a grammatical and skills approach to language learning, what happens when this step is missed by the facilitator is discussed next. When Zinzi asks 'What does stripped mean?' and the facilitator does not guide the participants to the literal meaning of the word 'stripped' in the English dictionary she misses an opportunity for learning. She assumes that because the students had stripped the wire for the experiment performed an hour ago, they understood the word and so she asked the students instead, 'What would be the isiXhosa equivalent of that?'. But by not looking up the English word 'stripped' which means 'to remove a layer', the students miss the explanation of the word which could have guided them more closely when they translated the word into African languages. When teachers switch from scientific English in the textbook to everyday language, there is often the danger that the learners will forget the scientific term. Since African language-speaking teachers often have to translate English science textbooks so that learners can understand the curriculum content, there is a greater possibility that the teachers will use their own approximate understanding of concepts and words. For example, Kagiso's closest synonym for stripped is chipped: He says, 'Chipped off, stripped is like chipped. *Ukucola* (to grind – isXhosa).' The literal meaning of chipped is 'breaking off or gouging out of a small piece' whereas stripped is 'to remove a layer' and his isiXhosa answer '*Ukucola*' means to grind. All Kagiso's answers directed learners away from the action of removing the layer of plastic coating to expose the copper wire that will conduct the electricity needed to create an electromagnet. Similarly, Lera, Thebo, Zara and Zinzi also rely on their everyday knowledge and translate stripped as 'pluck' (isiXhosa: *ukuxhwitha*; isiZulu: *ukuchutha*; Setswana: go *tlhoba*). While all the translations are probable answers, they are not appropriate to the context of this science activity. The potential for misunderstanding increases when instead of remembering stripped, the learners remember the teacher's translations 'chipped' or 'grind' or even 'pluck' which could lead to confusion and an incorrect answer in assessments that are written in standard English using scientific register.

Though the teacher in Dong's example demonstrates pedagogically how dictionaries and translation can be used to create a glossary in multilingual classrooms and how this benefits learning, there are other considerations when using language as a resource and delinking from Anglonormative ideology. In particular, one might challenge the dominance of English and consider how to use the students' languages as a resource alongside English in a way that benefits the language practices of the entire class. Asking students to look up the words in their language and write these next to the English word might save time and support individual learning but it also means that the teacher and the rest of the class do not need to engage with any other language besides English. Instead of telling the students which word to look up, the facilitator, Soraya asks the students to identify the words they find difficult to understand and thus gains a better understanding of how the metalanguage of science contributes to or hinders learning. The facilitator also draws on the language resources of all the students and the translations are listed below each other on the board so that all the students are given an opportunity to learn the term in each other's languages. When the students provide the translations, the facilitator is repositioned as the learner and there is a shift in power.

Dong's example and this case study thus allow for a closer look at how science teachers are also language teachers and brings to the fore the fact that when students are translating into their familiar language resources they are negotiating meanings, understandings and words. After the workshop when the facilitator was made aware that the translation was incorrect by an isiXhosa/English bilingual colleague, she followed Dong's example to first look up the English word 'stripped' – 'to remove a layer' – and then asked her colleague for an English/African language science dictionary to find the correct term. The correct isiXhosa translation of the term 'stripped' would be *'ukuhlubulula'* (to remove a layer).

Including the urban varieties and moving between varieties

Both Dong's example and the facilitator in this case study are asking students to translate from a standard variety of English to a standard variety of another language, in this case, isiXhosa, isiZulu and Setswana. However, in the South African context, especially in urban areas and surrounding townships, teaching and learning happen through translanguaging between African language/s and English, with the urban variety of the African language in common use.[9] In Transcript 1, for example, both Xara and Zinzi translanguage as they discuss translating the word 'stripped' into their home languages:

> Xara: Cause *Ngasu sa* the feathers (I have removed the feathers – isiXhosa)
> (hand movements mimic plucking)
> Zinzi: Exactly! And in isiZulu, *ukuchutha (to pluck – isiZulu)*[MC19]

To students and learners living in urban areas then, the standard versions of African languages can be as alien as standard English because they are immersed in multilingual cities inhabited by South Africans and Africans from diverse backgrounds. Below in Transcript 2, Lera (who is Setswana) provides an example of the meshed code of English and isiXhosa that makes up some of the urban variety of isiXhosa when she recalled working in the laboratory at university. Lera and Soraya speak about language use:

Transcript 2

>Lera: She'll want to say something to me like '*uyayibona* imicroscope' (you see the microscope) [laughing] so you can see, she speaks isiXhosa but then only said 'microscope' in English. Or we will do, we will do ...
>Soraya: So what is the equivalent for microscope?
>Lera: In isiXhosa? Yoooooh.
>Soraya: In Setswana?
>Lera: I don't know. I don't really know Tswana that deep so I'll also just use 'microscope'
>Soraya: Ok.

The inclusion of the urban variety is important because students may not be familiar with the standard variety, which impedes their learning. In Transcript 2 above, the use of the meshed code 'imicroscope' is both an example of translanguaging and part of the language mix that characterizes the urban variety and facilitates understanding between multilingual speakers, in this case Lera who is Setswana and her friend who speaks isiXhosa. Lera's admission 'I don't really know Tswana that deep so I'll also just use "microscope"' reveals how the dominance of English and a continuing lack of resources invested into the creation of books in African languages mean that a subtractive bilingual education system is the experience of most students and learners. Students have not learned scientific and academic terms in African languages because bilingual science dictionaries or books in African languages to explain these terms are not easily available. Lera's response 'Yooh' and 'I don't know' could further explain the students' initial silence and reluctance to engage in practices that require translation into scientific or disciplinary registers because they might not have had access to learning these terms in their own schooling. The translation exercise could be risky and have consequences such as a loss of face for both students and teacher. Similarly, in Transcript 1 Kagiso, who lives in an urban area struggles to spell *ukuxhwitha*. He spells it as *ukukwita* and Xara, who went to school in a rural area and knows isiXhosa well, teases him by saying, 'Kagiso is using the BEE spelling'. The 'BEE' Xara refers to is an acronym for Black Economic Empowerment and refers to African language speakers in urban areas who may have more opportunities for economic empowerment, but lack vocabulary and knowledge of the standard varieties of isiXhosa spoken in the rural areas and used in the few bilingual/multilingual books published thus far. Kagiso's use of the urban varieties and Xara's calling it 'BEE spelling' as well as Zinzi's translation of stripped as '*ukuchuta* (to pluck)' signalling her experience of plucking feathers provide examples of how people 'bring into contact different

Creating a multilingual word wall of scientific terms: 'Strip some wire'

Standard English	Urban Variety	Standard isiXhosa	Standard Afrikaans
strip/	istrip/	ukuhlubulula/	afstroop

"to remove a layer or layers of coverings"

Figure 7.5 Creating a multilingual word wall of scientific terms.

biographies, histories and linguistic backgrounds as they translanguage' (Blackledge and Creese, 2017: 253). Heteroglossic language practices such as translanguaging play a crucial role in communication, and the urban variety can act as a bridge between the English version and African language translation and is thus important to include it in the glossary. It is the movement between the different varieties that enables full conceptual understanding seen in the following translingual example: strip/istrip/ukuhlubulula/afstroop or 'strip (standard English)/istrip (urban isiXhosa)/ukuhlubulula (standard isiXhosa)/afstroop (Afrikaans)' (see Figure 7.5).

Conclusion

Our aim in this chapter was to describe and analyse two case studies of teacher education courses which explicitly delink from monolingual English practices, or Anglonormativity, by decentring English resources and foregrounding the use of language resources other than English. Through an analysis of the student's embodied language practices in case study 1, we have been able to develop insights into their language histories and ideologies. Monolingual language ideologies were challenged through an activity that required students to use isiXhosa and Afrikaans in small group work and in public presentation of that work to the whole class. In this case, the alignment of the lecturer's and the student's linguistic resources enabled Lisa's usually invisible linguistic resources to become an essential asset and visibly bolstered her confidence as she took up the position of knower and of teacher in relation to the rest of her class.

In the first case study, we used the social construction of named languages productively (in a form of strategic essentialism) to make visible linguistic resources that are usually excluded from formal university spaces. However, in the second case study we draw attention to the limitations of 'standard languages' and named language constructs. Soraya encouraged a mix of students from urban and rural areas, who had different linguistic repertoires, schooling and university experiences, to use as resources all the language varieties and registers available to them in their repertoires. As with the first case study, students' embodied histories are also seen to shape their language resources. Examples are: Xara's use of the playful metaphor 'BEE spelling' to reference Kagiso's urbanized isiXhosa and Lera using the more widely used descriptor of 'deep' Setswana to describe schooled, formal Setswana. This case shows the need to work across all registers and varieties to enhance conceptual understanding and language learning. Formal published glossaries that include only standard varieties of named languages and that pre-select the terms to be included have their limitations and do not necessarily delink from colonial language ideologies.

We believe we have shown how these two interventions in teacher education involve a double move:

1) enabling students to recognize (and often recover) their own linguistic resources and gaps as well as their own language ideologies;
2) enabling students to develop strategies to use these resources (i.e. their full linguistic and semiotic repertoires) for their own learning as well as for their teaching in schools.

Creating third spaces in which translanguaging is encouraged and monolingual English is backgrounded has enabled us to begin to disrupt the dominant hierarchies of language and culture that extend the colonial matrix of power in an elite university space in South Africa. As such we would argue that these cases have enabled acts of Linguistic Citizenship (Stroud, 2018) that are individually empowering as well as necessary first steps towards shifting restrictive monolingual ideologies of language.

Acknowledgement

Our work pays tribute to and builds upon the many NGOs, projects and work of researchers in South Africa who have published on and skilfully make arguments for social justice in language education.

Notes

1. Students here refers to those attending higher education institutions and learners to those attending schools.
2. The requirement for African language-speaking learners to study through the medium of Afrikaans ceased immediately thereafter.
3. Anglonormativity draws on the feminist–post-structuralist notion of heteronormativity which foregrounds the institutionalized normativity of heterosexuality and the far-reaching negative consequences for those who do not identify as heterosexual.
4. Under Apartheid, all South Africans were racially classified as 'coloured', 'black', 'white' or 'Indian'. It should be noted that in South Africa, the term 'coloured' has a different meaning to the way it is used in the United States and elsewhere. Here, it refers to people of mixed heritage, many descendants of slaves from South East Asia brought here during the colonial times, or descendants of contact between the indigenous inhabitants of southern Africa and colonial settlers who began arriving nearly 400 years ago. Despite their Apartheid and colonial histories, these racial labels continue to have considerable currency as markers of social identity in contemporary South Africa.
5. Neither isiXhosa nor Afrikaans is commonly used as a medium of instruction in English-medium universities such as UCT. Unlike isiXhosa, however, Afrikaans has historically been used as medium of instruction at a number of South African universities including Stellenbosch University, the University of the Free State and the University of Pretoria.
6. We have used pseudonyms for all students named in the chapter.
7. Acknowledgements to the artist, Julia Davies, for the line drawings in this chapter.
8. See also Versfeld (1995).
9. For some accessible and entertaining materials on multilingualism in the classroom cf. Achmat (1992) and Wescott (2004).

References

Achmat, Z. (1992), "Yo Dude, Cosa, Wena, Kyk A?" – *The Multilingual Classroom*. [Documentary Film]. South Africa: The National Language Project. Available online: https://www.youtube.com/watch?v=rhzhq46gLCo (date accessed 10 September 2020)

Anzaldua, G. (1987), *Borderlands/La Frontera: The New Mestiza*. San Francisco, CA: Aunt Lute Books.

Bailey, B. (2007), 'Heteroglossia and Boundaries', in M. Heller (ed.), *Bilingualism: A Social Approach*, 257–74. Basingstoke: Palgrave Macmillan.

Bhabha, H. (1994), *Location of Culture*. London: Routledge
Blackledge, A. and A. Creese (2017), 'Translanguaging and the Body', *International Journal of Multilingualism*, 14 (3): 250–68.
Busch, B. (2015), 'Expanding the Notion of the Linguistic Repertoire: On the Concept of *Spracherleben* – The Lived Experience of Language', *Applied Linguistics*, 38 (3): 340–58.
Dong, Y. R. (2011), 'Integrating Language and Content: How Three Biology Teachers Work with Non-English Speaking Students', in O. García and C. Baker (eds), *Bilingual Education*, 253–67. Clevedon: Multilingual Matters.
Flores, N. and O. García (2013), 'Linguistic Third Spaces in Education: Teacher's Translanguaging across the Bilingual Continuum', in D. Little, C. Leung and P. van Avermaet (eds), *Managing Diversity in Education: Languages, Policies and Pedagogies*, 243–56. Clevedon: Multilingual Matters.
Fuss, D. (1989), *Essentially Speaking: Feminism, Nature and Difference*. New York: Routledge.
Garcia, O. (2009), Bilingual education in the 21st century: A global perspective. Malden, M.A, Oxford: Wiley-Blackwells.
Garcia, O. and C. E. Sylvan (2011), 'Pedagogies and Practices in Multilingual Classrooms: Singularities in Pluralities', *Modern Language Journal*, 95 (3): 385–400.
Garcia, O. and Li Wei (2014), *Translanganguaging: Language, Bilingualism and Education*. Basingstoke: Palgrave Macmillan.
Gibbons, P. (2009), '*English Learners Academic Literacy and Thinking. Learning in the Challenge Zone*'. Portsmouth, NH: Heinemann.
Gutiérrez, K. (2008), 'Developing a Sociocritical Literacy in the Third Space', *Reading Research Quarterly*, 43 (2): 148–64.
Heugh, K. (2013), 'Multilingual Education Policy in South Africa Constrained by Theoretical and Historical Disconnections', *Annual Review of Applied Linguistics*, 33: 215–37.
Heugh, K., P. Plüddemann and A. Siegruhn, eds (1995), *Multilingual Education for South Africa*. Johannesburg: Heinemann.
Kapp, R. (1998), 'Language, Culture and Politics: The Case for Multilingualism in Tutorials', in S. Angelil-Carter (ed.), *Access to Success: Literacy in Academic Contexts*, 21–34, Cape Town: UCT Press.
Lemke, J. L. (1998, October), 'Teaching all the Languages of Science: Words, Symbols, Images, and Actions', in *Conference on Science Education in Barcelona*.
Makalela, L. (2015), 'Moving out of Linguistic Boxes: The Effects of Translanguaging Strategies for Multilingual Classrooms', *Language and Education*, 19 (3): 200–15.
Makoe, P. and C. Kinney (2014), 'Linguistic Ideologies in Multilingual South African Suburban Schools', *Journal of Multilingual and Multicultural Development*, 29 (3): 186–99.
Makoni, S. (1998), 'African Languages as Colonial Scripts', in C. Coetzee and S. Nuttall (eds), *Negotiating the Past: The Making of Memory in South Africa*, 242–8, Cape Town: Oxford University Press.

Maldonado-Torres, N. (2007), 'On the Coloniality of Being: Contributions to the Development of a Concept', *Cultural Studies*, 21 (2–3): 240-70. Available online: https://doi.org/10.1080/09502380601162548 (accessed 19 October 2017).

McKinney, C. (2017), *Language and Power in Postcolonial Schooling: Ideologies in Practice*. New York & London: Routledge.

Mignolo, W. (2007), 'Delinking: The Rhetoric of Modernity, the Logic of Coloniality and the Grammar of De-coloniality', *Cultural Studies*, 21 (2–3): 449–514. Available online: https://doi.org/10.1080/09502380601162647 (accessed 19 October 2017).

Mignolo, W. (2013), 'On Pluriversality', Available online: http://waltermignolo.com/onpluriversality/ (accessed 19 October 2017).

Ngũgĩ wa Thiong'o. (1986), *Decolonising the Mind: The Politics of Language in African Literature*. London: James Currey.

Pietikäinen, S. and A. Pitkänen-Huhta (2014), 'Dynamic Multimodal Language Practices in Multilingual Indigenous Sami Classrooms in Finland' in D. Gorter, V. Venotz and Jasone Cenoz (eds), *Minority Languages and Multilingual Education: Bridging the Local and the Global*, 137–57. New York: Springer.

Plüddemann, P. (2015), 'Unlocking the Grid: Language in Education Policy Realisation in Post-Apartheid South Africa', *Language and Education*, 29 (3): 186–99.

Soja, E. (1996), *Thirdspace: Journeys to Los Angeles and Other Real-and-Imagined Places*. Massachusetts, USA: Blackwell Publishers.

Spivak, G. C. (1988), 'Subaltern Studies: Deconstructing Historiography', in R. Guha and G. C. Spivak (eds), *Selected Subaltern Studies*, 3–34, Oxford: Oxford University Press.

Stroud, C. (2007), 'Bilingualism: Colonialism, Postcolonialism and High Modernity', in M. Heller (ed.), *Bilingualism: A Social Approach*, 25–49, New York: Palgrave.

Stroud, C. (2018), 'Linguistic Citizenship', in L. Lim, C. Stroud and L. Wee (eds), *The Multilingual Citizen towards a Politics of Language for Agency and Change*, 17–39, Clevedon: Multilingual Matters.

Stroud, C. and C. Kerfoot (2013), 'Towards Rethinking Multilingualism and Language Policy for Academic Literacy', *Linguistics and Education*, 24 (4): 396–405.

Versfeld, R. (1995), 'Language Is Lekker: A Language Activity Classroom', in K. Heugh et al. (eds), pp. 23–7.

Wescott, N. (2004), *Sink or Swim*. Tomix Productions: Cape Town. Available onliene: http://www.praesa.org.za/videos/ (accessed 10 September 2020)

8

When Linguists Become Artists: An Exercise in Boundaries, Borders and Vulnerabilities

Marcelyn Oostendorp, Lulu Duke,
Simangele Mashazi and Charné Pretorius

Introduction

It is widely acknowledged that learning occurs through a variety of modes including language, gesture, visual images, sound and physical performance. However, multimodal pedagogy has only recently emerged 'from the margins' of language-in-education and literacy research (Early, Kendrick and Potts, 2015: 447). To challenge this marginality, some researchers have used spaces outside of classrooms to communicate the value of multimodal pedagogy to the wider public. In 2012 and 2014, at regional conferences for English as a second language (ESL) teachers in Ontario, Canada, Stille and Prasad (2015) curated exhibitions showcasing multimodal texts designed by students and teachers. Holmes (2015) reports on projects which used multimodal pedagogy and displayed the physical or digital forms of assessment to the public. Following Stille and Prasad (2015) and Holmes (2015), this chapter reflects on an exhibition that was designed to showcase multimodal assessment for a postgraduate module titled *Re-imagining Multilingualisms*. It was originally envisaged that the exhibition would display assessment but has since become a point of reflection for us on aspects such as pedagogy, research, positionality and unexpected outcomes. This chapter is, therefore, written from the perspective of the lecturer. While we acknowledge that the student voice is of paramount importance in student-centred initiatives and interventions,[1] we are concerned that the voices of the lecturers, the designers of teaching and learning materials, are 'frequently ... silenced by policy and suppressed or distorted within educational research' (Hargreaves, 1996: 12).

For the purposes of this chapter, the processes of creating an exhibition are viewed through the theoretical lens of resemiotization (Iedema, 2001, 2003) situated within the larger framework of multimodality and multiliteracies (The New London Group, 1996).[2] This lens offers a way of retrospectively making sense of how the assessment pieces were turned into an exhibition. However, in addition to retracing the process, we also point out particular instances of discomfort or tension within it. Research on multimodal pedagogy tends to be 'celebratory' on the effects of such pedagogies.[3] For example, Stille and Prasad's (2015: 620) article ends as follows:

> The three exhibits featured in this article have been offered to provide insight into and inspiration for the development of coordinated and systematic inquiry into the engagement of students at all stages of language learning in creative, personally meaningful, and socially significant work through a range of multimodal tools as a way of enlarging the English language classroom in the 21st century.

As we ourselves have witnessed the positive effects of multimodal pedagogy on student voice and agency, we do not wish to disparage Stille and Prasad's view. Instead, we bring these moments of tension and discomfort into the conversation. Zembylas and McGlynn (2012: 41) state that 'a pedagogy of discomfort, as an educational approach, emphasizes the need for educators and students alike to move outside their "comfort zones"'. Based on this, we take the view that feeling out of place and uncomfortable can play a role in 'challenging dominant beliefs, social habits and normative practices that sustain social inequities and in creating possibilities for individual and social transformation' (Zembylas and McGlynn, 2012: 41). Specifically, we want to focus on the discomfort and vulnerabilities of the lecturers.

First, we sketch the context and background of the course which led to the exhibition, after which we present the theoretical framework. Then, we discuss the process of 'making an exhibition' through the lens of resemiotization. Lastly, we discuss moments of tension in lieu of theory on the pedagogy of discomfort (Zembylas, 2015; Zembylas and Papamichael, 2017).

Context and background

Almost all universities in South Africa have some section or department that offers linguistics, either as an independent discipline or as part of a language offering (for example, Afrikaans or isiXhosa). In the Western Cape, where this study is situated, three of the four universities have linguistics departments or sections.[4] These three universities also all have an honours programme which comprises coursework and the completion of a small research project. These honours courses are generally conducted through seminar-style teaching, which can be both lecturer- and student-led. Assessment tends to include standard practices such as seminar presentations and papers, examinations and research-based assignments.[5] This chapter reflects on a joint honours module designed and presented by Stellenbosch University (SU) and the University of the Western Cape (UWC), which attempted to 're-imagine' multilingualism(s) both in terms of the content offered and in the pedagogies which were used to teach the module.[6]

UWC opened its doors in 1960 as an institution designated for 'coloured' people during Apartheid. The institution initially had Afrikaans as the sole medium of instruction.[7] According to Wolpe (1995: 283), UWC was established to give education only in a few fields to 'meet the needs of the coloured people as defined by the Apartheid state and in accordance with the racial stratification system of the prevailing social order' as its goal. During the 1980s, the university repositioned itself and sent a clear signal to the Apartheid government when the then rector, Jakes Gerwel, in his 1987 inaugural address, declared that UWC should be the 'intellectual home of the left' and began admitting students classified 'African' in defiance of the Apartheid laws (Wolpe, 1995: 287). Students and staff are still predominantly 'black' (in the broader political sense of 'black'), and the medium of instruction is now English, although the official language policy of the university acknowledges multilingualism and makes some provision for teaching in Afrikaans and isiXhosa 'where practicable'.[8] Despite the lack of resources during Apartheid, UWC is now considered a research-intensive university and continues to strive to erase the perception that the institution is 'inferior' to the former white universities in the province.

Stellenbosch University, on the other hand, became a fully fledged university for white students in 1918. Every Apartheid prime minister up until Balthazar Johannes 'B.J.' Vorster, who became prime minister in 1966, attended the university.[9] SU continues to struggle to rid itself of the label of being a bastion of Afrikanerdom. The university is usually ranked second or third in the list of top South African universities, behind the University of Cape Town and/or the University of the Witwatersrand. The majority of SU's staff and students are white (https://www.sun.ac.za/english/Pages/Student-Profile.aspx), and the mediums of instruction are both English and Afrikaans. Vigorous debates around the language policy flare up every few years,[10] with some demanding that the university use Afrikaans as medium of instruction to a greater extent, while others call for English to be the only medium of instruction.[11] As can be gleaned from these short overviews, the two universities have traditionally served quite different populations, and each has its own challenges in establishing a post-Apartheid identity. It is exactly because of the differences between these two institutions that we believed that the joint course would make an impact and allow different student populations and lecturers to learn from each other.

The course was divided into five-day-long seminars alternating between the two campuses, with a focus on linguistic ethnography, visual arts methods for creating concepts, multilingual creative writing, semiotic landscapes, reimagining formal linguistics and Linguistic Citizenship. For four of these seminars, students were required to do a multimodal assessment based on the preceding seminar which routinely included a reflection and a multimodal task (see Figure 8.1) or a reflection in a multimodal format. Due to the nature of administrative processes, the course was credit-bearing only for the twelve SU honours students. In their case, it formed part of their compulsory base module, and they attended all of the sessions.[12] For the UWC students, this was an enrichment course which was open to all postgraduate linguistics students. The groups were not evenly matched in number. The attendance of the UWC students fluctuated depending on the topics, and they were always fewer UWC students than SU ones in the sessions. Four honours students from UWC attended all five of the seminars. In addition, some master's and doctoral students attended all or selected sessions for their own enrichment but they were not expected to complete the assessments.

The assessment pieces had to be presented in the form of a portfolio submitted at the end of the course. After the course had been completed, the

---

Search for any newspaper articles on 'Kaaps' or 'Afrikaaps' (at least five). Read through these articles and cut out words, sentences or images from these articles which make an impact on you. Create a collage with these cut-outs. Write a short reflection (maximum one page) on how you see Kaaps differently (or not) and why in view of the collage you made. Also, reflect on why you chose the words and images that you did.

OR

Reflect on your own relationship with any linguistic variety (this can be a variety with which you have an ambiguous, antagonistic, or close and warm relationship. It can also be a language of longing or desire). Try to express your relationship to this variety through any multimodal means (clay, collage, drawing, poetry, video, animation). Write a short reflection on the piece that you created, briefly explaining how through multimodal means you might have forged new relationships with this variety (or not).

Figure 8.1 Multimodal assessment task.

honours students had two weeks to revise and refine their portfolios, and they could consult us about their ideas. The submitted works included an array of multimodal forms comprising video installations, interactive pieces, posters, poetry, sculpture, collages, photographs and written reflections (see Figure 8.2). All of the SU students submitted complete portfolios, while only two UWC students submitted pieces for the exhibition.

The students' works were exhibited from 29 May to 1 June 2018 at the Gallery of the University of Stellenbosch (GUS). This gallery is housed in what was once a Lutheran church located in the historical core of the town. We installed the exhibition together with some of our students. We decided to organize the exhibition around the four seminars for which assessment was required. Friends with video-editing skills, technical knowledge and equipment assisted in setting up the exhibition. The exhibition officially opened on 29 May and on Thursday 1 June, we held a cocktail function as part of the monthly 'First Thursdays' event, during which iconic South African Hip Hop artist Emile YX? performed a set.[13] The evening was generally hailed as a success with a conservative estimate of 100 people in the gallery space. The following Monday, the exhibition travelled

Figure 8.2 Exhibited multimodal pieces.

to UWC where it was exhibited in the institution's library atrium for a month. The discussion in this chapter is, however, solely based on the exhibition that was held in Stellenbosch. In the following section, we first introduce multimodal pedagogy and then discuss the main analytical framework of the paper, namely resemiotization.

Multimodal pedagogy

The first real rallying cry for multimodal pedagogy was made by the New London Group in 1996. Their central argument was that the conceptualization and teaching of literacy should be expanded to include multiple discourses and modalities. This had to be done to acknowledge increasing diversity in all societies, and the rise of multimedia and digital technologies (The New London Group, 1996: 61). Although they call their approach 'multiliteracies', multimodal teaching and learning practices were the cornerstone of this conceptualization of literacy. The New London Group stated that, rather than focusing only on language, a pedagogy of multiliteracies 'focuses on modes of representation much broader than language alone'. In order to explicate what a multiliteracies approach looked like, they drew on a metalanguage 'based on the concept of "design"' (The New London Group, 1996: 73). This concept can be simultaneously used to identify the 'organisational structure of products [or] the process of designing' (The New London Group, 1996: 74). Design involves three elements: 'available designs, designing, and the redesigned'. Available design includes the resources available across semiotic systems as well as the conventions governing their use and the experience of the text producer with these resources (The New London Group, 1996: 74). Designing refers to 'the process of shaping emergent meaning [which] involves re-presentation and recontextualisation' (The New London Group, 1996: 75). Finally, the redesigned refers to the outcome of the designing process, which is always something new. It is usually an interplay between new elements and the available designs (The New London Group, 1996: 76). Subsequently, research on multimodal pedagogy has included work as diverse as the use of visual images in textbooks, multimodal approaches to student writing, and the use of gestures in the classroom by students and teachers.[14]

The South African context has produced several rich studies on multimodal pedagogies. The Wits Multiliteracies group – among others, Pippa Stein and Denise Newfield – was particularly influential.[15] In other parts of South Africa, scholars like Arlene Archer and Lucia Thesen contributed significantly to research on multimodal pedagogy, especially in higher education.[16] Early et al. (2015: 449) highlight the significance of this South African research in exploring 'cultural and linguistic diversity in multimodal meaning making'. Stein (2008: 3) argues that South Africa provides a poignant case study of a context where 'students from different language and cultural backgrounds negotiate ongoing tensions' between different knowledge-creating systems and cultures.

Transforming texts, transforming meanings

In research on multimodality, the reshaping, recontextualization and transformation of modalities, contexts, formats and meanings are theorized in a few different ways. In this paper, we use 'resemiotization' as an umbrella term to talk about all the ways in which texts and their meanings can be reshaped and transformed. Iedema (2003: 41) defined resemiotization as how 'meaning making shifts from context to context, from practice to practice, or from one stage of a practice to the next'. Initially, Iedema's work on resemiotization was ethnographic in nature and focused on various stages in a building project (for example, planning, meeting and drawing up of plans). Iedema (2001) showed through his close multimodal analysis how the building project relied initially on modes such as talk and gesture. He further observed that as the project progressed, more durable modalities such as writing became dominant (Iedema, 2001: 23–4). According to Iedema (2001: 26), 'organizationally relevant meanings are relegated from the relatively volatile sphere of embodied semiosis, into the naturalizing contexts of spatio-material semiosis'. By introducing resemiotization into the toolkit of multimodality, the historical and material natures of representation are foregrounded (Iedema, 2003: 50).

For us, the notion of 'resemiotization' broadly captures the kinds of recontextualizations and transformations that can be found in the way the exhibition was 'made'. However, some of the other terms within the toolkit of multimodality – which also speak to ideas of transformation, change and reshaping of meaning – can assist in highlighting in part how the assessment pieces were transformed into an exhibition. Bezemer and Kress (2008: 175) make a distinction between 'transformation' and 'transduction'. For them, transduction refers specifically to 'the move of semiotic material from one mode to another' (Bezemer and Kress, 2008: 175). Transduction is argued to bring about profound changes with some meaning-making potential being lost and others gained during the process. Transformation, on the other hand, is described as a change that occurs 'in the arrangement within one mode' (Bezemer and Kress, 2008: 175), meaning that the elements within a text remain the same but the structure changes.

Drawing on understandings of text transformations from multimodal discourse analysis, and from other fields such as sociolinguistics, linguistic anthropology and psychology, Prior and Hengst (2010) introduce the concept of 'remediation'. They state that 'remediation points to ways that activity is (re) mediated – not mediated anew in each act – through taking up the materials at hand, putting them to present use and thereby producing altered conditions for future action' (Prior and Hengst, 2010: 1). The emphasis on activity and social action is evident in their description of semiotic remediation as 'the diverse ways that semiotic performances are re-represented and reused across modes, media and chains of activity that is grounded in a dialogic understanding of semiotics that focuses on the situated and mediated character of activity, and that recognizes the deep integration of semiotic mediation with the practices of everyday sociocultural life' (Prior and Hengst, 2010: 6). Iedema (2010: 139), however, states that the difference between remediation and resemiotization is that 'semiotic remediation privileges the multiple and complex flows through which meanings are mediated and project one another' while 'resemiotization serves to highlight how practices capitalize on making meanings traverse across semiotic modes towards increasingly nonembodied (exosomatic) phenomena'. The primary difference between the two concepts thus seems to be a matter of focus.

A further concept that attempts to explain the reshaping of texts and meanings is 're-genreing', introduced by Fiona English in her 2011 monograph. Initially based on work on student writing in university contexts, re-genreing refers to the transformation of material into different genres or communicative formats, for example from textbook to student essay, to play, and the new meanings and engagements with knowledge that this opens for students. More recently, re-genreing has not only been used to refer to student writing, but knowledge production more generally. English (2018: 179) states that 'different genres help us to grapple with knowledge more effectively than relying on one alone'.

Resemiotization: From task to exhibition

In order to retrospectively structure our experiences of the exhibition, resemiotization offered what other possible theoretical frames did not – it enabled an analysis of the 'dynamics which resulted in socially recognizable and practically meaningful artefacts' (Iedema, 2003: 50), and not only on the modalities of artefacts themselves. Having an exhibition of student work (not a typical conclusion to a postgraduate course in linguistics!) offered us an opportunity to engage with the communities in which we were situated and to problematize institutionalized conventions of knowledge production and dissemination. An exhibition also allowed us to display the multimodal approach which had been taken towards assessment. Furthermore, it presented us with an opportunity to explore the potential that creative- and arts-based methodologies could add to academic research processes and pedagogies. Thus, an exhibition allowed us to showcase the potential of re-genreing to a wider audience.

Given that the course foregrounded the embodied and experiential aspects of multilingualism, it was important that the 'assessment' portion did not unnecessarily constrain the students' expression and reflection of what they had learned or experienced during the course. We wished to decentre language in processes of knowledge production and to problematize the textual boundaries of conventional academic practice. As a result, assignment guidelines were vague and encouraged students to draw on any semiotic resources which were available to them. This kind of approach is in line with the notion of 'authentic learning', as Herrington (2006: 2) states that 'the learning environment needs to provide ill-defined activities which have real-world relevance and which present a single complex task to be completed over a sustained period of time'.

In the following sections, we offer one concrete example of how a particular task was framed and reframed by us, reframed by the students and then exhibited. We focus on the task related to semiotic landscapes as this brought interesting reflections on how students related to various spaces within the town of Stellenbosch. This task, more so than the others, moved outside of the traditional classroom setting.

The task

For this specific task, the students were divided into three groups that each had a different activity to engage in and to complete. One group visited the area previously known as *Die Vlakte* ('The Flats'), an area from which coloured residents were forcibly removed during Apartheid after the area was declared white (Fransch, 2010). Some of the university buildings at SU, such as the Arts and Social Sciences building, were built in this area. Students were led on this tour by an individual whose family lived in *Die Vlakte* and was subsequently moved to another area. The second group visited Goldfields residence, the first university housing that was allocated for black students at SU. After the fall of

Apartheid in 1994, the residence became increasingly integrated, but it remains proud of its history in the struggle to desegregate the university and displays this history in the public spaces of the residence. Lastly, there was the 'Little Europe' group. 'Little Europe' refers to the tourist hub in central Stellenbosch, which usually includes Church Street, Dorp Street and certain parts of Ryneveld and Andringa streets. This area has many coffee shops, restaurants and curio shops. We have often heard students refer to this area as 'Europe' or 'Little Europe', hence the name of this task. This proved to be the most popular group with most students choosing to be in this group and to complete the related task. Due to space constraints, this is the sole task of this seminar that we focus on in this chapter.

In order to complete the task in Figure 8.3, students were required to use (1) language which occurred in the context of a lecture, (2) the accompanying linguistic materials, such as their course readers and personal notes, and (3) personal narratives, which they had constructed around these resources, and to transform and develop these into concretized and explicitly multimodal artefacts. Instructions for the tasks were given in writing and orally at the end of the first session of the seminar on semiotic landscapes. Students were then divided into groups of three or four, with all of the groups comprising a mix of UWC and SU students. Each group was assigned a different coffee shop.

Most students took photographs and wrote reflections on them. However, we also received reflections in the form of poetry and other multimodal artefacts that had been collected or created, such as takeaway boxes/coffee cups, or a map drawn of their journey through Little Europe. The words that the students captured differed quite significantly, and some students captured images rather than words. Although the written instructions stated that they should capture a word, we emphasized in our oral instructions that the students

---

'Little Europe': Embodied Linguistic Landscapes
- Students will be asked to walk around the main tourist area of Stellenbosch and have coffee at any location and observe the space.
- Take a photograph of a word you find in 'little Europe' that you believe is indicative of the place or encapsulates your experience in that space.
- Write a reflection/explanation on why you have selected that particular word (this could include your language experience, embodiment, etc.).

Figure 8.3 Little Europe task.

were also free to use other modalities. Through our oral interactions with the students, we were thus able to challenge the permanency of writing and recast the instructions in line with the spirit of the course. Thus, the available design elements for this assessment included the constraints of the assignment, the conventions associated with it as well as the 'discoursal experience of those involved in designing' (The New London Group, 1996: 75). One discoursal experience which we believe had a particularly profound influence on what was designed was the multilingual creative writing seminar preceding the semiotic landscapes seminar. For this seminar, we unexpectedly received quite a number of reflections in poetic form. Thus, the design here both reproduced and transformed 'given knowledge, social relations, and identities' (The New London Group, 1996: 75).

The meeting

Once we received all of the students' portfolios, executing the theoretical and conceptual aims that we had for the exhibition proved challenging. In the conceptualization stage(s) of the exhibition, exactly how we might 'redesign' (The New London Group, 1996) the opportunities offered by an exhibition as a 'linguistic' platform remained abstract. Along with the expected constraints of finding the time and space to realize our visions were the challenges that came with practically and pragmatically realizing the abstract, shifting and multiple meanings we wanted to embed in and extract from the exhibition as both process and product. Our main intention was to ensure that every student was adequately represented and that they all had the opportunity to take part as creators and curators.

In order to begin planning the finer details of the exhibition, we simply started by going through each portfolio and discussing possible emergent themes and ways of coherently organizing the material. It soon became evident that filling the large gallery space would be more complicated than we had anticipated. We arranged a meeting with Jason Richardson, our colleague from UWC who had been tasked with managing the submissions from UWC students and moving the exhibition to the UWC venue. During this meeting, we discussed the logistics of how we would (1) display the works, (2) host an opening evening function and (3) move the exhibition to UWC. This meeting obviously did not occur in isolation; many smaller, official and casual conversations about the exhibition and content of the course had occurred over the many months of the planning and running it. However, this meeting was significant as it marked a semiotic shift in the trajectory of the course: a resemiotizing move in which previously ephemeral meanings moved towards material realization.

Once we had looked over all the portfolios and discussed possible ways in which we might display them, it was decided that we would take some written pieces such as the reflections and poems and display them in more diverse materials, modalities and mediums. Both transformation and transduction (Bezemer and Kress, 2008) took place, with some pieces changing modalities (written poetry that we asked students to perform) and others being reshaped. The most significant change, however, was the changing of materiality; for example, parts of the submitted texts were written or printed into and onto a variety of mediums such as paint or chalk on cardboard or mirrors. While we felt that these resemiotizing moves would serve to enhance the overall aesthetic of a cohesive exhibition, we also knew that this was a contentious move as we were asking the artists to change their works, more specifically, if *we* could change their works. This meant that by privileging the semantic content of their work, some meanings – such as those captured by the visual dimensions of the original printed text – would be lost (for example, font size and colour), and others would be created depending on the particularities of how we chose to materially alter and display their works.

The making

To mitigate some of the effects that changing the works would have in terms of creative control, we invited all of the students to meet with us to discuss suggested changes and to participate centrally in the installation of the exhibition. This was minimally successful as only two of the twelve SU students were able to meet with us and participate in making decisions about how best to expand the material realizations of their texts. Over the week that followed, we used our own creative insights and talents to record, draw and print pieces for the exhibition. We were more successful in encouraging the students to take ownership of how the pieces were installed, with five students being actively part of the installation of the exhibition. Only on the day of the physical installation was the final overall aesthetic established. This week of meaning-making work demonstrates the way in which meanings were stabilized and resemiotized 'into more durable manifestations' (Iedema, 2001: 35), as the semiotic landscape of the exhibition became finalized and materially fixed based on the social, cultural and institutional context of an exhibition space.

From the beginning of the course, we felt it important that the approach we took to the exhibition should challenge the colonial paradigm in which the museum and gallery space was forged. We were interested in creating a space that challenged a totalizing, homogenizing approach to art, academics and display. We viewed creativity in the same way as Nelson and Johnson (2014: 1) did – as something which is 'not a special quality possessed by artists and designers'. Instead art 'comes about, when it does, in and through socially situated, integrative, transformative processes of meaning making, which are potentially available to all' (Nelson and Johnson, 2014: 1). We wanted to decentre the colonial gaze through language and its multiplicity. Therefore, the process of changing works to create a more coherent and aesthetically-pleasing exhibition became a balancing act, juggling opposing directives generated by external and personal pressures to celebrate the students' work, and put on the most academically successful exhibition as possible.

The display

In different parts of the gallery, we displayed the multimodal artefacts of each seminar. One part of the gallery was a dedicated poetry room, where a video with some of the poetry recordings performed by students played on repeat and where printed poetry was hung up in various parts of room. We decided that the semiotic landscape task on Little Europe should be displayed in the form of a coffee shop setting (see Figure 8.4). In this coffee shop, the photographs and poems were put up on the wall. We used different kinds of writing and materialities (black paper resembling a blackboard menu with the options written in chalk) which played with the aesthetics of a coffee shop. Exhibition-goers were invited to sit on the chair provided, as we wanted them to be aware of their bodies in this specific space. Another theme that we played around with was that of *decadence* – a word that was used by more than one group to describe their experiences in Little Europe. One way in which we did this was by 'oversaturating' a photograph of a group of street performers which was captured by one of the students. Thus, we juxtaposed the decadence of Little Europe with the itinerant poverty also found within the area.

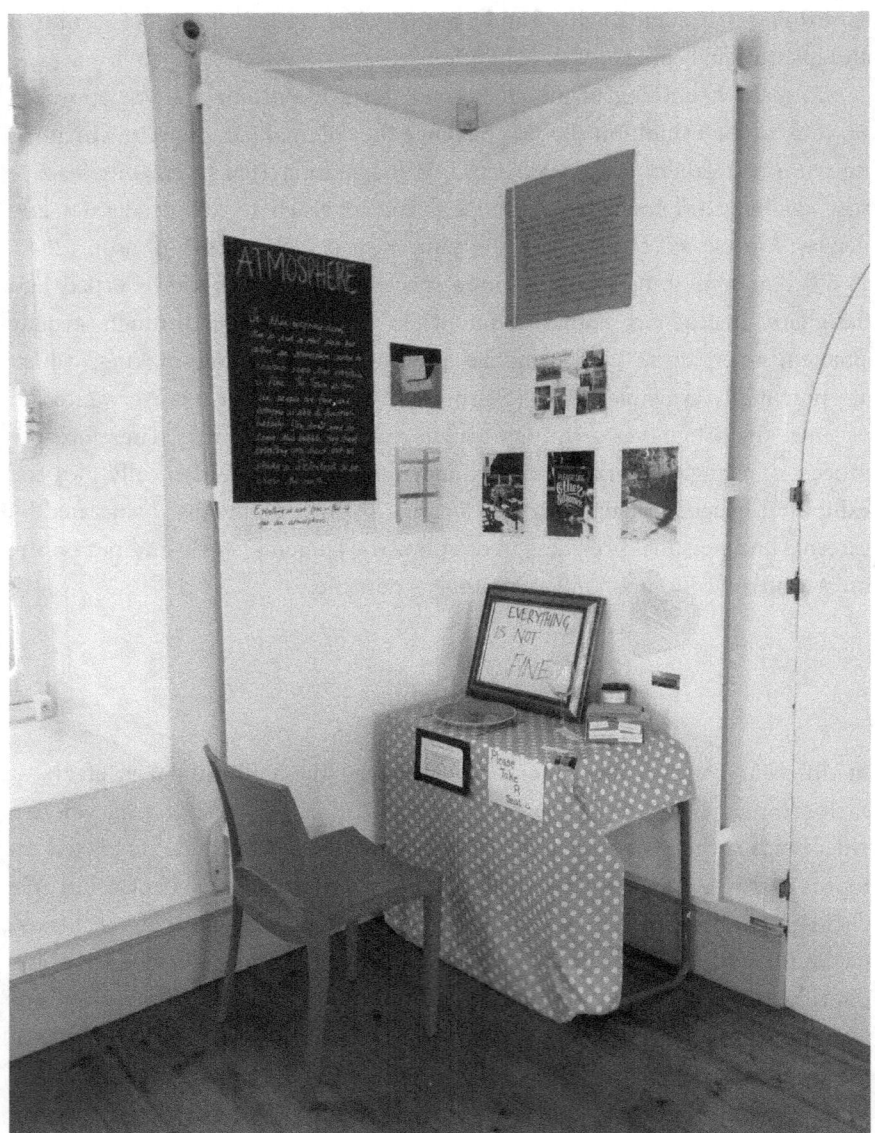

Figure 8.4 Little Europe display.

The exhibition

The exhibition attracted people of various ages and cultures, representing an array of languages. This included the students themselves, their friends, family, members of university management and, unexpectedly, a number of homeless people. During our cocktail function on the First Thursday evening, the first guest that arrived was a homeless person. He came in, we gave him something to eat and drink, and he looked around at the exhibition. He had a First Thursday programme for the evening and told us that he wanted to attend a talk by a famous photographer at one of the other galleries in town. Later that evening, a homeless woman came into the gallery. She danced while Emile YX? performed his set, then she had something to eat and started collecting empty bottles for recycling. We were all not quite sure how to handle the situation. Later on, in the evening, one of our students came up to us and said, 'I don't want to alarm you, but I think she has gone to fetch her friends.' The woman indeed came back, and a family who seemed to be living on the street joined her in the gallery. They also had something to eat and left shortly afterwards. This was one of the unexpected consequences of the exhibition – it was life-imitating art, with this juxtaposition of affluence and poverty also being a central theme in the Little Europe display. For all of us, this was one of the remarkable points during the exhibition. On the Saturday, the exhibition was taken down and moved to UWC.

The marking

A specific method for grading the assignments had remained unresolved for the duration of the course with some members of the team being completely against assessing the assignments. It seemed inherently uncomfortable to quantify the truths, vulnerabilities and experiences of the students manifested in their work. However, the structure of the honours module made it necessary to award a mark for the course. Ultimately, we decided to mark collectively. We went through each portfolio together and discussed what we felt the most appropriate method would be to determine a final mark for each student. After looking through all of the portfolios, it was evident that all of the students made a serious attempt to engage with the course and to use multimodal forms of making meaning. Because of this, we decided that each student would start on 50 per cent (a pass mark for the course) before any grading took place. From there, we assigned each student a mark for each of the seminar assignments. We discussed what we felt were the merits of each portfolio and decided collectively on a final mark for each portfolio based on content and form. This process relied on a series of subjective and contested agreements to establish what would become an institutionally categorized and recognized symbol – a value – representing a person's academic achievement. This resemiotizing move was possibly the most salient as it represents a significant move towards 'facticity' (Iedema, 2001: 25). All previously contested, negotiable and flexible meanings had now been materially realized and committed to in one final and singular *mark*.

The afterlife

Published articles on resemiotization often end their analyses with the officialization of processes – the filing of the report, the erection of the building or, in our case, with the final awarded mark. However, by drawing on the extended toolkit provided by multimodality research, we are able to discuss the afterlife of the exhibition in terms of remediation. After the exhibition, the marks were entered, released to the students and recorded on their study records.

We, the lecturers and the students, continue to interact with the semiotics created in and through the course and exhibition in different ways (see also Abrahams et al., 2019 and Bock et al., 2019) We have written this chapter about the exhibition, further resemiotizing it as 'research', rendering a multimodal experience in a print-dominant form. The materials produced for the exhibition have served as examples, precursors and ways to build on for the new assessment tasks for 2019. We have also discussed the assessment criteria and have decided to inform the students from the beginning how they will be assessed (unlike the previous year). We have had some discussions on self- and peer assessment as ways to further engage our students and challenge the top-down nature of assessment practices. This new, transformed meaning has become an available design, a new meaning-making resource (The New London Group, 1996) which will shape the new assessments created by students in years to come and the form of the exhibition. In 2018, the audience reacted in particular ways, and in 2019, we will get new reactions. The exhibition in 2019 will form part of an intertextual chain connected to the previous year's course and assessment whilst continuously pointing forward and anticipating new forms of engagement. As Prior and Hengst (2010) put it, the activities for 2019 will not be made anew but will be remediated and will produce new possibilities for future action.

Moments of discomfort

In this section, we focus on some of the tensions we have pointed out in the previous sections and the implications of this for multimodal pedagogy.

Linguists making artistic decisions

As we were making decisions about how best to display the students' work, we were confronted with the fact that none of us had any training as curators or artists. The desire to produce an exhibition which was 'artistic' was in tension with our desire to decolonize a gallery space as, invariably, our ideas of visual display are influenced by our previous (colonial) encounters with art. This uncomfortable interaction outside of our discipline allows for reflection on other more common processes about which we are not reflective. We are not used to making decisions on whether something is artistic enough but we routinely make judgements about other aspects of student work, such as whether something is academic or formal enough in 'normal' academic writing. We do this so often that we do not reflect on this. In addition, we felt increasingly uncomfortable about the significant role we as teaching staff played in deciding how the pieces should be displayed (especially after the exhibition), as we felt that this was exactly the kind of top-down approach that we had wanted to challenge. By crossing disciplinary boundaries and embracing multimodal pedagogy, we learned about 'the invisible ways in which we comply with dominant ideology' (Zembylas and McGlynn, 2012: 44).

Assigning marks

Another area in which we experienced tension and uncertainty was in awarding marks for the assessment. Firstly, some of us felt that marks should not be assigned, but we were forced by the structure of the honours programme to do so. We also remained unsure about how exactly to grade the work. Wyatt-Smith and Kimber (2009: 80) state that English teachers are usually 'experienced assessors of student reading, writing and speaking. Their ability to identify markers of quality in student work indicates not just their expertise in substantive discipline knowledge, but also their potential for inducting student novices into both knowledge of relevant assessment criteria and the rules for applying them.' In our case, we lacked experience in assessing multimodal work because of the dominance of writing at university. We could thus not be so sure that, as Wyatt-Smith and Kimber (2009: 80) state, we had 'the insider knowledge of what counts as quality', and that we could give good advice to students on how to improve their work. There was thus a constant tension between established norms and new ways of doing, and diversity and uniformity, which caused insecurities (and admittedly some mistakes) on our part in terms of how to handle this tension.

Conclusion

Multimodal pedagogy created an opportunity for us to admit to and encounter our own vulnerabilities. Stroud (2015: 35) argues that

> multilingualism comprises sites of vulnerability in the sense that no common ground can be assumed – all participants relinquish monologic control over the exchange and open themselves to the inevitable fact that the significance of any instance of language may evolve outside of the control or intentions of any one single participant at any one moment of interaction.

We argue here that it is not only multilingualism that captures this dimension of vulnerability, but also multimodal expression, as participants similarly relinquish monomodal control over the interaction and open themselves to new possibilities. The engagement with multimodality also opened new spaces of interaction outside of the usual classroom (for example, coffee shops, the exhibition site), and made for new social encounters (for example, students were 'forced' to interact with homeless people) which we were also not sure how to handle. The encounters around the exhibition allowed us as lecturers to get some way into realizing our 'unconscious privileges as well as the invisible ways in which they comply with dominant ideology' (Zembylas, 2015: 166). Moreover, we as lecturers were transformed by the process and through discomfort. Not only were material resources redesigned, but 'designing also transformed the designer' (New London Group, 1996: 76).

Notes

1. For more on the student perspectives of this project, see Bock, Abrahams and Jansen (2019), Abrahams et al. (2019) and Moolman et al. 2019.
2. The New London Group was a group of ten academics which included Courtney Cazden, Bill Cope, Norman Fairclough, James Gee, Mary Kalantzis, Gunther Kress, Allen Luke, Carmen Luke, Sarah Michaels and Martin Nakata. They met in 1994 in New London in the United States to discuss literacy education, and they coined the term 'multiliteracies'.
3. See Newfield et al. (2003) for an exception.
4. The four universities are the University of Cape Town, Stellenbosch University, the University of the Western Cape and the Cape Peninsula University of Technology (CPUT). CPUT does not offer linguistics as a subject.

5   The brief outline here of honours teaching in linguistics is based on the experience of the first author, who has taught honours courses at two of the four universities in the Western Cape, and is an external examiner/moderator of several honours courses at universities in South Africa.
6   This project was funded with the assistance of a Mellon Foundation's grant awarded within the program me *Unsettling Paradigms: The Decolonial Turn in the Humanities Curriculum at Universities in South Africa.*
7   'Coloured' is an Apartheid racial category used to refer to someone of mixed ancestry (including, but not limited to, the indigenous Khoi and San, Indonesian and Indian slaves, white European settlers and Bantu-speaking Africans). Like all racial categories, it is contested but is still used widely by official bodies, mostly for the purposes of redress.
8   'Black' here refers to everybody who is not white.
9   Notable SU alumni of this era include anti-Apartheid struggle heroes such as Beyers Naudé, a former Dutch Reformed Church minister, and Frederick Van Zyl Slabbert, who later became the leader of the Progressive Federal Party, the official opposition to the National Party during the late 1970s and 1980s. SU, however, is not generally perceived as the space in which their anti-Apartheid ideas were formed.
10 Recently, the constitutional court ruled in favour of the university's amended language policy which allows for the greater use of English (i.e. that everything that is in Afrikaans should also be available in English – but not necessarily the reverse).
11 See Williams (2018) for more.
12 Yearbook amendments at SU usually have to be submitted at least a year in advance, and there are specific cut-off dates by which these amendments need to be made. By the time the funding for this module was secured, the cut-off date had already passed, and amendments to the course could not be made.
13 On the first Thursday evening of every month, entrance to art galleries and some other institutions in Stellenbosch is free. In addition, these institutions usually host special guests or programmes and offer free wine and snacks. Many opening functions are held on these 'First Thursday' evenings as they attract bigger crowds.
14 See Bezemer and Kress (2008), Hood (2011) and Early, Kendrick and Potts (2015).
15 See Stein and Newfield (2008).
16 See, for example, Thesen (2001) and Archer (2006 and 2010).

References

Abrahams, L., K. R. Jansen, L. Julie, N. Mpuma and Z. Bock (2019). *Special Issue of Multilingual Margins: A Cat's Cradle*, 6: (1).

Archer, A. (2006), 'A Multimodal Approach to Academic "Literacies": Problematising the Visual/Verbal Divide', *Language and Education*, 20 (6): 449–62.

Archer, A. (2010), 'Multimodal Texts in Higher Education and the Implications for Writing Pedagogy', *English in Education*, 44 (3): 201–13.

Bezemer, J. and G. Kress (2008), 'Writing in Multimodal Texts: A Social Semiotic Account of Designs for Learning', *Written Communication*, 25 (2): 166–95.

Bock, Z., L. Abrahams and K. R. Jansen (2019), 'Learning through Linguistic Citizenship: Finding the 'I' of the Essay', *Multilingual Margins*, 6 (1): 72–85.

Early, M., M. Kendrick and D. Potts (2015), 'Multimodality: Out from the Margins of English Language Teaching', *TESOL Quarterly*, 49 (3): 447–60.

English, F. (2011), *Student Writing and Genre: Reconfiguring Academic Knowledge*. London: A&C Black.

English, F. (2018), '"It's Called Change": Regenring, Reconfiguring and Representation', *Journal of Writing in Creative Practice*, 11 (2): 171–80.

Fransch, C. J. (2010), '"We Would Have No Name": The Porosity of Locational and Racial Identities amongst the "Coloured Communities" of Stellenbosch, c. 1890–1960s', *African Studies*, 69 (3): 403–22.

Hargreaves, A. (1996), 'Revisiting Voice', *Educational Researcher*, 25 (1): 12–19.

Herrington, J. (2006), 'Authentic e-Learning in Higher Education: Design Principles for Authentic Learning Environments and Tasks', *E-Learn: World Conference on E-Learning in Corporate, Government, Healthcare, and Higher Education*, 2006 (1): 3164–73.

Holmes, S. (2015), 'Promoting Multilingual Creativity: Key Principles from Successful Projects', *Working Papers in Urban Language and Literacies*, paper 182.

Hood, S. (2011), 'Body Language in Face-to-Face Teaching: A Focus on Textual and Interpersonal Meaning', in S. Dreyfus, S. Hood and M. Stenglin (eds), *Semiotic Margins: Meaning in Multimodalities*, 31–52. London: Continuum.

Iedema, R. (2001), 'Resemiotization', *Semiotica*, 137 (4): 23–39.

Iedema, R. (2003), 'Multimodality, Resemiotization: Extending the Analysis of Discourse as Multi-semiotic Practice', *Visual Communication*, 2 (1): 29–57.

Iedema, R. (2010), 'Resemiotization of a Policy Initiative: Promoting Open Disclosure as "Open Communication about Clinical Adverse Events"', in P. A. Prior and J. A. Hengst (eds), *Exploring Semiotic Remediation as Discourse Practice*, 139–55. London: Palgrave Macmillan.

Moolman, K., N. Mpuma and L. Julie. (2019), 'Re-imagining the Writing Workshop: The Creation of Multilingual, Collaborative Poetry', *Multilingual Margins: A Journal of Multilingualism from the Periphery*, 6 (1): 15–35.

Nelson, M. E. and N. H. Johnson (2014), 'Editors' Introduction: Multimodality, Creativity and Language and Literacy Education', *Pedagogies: An International Journal*, 9 (1): 1–6.

Newfield, D., D. Andrew, P. Stein and R. Maungedzo (2003), '"No Number Can Describe How Good It Was": Assessment Issues in the Multimodal Classroom', *Assessment in Education: Principles, Policy & Practice*, 10 (1): 61–81.

Prior, P. A. and J. A. Hengst, eds (2010), *Exploring Semiotic Remediation as Discourse Practice*. New York: Palgrave Macmillan.

Stein, P. (2008), *Multimodal Pedagogies in Diverse Classrooms: Representation, Rights and Resources*. London: Routledge.

Stein, P., and D. Newfield (2006), 'Multiliteracies and Multimodality in English in Education in Africa: Mapping the Terrain', *English Studies in Africa*, 49 (1): 1–21.

Stille, S. and G. Prasad (2015), '"Imaginings": Reflections on Plurilingual Students' Creative Multimodal Works', *TESOL Quarterly*, 49 (3): 608–21.

Stroud, C. (2015), 'Linguistic Citizenship as Utopia', *Multilingual Margins: A Journal of Multilingualism from the Periphery*, 2 (2): 2–22.

The New London Group (1996), 'A Pedagogy of Multiliteracies: Designing Social Futures', *Harvard Educational Review*, 66 (1): 60–92.

Thesen, L. (2001), 'Modes, Literacies and Power: A University Case Study', *Language and Education*, 15 (2–3): 132–45.

Williams, S. L. (2018), 'The Discursive Construction of the Language Policy Debate at Stellenbosch University: An Investigation of the Cape Times and Die Burger', MA dissertation, Stellenbosch University, Stellenbosch.

Wolpe, H. (1995), 'The Debate on University Transformation in South Africa: The Case of the University of the Western Cape', *Comparative Education*, 31 (2): 275–92.

Wyatt-Smith, C. and K. Kimber (2009), 'Working Multimodally: Challenges for assessment', *English Teaching: Practice and Critique*, 8 (3): 70–90.

Zembylas, M. (2015), '"Pedagogy of Discomfort" and Its Ethical Implications: The Tensions of Ethical Violence in Social Justice Education', *Ethics and Education*, 10 (2): 163–74.

Zembylas, M. and C. McGlynn (2012), 'Discomforting Pedagogies: Emotional Tensions, Ethical Dilemmas and Transformative Possibilities', *British Educational Research Journal*, 38 (1): 41–59.

Zembylas, M. and E. Papamichael (2017), 'Pedagogies of Discomfort and Empathy in Multicultural Teacher Education', *Intercultural Education*, 28 (1): 1–19.

9

Decolonizing Linguistics: A Southern African Textbook Project

Zannie Bock

Introduction

The textbook project was never planned as a 'decolonial' project. The idea was sparked in 2010 by a random conversation with a publisher from a local publishing house who asked me to review a proposal for an introductory text on linguistics and to indicate whether our department (the Linguistics Department at the University of the Western Cape) would consider prescribing it for our huge first year classes. 'Oh, no', I said (somewhat dismissively), on looking at the outline, 'this is far too boring, we do much more interesting things with our first years!' 'Well, send me a proposal for your course', she said. And so 'a seed was planted' and the textbook project began to grow.

The project took three years to come to fruition, and initiated a process of collaboration and curriculum renewal in our department which had a number of unexpected and positive outcomes. Because the entire teaching staff was involved, it had a profound effect on the department, both in terms of building a shared intellectual project and collective professional identity, and in terms of strengthening learning and teaching in our undergraduate programme. Following a pilot version in 2013, the first edition of *Language, Society and Communication: An Introduction* was published in 2014, and is currently being used in our undergraduate programme, as well as in a number of universities

To my co-editor, Gift Mheta, and all authors, a thousand thanks, may the seeds continue to grow and flourish: Bassey Antia, Felix Banda, Manne Bylund, Dinis Da Costa, Zodwa Dlayedwa, Paul Duncan, Charlyn Dyers, Fiona Ferris, Niklaas Fredericks, Kathleen Heugh, Thokozani Kunkeyani, Nobuhle Luphondo, Lynn Mafofo, Kelvin Mambwe, Sibonile Mpendukana, Matthys Odendal, Marcelyn Oostendorp, Amiena Peck, Ellen Simon, Anne-Marie Simon-Vandenbergen, Chris Stroud, Quentin Williams and Hermann Wittenberg.

throughout southern Africa and beyond. A second edition was published in 2019 (see Bock and Mheta, [2014]2019).

This chapter uses a decolonial lens to reflect on the process of writing the textbook. In addition to considering the ways in which the textbook attempts to develop a local linguistics curriculum, it explores the complex and challenging process of co-authoring a textbook with twenty-five authors, eleven of whom were doctoral students at the time and relatively inexperienced writers. Drawing on interviews and written correspondence with these authors, as well as my own notes and reflections as project co-ordinator and co-editor, this chapter describes how the collaborative writing process enabled a 'praxis of fissure' (Walsh, 2014) which opened up alternative modes of academic practice ('cracks') and had, I will argue, the effect of constructing 'epistemic authority' (Chandoke, 2003) and of building local value and pride. In her *Pedagogical Notes from the Decolonial Cracks*, Walsh (2014) writes:

> *In and of themselves, the cracks ... denote little more than apertures or beginnings. While they may weaken and fracture the hegemonic whole, their effect is dependent upon what occurs within the fissures and crevices, on how the seeds planted, sprout, flourish, and grow, on how they extend ruptures and openings.*

In a sense, the context in which we teach is also a 'crack', a relatively under-resourced historically black university in post-Apartheid South Africa. This chapter includes a description of this context (Section 2), and the ways in which the textbook was a response to, as well as constrained by this setting. It then reflects on how the project served to shift, in Mignolo's (2009: 4) words, both the 'terms of the conversation' (Section 3) and the 'content' (Section 4), by focusing on how the textbook attempted to re-centre local knowledge and voices in both its academic writing practices and its curriculum content. Adopting this perspective, I argue, helps us to understand and validate this authoring process as an alternative mode of practice: firstly, in the sense of including multiple authors, many of whom were novice writers; and secondly, in the sense of acknowledging how a text and project like this can build academic capacity and voice,[1] even though it carries no 'institutional reward' for its authors in terms of recognition by quality assurance regimes, such as the accredited publication lists. I conclude by reflecting on what this project demonstrates about 'transforming academic curricula' and argue that changing the 'terms' may be a prerequisite for changing the 'content'. I argue that the creation of 'participatory spaces' (Kerfoot, 2011) in academia that encourage collaborative and mentoring relations, and build the confidence, pride and agency of (new) knowledge producers, may be a first step to shifting disciplinary paradigms.

A decolonial lens

Decoloniality has been a topic of scholarly concern and local activism since the historic Bandung conference of 1955 (Baker, 2014). Much of the groundwork has been laid by scholars such as Walter Mignolo, Boaventura de Sousa Santos, Lynn Mario Menezes de Souza, Catherine Walsh and others. In developing his approach to decoloniality, Mignolo (2009, 2013) writes about the need for 'epistemic disobedience', which, he argues, entails delinking from the dominant Euro-American-derived epistemologies by changing both the *content* and the *terms* of the disciplinary conversation. In relation to higher education, changing the *content* can be understood as a call to critically interrogate those epistemologies which are valued and included in the curriculum. It means recognizing that many knowledges – and languages – have been made invisible or 'non-existent' (Santos, 2012) because they have been relegated to the status of the 'local and particular'. Thus epistemic disobedience requires critically confronting the more powerful (Western) knowledge traditions and recentring those languages, epistemologies and practices which have historically been marginalized or silenced.

Mignolo (2009, 2013) further argues that the process of 'delinking' from the grand narrative of Western modernity entails changing 'the terms of the conversation'. His argument rests on the premise that all knowledge is shaped by the context in which it is produced. However, this situatedness is often concealed by the fiction of the 'detached observer' whose assumed neutrality serves to hide the extent to which he or she 'controls the disciplinary rules and puts himself or herself in a privileged position to evaluate and dictate' the conversation (Mignolo, 2009: 4). Asking questions about *who* produces (or consumes) *what* knowledge, *when*, *where* and *why*, argues Mignolo (2009), serves to shift attention from the 'enunciated' (or 'the known') to the 'enunciator' (or 'knower'). It is about opening up epistemic sites that have been negatively shaped by colonialism and modernity and making visible (or audible) the experiences, insights and perspectives of people who live and work in these spaces.

For Boaventura de Sousa Santos (2012), decoloniality is about developing theories which are anchored in an understanding of the world as infinitely diverse. There is, he argues, an 'immensity of alternatives of life, conviviality and interaction with the world' not recognized by northern theory (2012: 51). For him, the construction of southern epistemologies includes four core tenets: the sociology of absences, the sociology of emergences, the ecology of knowledges and intercultural translation. By a *sociology of absences*, he refers to 'research that aims to show that what does not exist is actually actively produced as non-existent' when 'monocultural rationality' exercises five logics which produce the Other as 'ignorant, backward, inferior, local or particular, and unproductive or sterile' (2012: 52). The *sociology of emergences* is a complex notion that includes a way of thinking about the future as a space of 'plural and concrete possibilities, Utopian and realist at one time, and constructed in the present by means of activities of care' (2012: 54). It requires 'speculativeness' or a belief in the possible (2012: 54) and 'an anticipatory consciousness' built on an understanding of capacity and potentiality (2012: 55). By *ecology of knowledges*, Santos stresses that theory building should begin with the principle that all kinds of knowledge are by nature incomplete and it is therefore necessary to engage in 'epistemological dialogue and debate among them' (2012: 58). Santos's fourth and final core tenet is *intercultural translation*, which refers to the need to 'translate' between different schools of thought (e.g. European vs African philosophical traditions) in order to allow 'mutual intelligibility among the experiences of the world' (2012: 58). Such a procedure, he argues, 'does not endow any set of experiences with the statute either of exclusive totality or homogenous part' (2012: 58) but 'stems from the idea that all cultures are incomplete and may, therefore, be enriched by engaging in dialogue with or confronting other cultures' (2012: 60).

In South Africa, recent student protests and calls to 'transform' tertiary education and 'decolonize the curriculum' have ignited heated debates on how to reimagine universities as inclusive spaces in which people (black students in particular) can feel 'comfortable' and develop a sense of ownership (e.g. Mbembe, 2015; Morreira, 2017; Ndlovu-Gatsheni, 2013). It should be noted that many of these concerns are not new as local scholars have for decades been working on how to transform the inherited structures of power in academia so as to enable greater access, inclusion and participation (e.g. Angélil-Carter, 1998; Thesen and Van Pletzen, 2006). However, it could also be argued that while many of these efforts were directed at giving students access to the existing (Eurocentric) 'powerful knowledge' (Young, 2009), recent calls for curricular transformation have called into question what *constitutes* that powerful knowledge. (See Sebidi and Morreira, 2017, for an example of a project which begins to question the inherited canon in a Sociology undergraduate course, and shows how reflexivity and contextualized teaching can assist students to engage with this body of thought, thereby giving them access to the powerful knowledge that comes with familiarity with this theory-dense canon.)

Similarly, ways of understanding language and its role in education have also been a focus of local research for many years (Stroud and Kerfoot, 2013). The notion of Linguistic Citizenship, as developed by Stroud (2001, 2009, 2015) and others (e.g. Stroud and Heugh, 2004; Williams and Stroud, 2015), has particular resonance with decolonial theory, as it challenges dominant notions of language as separate, bounded entities, and seeks to conceptualize it 'in ways that can promote a *diversity of voice* and contribute to a *mutuality and reciprocity* of engagement across difference' (Stroud, 2015: 20, italics in original). Based on an understanding of language as 'constructed and contested' (2015: 23), Linguistic Citizenship conceives of language as a semiotic resource which speakers use and reconfigure 'through the creation of new meanings, the repurposing of genres and the transformation of repertoires' (2015: 25). By disrupting normative (often standard) language ideologies, Linguistic Citizenship (as a lens) draws attention to the diverse, creative and dynamic ways in which people use their linguistic resources to assert their agency and voice; in other words, to act and be heard as citizens. For Stroud (2009), citizenship discourses are the medium through which politics is enacted, including the potentiality 'to bring about alternative worlds' and a sense of 'utopian surplus' (Stroud, 2015: 23). Stroud illustrates his ideas with reference to a film on Afrikaaps, 'a local and racially stigmatised variety of Afrikaans' (2015: 26; see Chapter 2, this volume, for a fuller description of the Afrikaaps example). The film begins by tracing the emergence of Afrikaaps as a contact variety in the early settler colony of South Africa (a history invisibilized by the dominant narratives of white Afrikaans), and then records the responses of speakers of Afrikaaps to this film, showing how the legitimation of their language engenders pride and a new-found sense of ownership. This *linguistic reconnect* of self and language through Afrikaaps, argues Stroud (2015), is represented 'bodily' by participants in the film through dance, gesture and facial expressions, as well as in their heightened emotion, described as 'an ecstasy of liberation, dignity, autonomy, agency and inclusivity' (Stroud, 2015: 32). It is in moments such as these, suggests Stroud (2015: 34), that we see the 'utopian dynamic' of Linguistic Citizenship, where new kinds of knowing premised on the 'negotiation of difference' (rather than the 'imposition of commonality', or inferiority) become possible.

In a second case study of Linguistic Citizenship in action, Kerfoot (2011) records how a capacity building programme for adult educators in the Northern Cape in the late 1990s enabled these educators to create and run their own community workshops, in which they took participants through a problem posing cycle of identifying, analysing and developing 'action plans' to address social issues in their communities. She argues that these workshops created *participatory spaces*, which she defines, after Cornwall (2002), as neither neutral nor separable from broader structures of power, but as offering on these occasions, the possibility of transformative practice. She contends that it was the educators' grasp of the 'discourses of participatory development' (e.g. critical contextual analysis, drafting agendas, chairing meetings, negotiating, listening, resolving conflict) which they had acquired on the capacity building programme that enabled them to create these participatory spaces. She further argues that a major factor in their success rested on their ability to shape these discourses to local conditions and to recontextualize them in different semiotic modes (e.g. speech, song, image, gesture, writing). It was, she continues, both the opportunity to select 'sign complexes which legitimized local language varieties, re-organized language hierarchies, and de-emphasized written text as the semiotics of power' (Kerfoot, 2011: 98), and the chance to resemiotize these meanings in different moments of practice, which could be said to have succeeded in validating what Chandoke (2003: 186) calls the 'linguistic and epistemic authority' of subaltern actors, and in mobilizing collective agency (Kerfoot, 2011: 98). In other words, this participatory space enabled a reconfiguring of meaning in local terms, thereby serving to build agency and voice – and promote and enact a form of Linguistic Citizenship.

The concepts of Linguistic Citizenship, particularly its 'utopic dynamic' as well as the notion of a 'participatory space', offer a framework for understanding the textbook authoring process. They resonate, I would argue, with Santos's sociology of emergences, or a way of thinking that enables a belief in capabilities, potentialities and future possibilities. In this chapter, I will argue that the textbook project created a participatory space which enabled authors to work together in ways which legitimated them as writers and knowledge producers. While the most visible outcome of the project was a material artefact, a textbook, the process generated a number of unanticipated outcomes. Most significantly, it enabled participants to imagine themselves differently, as emerging writers and academics, thereby building confidence in their own agency and voice.

Responding to a need

Contemporary decolonial scholars pay tribute to the contribution of early thinkers like Paulo Freire (1970), whose work on participatory education inspired grassroots literacy movements across the world (Kerfoot, 2009; Walsh, 2014). A core principle in his methodology was the need for pedagogic interventions to be situated in the everyday struggles of learners and responsive to their needs and aspirations. The textbook project was a response to a particular context and set of needs, as outlined below.

The site for the development of the textbook is the University of the Western Cape (UWC), a relatively marginal tertiary institution given its geo-historical position. Not only is it in the geo-political south, but it has had to deal with the legacy of being an historically black university, and therefore perceived as 'inferior' when compared with many of the better resourced 'formerly white' universities in South Africa. UWC was established for 'coloured students' in 1960 as part of the Apartheid grand plan of separate education for separate races.[2] In the 1980s, under the leadership of a particularly visionary and progressive rector, the university defied government legislation and opened its doors to black (African) students for whom there was no designated institution of higher learning in the region. Despite the dismantling of the Apartheid laws post-1994, the composition of the student body has remained predominantly 'coloured' and 'black', with a growing number of postgraduate students from African countries to the north. Given the inherited Apartheid structures of race and class, students have traditionally come from working class or less economically privileged homes, often having had limited access to the better resourced schools in the formerly white residential areas, although this demographic is shifting in the post-Apartheid era as the middle class is increasingly de-racialized. While the medium of education at UWC is English, the students are typically multilingual: the majority of coloured students speak English and Afrikaans (and local varieties of these languages), and black students generally speak one or more African languages, plus English and sometimes Afrikaans. Given this student population, access to tertiary study has always been constrained by a combination of factors, most significantly, the high financial costs and the relative under-preparedness of students for academic study through English in a higher education sector that is still largely shaped by Western academic norms.

Firstly, our teaching programme has historically made use of texts written in the global north (e.g. Fromkin and Rodman, 1983; Yule, 1996). For students in southern Africa, the languages and contexts that these books profile are often remote and disconnected from their lived experiences. Thus the textbook project was initially a response to the need for theoretically 'up-to-date', contextually relevant materials which spoke to our undergraduate students' multilingual and southern African experiences.

Secondly, many of the students found (and continue to find) the average academic textbook (imported from the global north) unaffordable. This, combined with the lack of contextual relevance, has given rise at UWC to a tradition of 'workbooks', whereby the lecturers compile course readers with selected prescribed readings and study questions (with the university carrying the copyright costs). The textbook was thus an attempt to provide first year students with a published text (as opposed to photocopied workbooks), thereby exposing them to an affordable, yet professionally edited, academic text in English.

Thirdly, given our high student enrolment and a history of underfunding of our institution, we have over the years had to rely on a large contingent of contract lecturers (mostly doctoral students) and postgraduate student tutors to staff our programme. This has resulted in a high turnover of staff, whose primary focus was the completion of their own degrees, and who had limited investment in revising and upgrading modules and workbooks.

Thus the development of our own textbook served to address these concerns by providing a quality teaching resource which offered locally relevant content and ensured consistency from year to year in a context of changing staff and constrained resources. The cost, while still a challenge for many students, is lower than the imported texts we had relied on previously. In terms of improving the quality of teaching and learning, the lecturers are able to follow the textbook closely and this serves as a critical support to the students, as indicated in this email written to a lecturer on the first year module near the beginning of the year:

> Date: Thu, Feb 14, 2013 at 12:34 AM
>
> Hi Mam,
>
> I apologise for sending this e-mail this time of the morning. I bought the Linguistics book yesterday and I have been trying to study the book, getting more information on the work we did in lectures. I now have no reason for coming to see you because I finally understand fully what is going on. What I'm trying to say is that I would like to cancel my appointment with you because I am settled now. This book is being useful, now I am on track.
>
> Thank you,
>
> Regards,
> RXXX

Changing the terms

For Mignolo (2009, 2013), changing the *terms* of the disciplinary conversation entails focusing on the 'knower' (as opposed to the 'known') and recognizing that the former is inherently subjective and always implicated within a 'geo- and bio-graphic politics of knowledge' (2009: 4). This focus throws into relief the issue of audibility: who gets to define the curriculum, whose voices are deemed legitimate for knowledge creation and whose are silenced. For Munroe et al. (2013), decolonial education means turning students into knowledge producers and curriculum makers by actively involving them in the processes of knowledge production. Thus changing the terms of the conversation, I would argue, includes critically interrogating who gets to participate as curriculum makers, whose perspectives and linguistic varieties are heard as credible, and how people (students, lecturers and disciplinary experts) relate as producers of knowledge.

The textbook project deliberately set out to be multi-vocal and inclusive, and this, I would argue, is the most significant way in which it served to shift the terms. It was planned as a collaborative departmental exercise with more senior staff forming an editorial collective and taking on roles as mentors and co-authors. In this way, I would argue, it served to model an alternative mode of academic practice, namely one in which the focus was the development of a collective product, rather than a research project or paper for individual advancement. In line with this intention, we agreed that all author royalties should be paid into a departmental account earmarked for research and development.

The project involved twenty-five authors who represented a range of voices, in terms of both their pan-African diversity and levels of expertise. It included the entire teaching staff, as well as a number of people associated with the department as past staff members, extraordinary professors and research fellows. Given our reliance on contract staff, eleven of the authors were doctoral students at the time, representing six different African countries: South Africa, Zimbabwe, Zambia, Malawi, Angola and Namibia. To accommodate this diversity, we developed a 'polyphonic' book structure: the final manuscript consisted of nineteen chapters and ten case studies, many of the latter profiling the research of the doctoral authors. For most of the latter, their chapter or case study was their first publication, their experience having been limited to writing thesis chapters for their academic supervisors. A major outcome of the project was therefore the professional development of these authors, as detailed below.

The manuscript for the pilot edition took two years to develop, with the first edition published a year later. The writing process included a series of workshops and editorial feedback meetings, initially to plan the content and develop a common chapter structure and style, and then to give feedback on individual chapters. All the chapters were peer reviewed, and the final text and study questions were also critically interrogated from a teaching and learning perspective by an experienced external reviewer. In addition, we elicited student and tutor feedback (on the pilot text) using group discussions and written questionnaires.

From my perspective as project co-ordinator, the collaborative authoring was the most interesting as well as the most difficult aspect of the process, and the remainder of this section reflects on the challenges of this process. It is based on notes and records I kept throughout, as well as two focus group interviews I conducted with six of the doctoral authors at the end of the writing process. The interviews took place in October 2013, once the revisions on the pilot edition were complete. The open-ended format included questions such as: What challenges did you experience as an author? What do you see as some of the achievements? What factors made writing your chapter easier or more difficult?

Four 'challenges' emerged as common, namely: (1) the difficulty of meeting deadlines given the very real time constraints writers experienced as a result of juggling their multiple roles as PhD candidates, contract lecturers and textbook authors; (2) the challenge and unfamiliarity of writing in a 'simplified' style for a first year student audience; (3) the extent to which they had 'underestimated the writing process'; and (4) the demands of writing collaboratively. However, all interviewees also claimed that being part of the project had been instrumental in improving their own academic writing. On reflection, they attributed this growth to the *very same factors* they had identified as 'challenges'.

While all interviewees admitted that time constraints had often affected the quality of their drafts, they also acknowledged that it was the deadlines (and reminders) which spurred them into action. As K explained: 'Personally, I think if you had not been knocking on our doors and sending emails and so on, that textbook was not going to be here today.'

They identified the imperative to recast their academic knowledge in a more pedagogic style suitable for a first-year audience as the most difficult challenge. As S commented:

> so how do you move away from academic writing to writing something, you know, in a way that would also make them, you know, whoever is reading the chapter to understand the concepts academically, but we are not using academic writing.

At the same time, this process of recasting for a different audience enabled interviewees to become more critical of their own writing. In the words of D, another author: 'It taught me to be more critical of my own work and place myself more as a student.' Others spoke about how the need to be 'more accommodating' in their style had forced them to become much more aware of the writing process and had therefore improved their own academic writing.

In decolonial terms, one could argue that this was a process of 'translation', from a complex academic register, to a more accessible, everyday one. In fact, one could take this further and argue that challenging the unnecessarily dense register that characterizes some academic writing is part of dismantling these dominant knowledge hierarchies which often serve to exclude those still on the 'outside' and maintain an 'elite' of experts (Shannon Morreira, personal communication). Perhaps, like the participants in Kerfoot's (2011) study, it was the shifting across registers which enabled them to grow as writers. The interview data certainly suggest that it was the act of shifting registers that catalysed the interviewees' development as writers.

The interviewees also acknowledged that they were unprepared for the rigours of taking a text from first draft to publication. As S put it: 'I underestimated the writing process'. However, they also all said that the process of feedback and drafting had had a positive impact on their own academic writing. Receiving feedback at various points from the editorial committee and external reviewers, as well as the intensive feedback from the editors, who also, at times, had to reorganize and overwrite sections of their chapters, pushed them to rework their writing in a way they had not previously experienced. So while they found some of the feedback from reviewers discouraging, and were sometimes very frustrated by the 'red marks' of the editor's track changes, they ultimately appreciated this as a necessary part of producing a text of quality. As S explained:

> For me I think the most important lesson that came out of that is that it is not your idea, you know, that matters the most, it's the language that makes the idea live. So writing, you can have a million beautiful ideas but if your writing doesn't capture those ideas, those ideas are as good as no idea at all … You know, for me that was the biggest thing that, you know, you have it in your head you can see it but then, you know … The road towards the idea that is the most important thing.

And K and T elaborate:

> K: it was a learning process, it was so enriching that some of our writing styles have been – have changed slightly (laughter) due to er people like you and ==
> T: == we have learnt how to write ==
> K: == WE'VE LEARNT HOW TO WRITE

The interviewees also indicated that they now wrote more carefully and checked technical details more thoroughly (e.g. references, quotations) as a result of having to respond to all the author queries in the final stages of production.

We (the editorial team) also underestimated the extent of revisioning that would be necessary. Although we organized workshops throughout the writing process, these focused on content rather than process (see next section for a discussion of the content). The single workshop we organized towards the end on how to strengthen the teaching and learning aspects of the textbook (e.g. drafting effective study questions) proved very popular. In retrospect, we should have had more workshops on the writing process itself (not just on chapter content) as well as regular meetings with the whole team to reflect on progress.

It was not only the doctoral students who developed as writers – all staff members experienced a learning curve, especially where we worked collectively. Six of the chapters were co-authored by two, three, and in one case, four people. The process of co-authoring proved hugely challenging: some chapters were co-authored from the beginning; others became co-authored when new people were brought in to provide a particular kind of expertise or to assist a less experienced author. Not only were the logistics of this testing (due to time or geographical constraints), but the difficulties of finding a common vision and style for these chapters also proved daunting. In addition, the ethics of co-authorship were challenging and required us to work through questions such as: Who is an author? Who can overwrite whom? Who takes responsibility for 'blending' the different contributions into a coherent text? How are differences resolved?

However, despite many frustrations along the way, the interviewees evaluated the process overall as enriching, as indicated by the following extracts:

F: it's very difficult to sit independently and write and then you send it to someone else and then they edit and they sometimes mess up, sometimes they make marvellous contributions … so I think the process it made us think it made me think realistically about my work, the work that I've produced you know, everything I write no matter how good the ideas are, sometimes good ideas just have to be left out for somebody else.

D: So in my case I think another challenge was actually seeing you sit there and you write, you spend so much time writing something and then when you give to your colleague they just chop it … then you wonder what happened there, then you see your ideas now scattered but actually I mean if you look carefully you find that your ideas have become more solid even though they've been chopped in different places.

In this way, the project created a participatory space in which new roles and ways of relating could be established (Kerfoot, 2011). The fact that each co-authoring team included at least one experienced academic created opportunities for mentoring that enabled new ways of relating. In the words of K (in written correspondence):

> The idea to blend emerging authors with senior ones (which is rarely practised on projects of that magnitude) was a brilliant one. It implicitly provided us an opportunity to learn a number of things from them.

And F comments that one of the things she appreciated was the chance to form 'different kind of relationships with colleagues' where

> we would give insights on different things or L would ask me something about her chapter and I would ask her something about my chapter and in this way we learnt a lot more.

In the end, for the co-authored chapters, we had to agree on a first author who would take responsibility for pulling the entire chapter together and work with the editor through the process of final drafting, checking and proofing. To guide us through this process, we developed a co-authorship policy to assist with issues such as the crediting of different contributions. While our policy was based on that of the highly regarded International Committee of Medical Journal Editors (ICMJE), it is more generous given our commitment to inclusivity. For example, we defined an author as 'someone who has made an intellectual contribution to the text, either by writing substantial parts of it OR by providing critical/creative input as to contents, structure and/or argument'. (The ICMJE requires BOTH criteria.) In a context where some authors have insider access to languages and communities which are the focus of research, these inclusive criteria become significant. We further agreed that even if an author's contribution was almost entirely overwritten by a subsequent co-author, he or she would be retained as one of the authors on the chapter. (Similar concerns are explored by Devisch and Njamnjoh (2011) who contest the idea of the expertise as located within the 'individual expert' – along with academic publishing quality assurance mechanisms, promotion criteria and so on – and argue instead for what they call mutually enriching 'co-implication', namely that all knowledge, in their case, anthropological, is co-produced between informant and researcher, or in this case, between co-authors.)

The co-authoring was the most difficult aspect of the entire project, and, in retrospect, it would have been wise to workshop this issue carefully at the beginning. However, even then, all the difficulties and sensitivities may not have been avoided. Issues would still have needed consideration on a case by case basis, and the various merits of each person's contribution would still have needed discussion with all relevant parties.

The process of co-writing with such a diverse group of authors can be seen, I would argue, as a form of delinking from the dominant modes of academic textbook production: what Walsh refers to as a 'praxis of fissure' or a 'pedagogy from the cracks'. This alternate and inclusive mode enabled the creation of a new community of knowledge producers and was a significant factor in building confidence, epistemic authority and pride (see last section for more detail). Furthermore, changing the terms in this way is, I would argue, a precursor to changing the content. The extent to which we were able to do the latter is detailed in the following section.

Changing the content

A key aim of decolonial pedagogy is the call to change the content by critiquing the dominant (Euro-American) epistemologies that shape the discipline, and by recentring local and/or marginalized languages and knowledges. The textbook project began to shift the content in at least three ways: Firstly, it is the first southern African introduction to linguistics, language and communication which takes as its primary frame of reference of the region's immensely rich and complex linguistic heritage. It introduces students to established theoretical concepts and frameworks in linguistics, but illustrates these with local, southern African content, much of it drawn from the authors' own research projects. Secondly, it seeks to promote a 'linguistics from the South', not only in terms of contextualizing knowledge in southern African terms, but also in the sense that it is premised on the understanding that 'multilingualism is the norm'. Various chapters draw attention to the constructed nature of language, and how the colonial powers and European missionaries used the creation of separate, codified African languages and orthographies as part of their project of containment and control. Lastly, it pushes the boundaries of more traditional curricula by introducing students to a range of innovative fields in linguistics, including social media communication, branding, graffiti and linguistic landscapes.

Given that a textbook typically aims to give students access to what Young (2009) refers to as 'powerful knowledge' within the discipline, it covers a number of topics which are the mainstay of linguistics textbooks internationally.

However, it tries, where possible, to situate these concepts in contexts that could be familiar to southern African students. For example, 'core' topics, such as language typologies and standardization, which are usually (in Western produced textbooks) exemplified with reference to the Indo-European language family and the history of English, are illustrated in this textbook with reference to the Niger-Congo and Khoisan language families, and the standardization histories of the southern African languages of Tshivenda, Sesotho and Afrikaans, among others. Case studies which draw on students' own research illustrate concepts such as language loss among speakers of Nama, or explore the role of the missionaries in the standardization of African languages. It is also the first time that a textbook has attempted to introduce the fundamentals of language description from both a Bantu and an Indo-European (English, Afrikaans) perspective and to provide illustrative examples in a range of southern African languages.

In this way, the textbook seeks to introduce students to what is traditionally considered canonical disciplinary knowledge, at the same time that it centres southern Africa's rich linguistic heritage. By 'making visible' languages such as isiXhosa, Xitsonga, Nama and ciBemba, it seeks to legitimize their place in the ecology of languages and affirm their value as worthy of academic study. Using examples from familiar languages also assists with learning, as evidenced by the following comment from a tutor in 2014: 'The textbook provided examples with African languages, which made it easier to explain to the students, because *we* understand it.' (author's emphasis)

While it could be argued that the content does not go far enough in terms of reconceptualizing linguistics from a southern (African) perspective, it had to balance this imperative with the need to equip students with knowledge which is sufficiently 'global' to enable them to 'compete' on a larger stage (Sebidi and Morreira, 2017; Young, 2009). It could also be argued that it reinforces the hegemony of English given that this is the language of publication. But once again, given the national (and global) demand for English, which in South Africa is associated with economic opportunity and social mobility, the language policy of UWC and the constraints on publishing multilingual texts, the adoption of a different medium did not seem possible. As Ndlovu-Gatsheni (2013) argues, transforming the curriculum in South African higher education requires finding creative ways to blend Euro-American and African epistemologies, while recognizing the need to decolonize the curricula, pedagogies and institutional cultures. In other words, the process of decolonizing the curriculum involves a dialogue (and, one could add, 'trade off') between different kinds of knowledge, processes and practices.

Building epistemic authority and local pride

Santos (2012: 54–5) describes the 'sociology of emergences' as a way of thinking that enables 'speculativeness', or a belief in future possibilities, as well as 'anticipatory consciousness' which is built on an understanding of capacity and potentiality. It is, he argues, about replacing the 'axiology of progress' with the 'axiology of care' (2012: 56). In other words, it is about believing in our agency and ability to act on the world from an ethical position of agency and custodianship. As Kerfoot (2009: 36) argues, citizenship agency is integrally related to consciousness, and to act as a citizen requires first a sense of agency and the belief that one can act. In this chapter, I have argued that the value of the textbook project lies as much in the process as in the final product, and that this process had unexpected and positive outcomes. In addition to affirming local languages and knowledge, it gave the authors a belief in their own potentiality as academics and knowledge producers, and enhanced their status as role models in the eyes of their students. In a context like South Africa, the significance (for students) of seeing young black and coloured lecturers in the role of experts cannot be underestimated, as illustrated by the following interview data:

> F: the students have made comments such as oh Miss F … wrote the chapter and you could see that they were very excited about seeing the authors and working with texts that you've created, so for me that was a very big achievement.
>
> D: you see the chapter is there now and the students are saying yoh you know when you standing there teaching the students give you a kind of different respect when they see that what you teaching is something you created, you were part of that creation. Ja well I think its ja I feel good, I feel proud.

Other interviewees report on how proud they felt when, on their return to their home universities after graduation, their colleagues and students were 'so excited' to see in print not only their own languages, but also 'one of their own appear between pages'. In this way, the process helped to build the 'epistemic authority' of local knowledge producers.

Associated with their status as role models, I would argue that the textbook project gave both the authors and their students a sense of 'euphoria' (Stroud, 2015: 34), a feeling that they (and their language repertoires and ideas) could be 'otherwise' (2015: 35). This emotion is variously referred to in the interview data as a sense of 'achievement', 'reward', 'enrichment' and 'pride':

L: the chapter ... that was a big **achievement** ... and it's really my first publication.
F: the process was sometimes very tough but then in the end the product ... was very **rewarding**.
K: it was a learning process, it was so **enriching**.
D: I mean you feel **proud** that ... ja it's something of yours is there, some hard work.

One very encouraging and unexpected outcome was the impact it had on the career development of one of the authors from a neighbouring country, who sent me the following email:

Let me announce that the efforts we put in the book were recently acknowledged by my university through a rise in rank from lecturer 2 to 1. This rise also means a rise in my salary ... I am smiling!! I never thought this work could reward me in this wonderful way.

At least in this context, his chapter was not devalued by quality assurance processes which reject textbooks as accreditable research outputs, even when they include a wealth of original material and engage with the epistemic foundations of the discipline itself. A decolonial approach in higher education should surely re-evaluate the current rather narrow criteria for acknowledging and rewarding excellence in research.

This chapter has explored the multiple ways in which this project 'was' and 'is' – in terms of voice, perspective and process – a polyphonic project. However, it is not only the authors who have experienced this audibility. By demonstrating how local knowledge and practices can be incorporated into university curricula, the textbook also opened the way for students to re-appraise their own linguistic and cultural inheritances and experience a sense of 're-connect' (Stroud, 2015) with these resources. Many first year students have commented on their pleasure and pride in finding their own sociolinguistic realities represented in a published set text. As one first year student so succinctly expressed in a written course evaluation:

The course has taught me about the importance of my culture, language and my identity as an individual, to make my own choices and believe in myself.

Conclusion

This chapter has used a decolonial lens to explore the authoring process of a departmental textbook. Working with Santos's sociology of emergences, it argues that the project created a participatory space which enabled emerging academics to develop as writers and knowledge producers. It suggests that a key aspect of this growth can be attributed to the shift in register that writing for a first year audience required, and that writing collaboratively allowed new and enriching collegial relations to emerge. It further traces how the experience of bringing the text to publication engendered a sense of confidence and pride (or in Stroud's terms, 'euphoria'), a prerequisite for the development of voice and epistemic authority. For this reason, this chapter has argued that decolonizing academic curricula depends on *first* changing the *terms* of 'who produces what knowledge for whom, how, when and why'.

To return to the metaphor of the crack: the textbook is only a beginning, a seed which has sprouted and continues to grow. While it may not extend the cracks as deeply as some would like, 'it does open and enable an envisioning and engendering of different paths and/as cracks, that may – or may not – lead toward decolonial horizons' (Walsh, 2014).

> The decolonial comes not from above but below, from the margins and borders, from the people, communities, movements, collectives who challenge, interrupt, and transgress the matrices of colonial power in their practices of being, action, existence, creation, and thought. The decolonial, in this sense, is not a fixed state, status, or condition; nor does it denote a point of arrival. It is a dynamic process always in the making and re-making given the permanence and capacity of reconfiguration of the coloniality of power. It is a process of struggle not just against, but also more importantly for – for the possibility of an otherwise. A process that begets movement, invites alliance, connectivity, articulation, and interrelation, and strives for invention, creation, and intervention, for radically distinct sentiments, meanings, and horizons. (Walsh, 2014)

Notes

1. Here, 'voice' is understood as the capacity to be heard and make oneself understood (Blommaert, 2005).
2. It should be noted that in South Africa, the term 'coloured' has a different meaning to the way it is used in the United States and elsewhere. Here, it refers to people of mixed heritage, many descendants of slaves from South East Asia brought here during the colonial times, or descendants of contact between the indigenous inhabitants of southern Africa and colonial settlers who began arriving nearly 400 years ago. Under Apartheid, all South Africans were classified either 'coloured', 'black', 'white' or 'Indian'.

References

Angélil-Carter, S. (1998), *Access to Success: Academic Literacy in Higher Education*. Cape Town: University of Cape Town Press.

Baker, M. (2014), 'Decolonial Education: Meanings, Contexts, and Possibilities', Unpublished Paper. Interpreting, Researching, & Transforming Colonial/Imperial Legacies in Education, American Educational Studies Association, Annual Conference, Seattle, Washington, 31 October to 4 November 2012. Available online: https://www.academia.edu/3266939/Decolonial_Education_Meanings_Contexts_and_Possiblities (accessed 10 March 2017).

Blommaert, J. (2005), *Discourse: A Critical Introduction*. Cambridge: Cambridge University Press.

Bock, Z. and G. Mheta. ([2014] 2019), *Language, Society and Communication: An Introduction*. Pretoria: Van Schaik Publisher.

Chandoke, N. (2003), *The Conceits of Civil Society*. Delhi and Oxford: Oxford University Press.

Cornwall, A. (2002), 'Making Spaces, Changing Places: Situating Participation in Development', IDS Working Paper 170, Brighton: Institute of Development Studies.

Devisch, R. and F. Nyamnjoh, eds (2011), *The Post-colonial Turn: Re-imagining Anthropology and Africa*. Bamenda, Cameroon: Langaa Research

Freire, P. (1970), *Pedagogy of the Oppressed*. New York: Continuum.

Fromkin, V. and R. Rodman. (1983), *An Introduction to Language*, 3rd edn, New York: Holt, Rinehart and Winston. International Committee of Medical Journal Editors. Available online: http://www.icmje.org/ethical_1author.html (accessed September 2012).

Kerfoot, C. (2009), 'Changing Conceptions of Literacies, Language and Development: Implications for the Provision of Adult Basic Education in South Africa', PhD dissertation, Stockholm: Stockholm University.

Kerfoot, C. (2011), 'Making and Shaping Participatory Spaces: Resemiotisation and Citizenship Agency in South Africa', *International Multilingual Research Journal*, 5: 87–102.

Mbembe, A. (2015), 'Decolonizing Knowledge and the Question of the Archive', Public lecture. Available online: http://wiser.wits.ac.za/system/files/Achille%20Mbembe%20-%20Decolonizing%20Knowledge%20and%20the%20Question%20of%20the%20Archive.pdf (accessed April 2016).

Mignolo, W. (2009), 'Epistemic Disobedience, Independent Thought and De-colonial Freedom', *Theory, Culture and Society*, 26 (7–8): 159–81.

Mignolo, W. (2013), 'Geopolitics of Sensing and Knowing: On (De)Coloniality, Border Thinking, and Epistemic Disobedience', *Confero*, 1 (1): 129–50.

Munroe, E. A., L. Lunney Borden, A. Murray Orr, D. Toney and J. Meader. (2013), 'Decolonizing Aboriginal Education in the 21st Century', *McGill Journal of Education*, 48 (2) (December): 317–38.

Morreira, S. (2017), 'Steps towards Decolonial Higher Education in Southern Africa? Epistemic Disobedience in the Humanities', *Journal of Asian and African Studies*, 52 (3): 287–301.

Ndlovu-Gatsheni, S. (2013), *Empire, Global Coloniality and African Subjectivity*. New York and Oxford: Berghahn Books.

Santos, B. de S. (2012), 'Public Sphere and Epistemologies of the South', *Africa Development*, 37 (1): 43–67.

Sebidi, K. and S. Morreira. (2017), 'Accessing Powerful Knowledge: A Comparative Study of Two First Year Sociology Courses in a South African University', *Critical Studies in Teaching and Learning*, 5 (2): 33–50.

Stroud, C. (2001), 'African Mother Tongue Programs and the Politics of Language: Linguistic Citizenship versus Linguistic Human Rights', *Journal of Multilingual and Multicultural Development*, 22: 339–55.

Stroud, C. (2009), 'A Postliberal Critique of Language Rights: Toward a Politics of Language for Linguistics of Contact', in J. E. Petrovic (ed.), *International Perspectives on Bilingual Education: Policy, Practice and Controversy*, 191–218. New York: Information Age Publishing.

Stroud, C. (2015), 'Linguistic Citizenship as Utopia', *Multilingual Margins*, 2 (2): 20–37.

Stroud, C. and C. Kerfoot (2013), 'Towards Rethinking Multilingualism and Language Policy for Academic Literacies', *Linguistics and Education*, 24: 396–405.

Stroud, C. and K. Heugh (2004), 'Language Rights and Linguistic Citizenship', in J. Freeland and D. Patrick (eds), *Language Rights and Language Survival*, 191–218, Manchester: St Jerome.

Thesen, L. and E. van Pletzen, eds (2006), *Academic Literacy and the Languages of Change*. London: Continuum.

Walsh, C. (2014), 'Pedagogical Notes from the Decolonial Cracks', *Decolonial Gesture*, 11 (4). Available online http://hemisphericinstitute.org/hemi/en/emisferica-111-decolonial-gesture/walsh (accessed 12 May 2016).

Williams, Q. and C. Stroud (2015), 'Linguistic Citizenship: Language and Politics in Postnational Modernities', *Journal of Language and Politics*, 14 3: 406–30.

Young, Michael (2009), 'Education, Globalisation and the "voice of knowledge"', *Journal of Education and Work*, 22: 3, 193–204.

Yule, G. (1996), *The Study of Language*, 2nd edn, Cambridge: Cambridge University Press.

10

Afterthoughts: Multilingual Citizenship, Humans, Environments and Histories

Duncan Brown

The higher education context globally is currently characterized by debates about anticoloniality or decoloniality (depending on which theorists one endorses), in relation to syllabi, pedagogies and the ideological orientations of degree programmes and academic departments. In their simplistic manifestations, these frequently amount to calls for the replacement of one set of authors with another ('white Northern' replaced by 'black Southern') or the replacement of one set of theorists by another (along the same principle). While there is some merit to these approaches, they frequently leave much of the higher education landscape fundamentally unchanged, because beyond largely rhetorical calls for the introduction of African/indigenous languages into education (usually made in English), they ignore deeper and more far reaching questions of the assumptions, modes of apprehension and ontologies of thought embedded in the languages and discourses through which we seek more adequately to engage with the particularities of our Southern contexts. In this chapter, I seek to explore questions of multilingualism and multivocality in relation to probably the most pressing global challenge we face: climate change, and our understandings of human-environmental relations.

At face value, citizenship, whether multilingual or otherwise, is something few people would readily associate with ecologies or biological systems. It seems to speak to the institutions of the public, social and political, to governance and legislation, rather than ecosystems or biodiversity. And yet, as the philosopher Holmes Rolston (1988: 3) reminds us:

> Humans depend on airflow, water cycles, sunshine, photosynthesis, nitrogen fixation, decomposition, bacteria, fungi, the ozone layer, food chains, insect pollination, soils, earthworms, climates, oceans, and genetic materials. An ecology always lies in the background of culture, natural givens that support

everything else. Some sort of inclusive environmental fitness is required of even the most advanced culture.

'Citizenship', in its broadest sense of the right to belong and the responsibility not to cause harm, proves on more careful consideration to be intimately bound up with questions of how humans relate to 'other' species and the environments that we share with them. In particular, 'multilingual citizenship', tied as it is to issues of epistemological access to or denial of 'other modes' of knowing, to negotiating or suppressing difference, proves crucial in making sense of environments, their characteristics and their processes. In this chapter, I consider some implications of multilingual citizenship for thinking about environmental issues,[1] both historically and in the present, including the ways in which expanding or contracting the multilingual may relate to ownership, access or political control. The sociologist Boaventura de Sousa Santos reminds us that 'social injustice is grounded in cognitive injustice' (2012: 57), and I focus in the latter part of the chapter on questions of mono- and multilingualism, colonization and decolonization. The examples I use are deliberately disparate in terms of geographical location and historical period, to suggest the possibilities of multilingualism in divergent contexts.

* * *

Scotland is known for many great things, not least among them its whiskies, but not for its fine weather. Anyone reading Ian Rankin's Detective Inspector Rebus series of novels, for example, which are set for the most part in Edinburgh, will note the range of words or expressions used to differentiate qualities and characteristics within the category of what would probably be called 'rain' by most non-Scots. Chris Robinson and Eileen Finlayson's book *Scottish Weather* (2008) is a compendium of terms or expressions used by Scottish speakers of English to describe weather (mostly bad), and in some cases, by metaphorical extension, human behaviours. Some notable examples are:

> blatter: to rattle, beat violently (often used of rain or hail); a violent rain or hailstorm. A period of sunshine during unsettled weather, or a moment of joy in troubled times may pessimistically be called the 'blink afore the blatter'.
> dreep: a light, steady fall of rain.
> dreich: dull, dreary, gloomy weather.
> feechie: foul, dirty, rainy and puddly. Feechie can be used for anything messy or unpleasant. Feech! is an exclamation of disgust.

onding: a heavy fall of rain or snow, a downpour. *Ding* is a verb meaning to beat or strike with heavy blows. So a real *onding* of rain has some real force behind it. *Onding* can also be used figuratively to mean an assault, attack, onset, outburst of noise, talk, etc. (Robinson and Finlayson, 2008)[2]

While the extent of such language may be daunting for non-Scots, the point is in fact not to obscure, but to distinguish or elucidate; to provide ways of describing the multiple manifestations of Scottish weather.

Anyone reading George Monbiot's remarkable book on 'rewilding', *Feral: Rewilding the Land, Sea and Human Life* (2013), will be struck by his routine use of words such as *carr*, *fridd* or *brae* in describing landscape (49, 65, 150). These would probably be unknown to most readers, but Monbiot uses them to differentiate particular features of the landscape because they are appropriate. He is, in an important sense, engaging with the notion of Linguistic Citizenship, 'the experiences people may have of language practices and representations that capture – however fleetingly – a different significance of language to life, and life to language' (Stroud, 2018b: 23). He is seeking nuanced and intimate ways of naming and apprehending the environments in which we live: a language that can register the kind of 'dwelling' perspective suggested by the anthropologist Tim Ingold (2000).

The environmental writer Robert Macfarlane has for many years been concerned with collecting unusual words for landscapes, plants, animals or weather conditions. In this regard, he recalls having been given 'an extraordinary document' in the coastal township of Shawbost on the Outer Hebridean island of Lewis. It was entitled 'Some Lewis Moorland Terms: A Peat Glossary', and included 120 Gaelic words or terms for the local landscape (Macfarlane, 2015b). Some examples that catch Macfarlane's imagination are:

coachan: a slender moor-stream obscured by vegetation such that it is virtually hidden from sight
feadan: a small stream running from a moorland loch
fèith: a fine, vein-like watercourse running through peat, often dry in the summer
rionnach maoi: the shadows cast on the moorland by clouds moving across the sky on a bright and windy day
èit: the practice of placing quartz stones in streams so that they sparkle in moonlight and thereby attract salmon to them in the late summer and autumn
teine biorach: the flame or will-o'-the-wisp that runs on top of heather when the moor burns during the summer. (2015b: 1)

In these and many other examples cited in this chapter, the ability of a single word to capture a feature of landscape, concept, practice or visual image that requires definition in a sentence or even a paragraph in another language is extraordinary. As Macfarlane comments, 'Words are grained into our landscapes, and landscapes grained into our words' (2015b: 3).

At around the same time that the 'Peat Glossary' suggested a range of additional terms to Macfarlane, the *Oxford Junior Dictionary* was doing the opposite. Oxford University Press admitted that it had deleted from the new edition of the dictionary a range of words that 'it no longer felt to be relevant to a modern-day childhood', including 'acorn, adder, ash, beech, bluebell, buttercup, catkin, conker, cowslip, cygnet, dandelion, fern, hazel, heather, heron, ivy, kingfisher, lark, mistletoe, nectar, newt, otter, pasture and willow'. In their stead had been added, 'attachment, block-graph, blog, broadband, bullet-point, celebrity, chatroom, committee, cut-and-paste, MP3 player and voice-mail' (Macfarlane, 2015b: 1). (That was about eight years ago, and I wonder now whether anyone still uses MP3 players, though I hope the otters, kingfishers and herons will be around for millennia to come.) Macfarlane laments:

> [I]t is clear that we increasingly make do with an impoverished language for landscape. A place literacy is leaving us. A language in common, a language of the commons, is declining. Nuance is evaporating from everyday language, burned off by capital and apathy ... The terrain beyond the city fringe is chiefly understood in terms of large generic units ('field', 'hill', 'valley', 'wood'). It has become a blandscape. We are *blasé*, in the sense that Georg Simmel used that word in 1903, meaning 'indifferent to the distinction between things'. (2015b: 3)

It is an impoverishment not limited to English, he notes, but evident also in Irish and Gaelic. He does, however, report substantial public outcry to the dictionary deletions, and several projects to counter such moves, including that by Monbiot himself (3).

In response to the sentiments expressed above, as well as the resources of the 'Glossary' and the substitutions of the *Dictionary*, Macfarlane set out on his own project of collecting terms for place and landscape, which eventually appeared as *Landmarks* (2015a), a book comprising nine individual glossaries with commentary on particular writers who have significantly engaged place and environment in their work. He notes that the words are those used by people who read the landscape, mainly for work, but also for leisure: crofters, fishermen, farmers, sailors, scientists, miners, climbers, soldiers, shepherds, poets, walkers and the like (2015b: 1). In this regard, he says, 'I became fascinated by those scalpel-sharp words that are untranslatable without remainder. The need for precise discrimination of this kind has occurred most often where landscape is the venue of work' (2015b: 2).

The terms and their definitions are often evocative and delightful. *Ammil* is a 'Devon term for the thin film of ice that lacquers all leaves, twigs and grass blades when a freeze follows a partial thaw'. *Pirr* is a Shetlandic word meaning 'a light breath of wind, such as will make a cat's paw on the water'. *Zwer* is the onomatopoeic word for 'the sound of a covey of partridges taking flight' in Exmoor, and *crizzle* in Northamptonshire dialect describes the freezing of water, evoking 'the sound of a natural activity too slow for human hearing to detect' (2). Others are, as Macfarlane reminds us, 'ripely rude'. The West Country term for 'a very substantial cowpat' is *turdstool*. *Ujller* is the Shetlandic term for the 'unctuous filth that runs from a dunghill'. And should Gerard Manley Hopkins have wanted an alternative dialect term for a kestrel in the title of his poem 'Windhover', he could have opted for *wind-fucker* (2).

Macfarlane's accounts of the extraordinary intricacies of language, place and identity in the work of particular writers are for me especially compelling. Norman MacCaig's plea in his Luskentyre poem – 'Scholars, I plead with you,/ Where are your dictionaries of the wind, the grasses?' – in fact proves to be a spur for the entire project (1). Tim Robinson, who spent forty years writing, painting and mapping the west of Ireland, remarks that 'the landscape speaks ... Irish'; and he refers to the 'language we breathe' as providing 'our frontage onto the natural world' (2).

If all of this sounds overly Eurocentric, Macfarlane refers to a project that he encountered that is similar in aim to his, but massively more expansive in scope, by a scholar living in Qatar. Abdul Hamid Fitzwilliam-Hall (a multilingual citizen's name if ever there was one) has been working on a study, which at the time Macfarlane encountered it, included 140 languages, contained '50,000 separate terms or headwords' and spanned 3,500 pages (4). It is apparently, and unsurprisingly, still in progress ...

I need to add a caveat here, one of which Macfarlane was aware, as indicated by his inclusion of current urban neologisms. Drawing attention to words or phrases that are rapidly being lost is not to advocate that we all adopt a quaint form of antiquated speech, the sort of archaic, bucolic language for which the Irish poet Seamus Heaney's early poems were unjustly caricatured. It is simply to recognize that with the loss of such terms, we are losing our ability to read and understand the environments in which we live, and the biological systems on which we depend for our sustenance, however far along the food chain we might think we are. Whether one calls it a *fèith* or not, for example, it is important to notice whether the moorland stream, which may dry up in summer, is now always dry, and what that means, or to register that no one bothers with *èit* any more in the local river, as the salmon runs have stopped. Recognizing the value of non-metropolitan languages, which is key to the notion of multilingual citizenship, is also to refuse to consign them only to a place in history which is assumed to have been surpassed in the teleological rush towards the metropolitan languages of power, technology and capital (in this case English), more of which below.

A term coined for weather more recent than some of Macfarlane's examples came from two Australian scientists studying the smells of wet weather. In an article in the influential journal *Nature* (7 March 1964), Isabel Bear and Richard Thomas introduced the term *petrichor* to describe the evocative smell of rain falling on warm ground (Poynton, 2015). The term is derived from the Greek words *petra* (stone) and *ichor* (the blood of the gods in Greek mythology) (2015: 1). The pair of scientists discovered that the smell was the result of moisture entering porous rocks and causing the release of miniscule amounts of yellowish oil, which produces the distinctive smell. The wind, which often accompanies rain, helps to disseminate the smell (2). We are smelling the oil from the stone, or the 'blood of the earth'. It is a smell deeply familiar to almost all of us, and apparently causes cattle in drought-stricken areas to become restless, presumably in anticipation (2).

* * *

Language does not only contribute to apprehensions or misapprehensions of landscape or environment. As Leon de Kock (1993) has argued in his essay entitled 'The Land and its Appropriation by "English"', it may also be fundamental to attempts to change patterns of land ownership and usage, and instrumental in processes of dispossession. It can 'dewild' or 'reculture' it. Nineteenth-century missionaries in the Eastern Cape were at pains to rename and reconceptualize African relationships with the land as part of the 'civilising' project of Christianity. In so doing, they engaged in a form of what Stroud, quoting Santos (2010), refers to as 'an effective form of *epistemicide* ..., that is, the eradication of a body of knowledge through epistemic violence' (2018b: 34).

As De Kock (1993: 208) points out, the initial model was that of the 'civilised haven' of the mission station surrounded by the 'savage terrain' around it. But with the expansion of mission activities and presence, the large mission stations became educational, spiritual and economic centres of their own, domesticating the surrounding regions. Fundamental to this process was the 'dewilding' of landscape and the language used to describe it, and the regulation, settling, cultivation and mapping of terrain to create 'orderly communities'. As the anthropologist Jean Comaroff has argued, 'agrarian metaphors came to pervade the evangelists' vision of a Christianized Africa: it was a "wilderness" to be turned into a "fruitful field"' (1985: 138). The missionary W. R. Thompson said in his report to the Glasgow Missionary Society in 1827, for example:

> It is a comfort to me that I can shew brickmakers, thatchers, sawyers, ploughmen and jobbers at ditching, hedging and field work, who do wonderfully well considering the master they had to instruct them. Where formerly a wilderness of long grass was, and the soil never turned up since the Flood, we now have growing many of the necessaries, and even some of the luxuries, of life. A neat little village has been formed, inhabited by those who a little while ago roamed the world at large, as wild and savage as their old neighbours, the lions and tigers of the forest ... If you except the black faces, a stranger would almost think he had dropped into a little Scotch village. (Shepherd, 1940: 67)

While the approach of the missionaries might have been rather more ameliorative, at least on the surface, colonial authorities were more aggressive and bellicose in asserting control of language and subjects. Sir Harry Smith illustrates this in his statement to the defeated Xhosa after the War of the Axe (1846–7), in rhetoric that echoes the creation narrative in Genesis:

> Your land shall be marked out and marks planted that you may all know it. It shall be divided into counties, towns and villages, bearing English names. You shall all learn to speak English at the schools which I shall establish for you ... You may no longer be naked and wicked barbarians, which you shall ever be unless you labour and become industrious. You shall be taught to plough; and the Commissary shall buy of you. You shall have traders, and you must teach your people to bring gum, timber, hides etc. to sell, that you may learn the art of money, and buy for yourselves. (Quoted in De Kock, 1993: 209)

In such contexts, English became a means of shaping understandings of human relations with landscape along European lines. It became complicit with, even instrumental in, initiating a process of land dispossession, which was to culminate in the notorious Land Act of 1913, through which the Union Parliament allocated 87 per cent of South Africa to white ownership.

* * *

As the statements quoted above from W. R. Thompson and Sir Harry Smith suggest, the landscape named and fashioned by English is modelled on that of the island where that language originated. What it cannot name or apprehend is dismissed as 'wilderness' that must be suppressed. English, in fact, turns out to be a rather poor language for engaging with African landscapes. The history of South African literature in English reveals many examples of the ways in which authors have turned to Afrikaans and appropriated its terms for the South African landscape – *veld, koppie, berg, kloof, donga* (via isiXhosa), *spruit*, to name a few. In many cases, these usages reflected attempts to write more 'authentically' in South African voice, and Afrikaans gave name to the movements, titles or journals that engaged in non-English appropriations: *Voorslag, Donga, Sjambok, the Veldsingers, Trek* or the *Purple Renoster*.

But it is certainly the case that Afrikaans has provided a rich resource of terms for speaking about the South African landscape in ways that English apparently does not. Some of the better-known terms are listed below. Part of the difficulty in engaging with such terms, though, is that their dictionary definitions seek English-word equivalents, which means that the idiomatic fullness of the term is frequently lost. To illustrate the point from another language, isiXhosa, *ukutshotshobela* is probably best translated as to 'wriggle/squirm closer to the fire on your bum', although Kropf in his famous 1915 dictionary rather prudishly defines it as 'to draw near (to the fire)'.[3] To return to Afrikaans, however, in the first example below, for instance, defining a *kloof* as a 'gulch' seems particularly unhelpful. In such cases, I have sought where possible and appropriate to offer slightly more expansive and suggestive definitions. It is also striking how many Afrikaans words have entered South African English (and in the case of 'trek', global Englishes), so that the same word is offered by dictionaries as the Afrikaans term and English translation (*kloof* – kloof; *veld* – veld; and so on).[4] Here are a few examples:

> Kloof: kloof, gulch, ravine or gorge; 'daar lê 'n kloof tussen hulle' – 'there's a gulf between them'. If you are at the bottom of the ravine or kloof, you may refer to the line of exposed rock at the top as the 'kloof'; or if you are near the bottom of a hill or mountain, and there is an exposed line of overhanging rock some way up the slope, providing shade and shelter, that could also be a 'kloof'; then the exposed rock line at the top would in contrast be the 'krans'. 'Kloof' is also anglicized (to rhyme with 'hoof') as in the geographical name for the suburb just inland from Durban through which 'Kloof Gorge' runs.
> Bult: knoll, hummock, hill(ock); ridge, rise, rising ground; 'dis net oor die bult' – 'it's a stone's throw away'; 'ons is oor die bult' – 'we are over the worst/we have weathered the storm'. It is usually used to refer to a flattish ridge, which can be quite substantial in height but is not very steep in ascent.

Fynbos: scrub, shrub, fynbos, especially of the *Euryops* genus. It is apparently of Dutch origin referring to the fine (fyn)/small leaves and flowers of the Western Cape coastal vegetation; as much in usage in English as in Afrikaans.

Hoek: simply means 'corner' or 'turning'. It appears in numerous place names – Keiskammahoek; Bulhoek – in which it refers to a sheltered, flattish place suitable for human habitation (on a small scale) amid mountainous terrain. I cannot think of an analogous English term.

Nek: literally, 'neck'; but by association mountain pass or saddle (as in Brook's Nek; Naude's Nek). Possibly originates from pre-pass days, when the *nek* was the only route across a mountain range. More than just a 'pass': a steep road snaking through a mountain range. To say that you had driven to the town of Rhodes via 'Naude's Nek' in the rain is to evoke in the mind of the listener a sense of heart-in-mouth trepidation. 'Naude's Pass' does not do the same.

Vlei: hollow, marsh, swamp, bog, quagmire, slough, moor, small lake. Most frequently used for something referred to as a wetland, or to a shallow body of water with vegetation surrounding it or in it, the kinds of marginal bodies of water that abound in this water-scarce country. Would not be used to refer to a body of water of substantial depth. 'Lake' and 'dam' are too expansive; 'marsh' does not suggest the free-standing water in a vlei.

Vlakte: plain or flat stretch of land. A defining feature of the South African landscape in the old national anthem, 'Die Stem'. A vlakte would be a good place to cultivate crops, or to allow livestock to feed safely. It is associated with expanse, but also in poetry with desolation.

Windstil: calm or windless. Wonderfully oxymoronic expression, which suggests both wind and stillness, so that one appreciates better the relief from the wind.

Fontein: fountain; spring. Also used in the same way as *oog* or *bron* to refer to the source of a river. A *fontein* can be an important water source, rather like a well, hence its frequent appearance in place names, as it provided the reason for settling there (Rietfontein, Bloemfontein, etc.).

Wild: game, wildlife, venison, chase, quarry. The term has a similar breadth and emphasis on function as the African term *nyama*, discussed in the next section. Interestingly, as an adjective applied to humans, the meaning is generally negative.

* * *

I want to turn now to African languages in my consideration of multilingual citizenship and environment. Writing about representations of landscape in the southern African context, Elsie Cloete (2015) has explored the contrasting possibilities and limitations of African and European languages (primarily English) in understandings of environment, both historically and in the present. She offers keen observations on widely differing assumptions about human-environmental relations in different language systems and their political and economic implications; and she shows in this regard just how poor English is as a language to engage with African landscapes.

Cloete points out that many African languages use the term *nyama* (meat), or a variation of this term, to refer to a wide range of wild animals: for example, *mnyama* (Kiswahili); *inyama* (isiZulu; isiXhosa; Xitsonga); *nama* (tshiVenda; siPedi) or *nyamatsane* (Sesotho/Setswana) (2015: 26). This is not to suggest that animals were not identified by species – they were – but that they were also generically lumped together as food resource. The tendency to prize use over taxonomy is something we will encounter a little later in African descriptions of landscapes. Cloete points to the irony that the word *nyama* 'became locked in the printed medium of indigenous-language dictionaries in the nineteenth and early-twentieth centuries at almost exactly the same time that colonial authorities declared that wildlife as a source of meat for indigenous Africans was illegal' (27). While 'game meat' had previously been a food resource for African and Khoisan/Khoikhoi peoples, it became legislatively off limits. As Cloete points out, even now:

> A man who is caught trapping an antelope to feed his starving family will be charged under current law. In his defence, he will have no legal recourse to a counter-memory or meaning-system from the past and which is available in his own language. In the twenty-first century, *nyama* represents an unacknowledged 'extinction of experience' and will not be legally viewed as an intrinsic part of a cultural history. (27)

One could compare the experience of the nineteenth-century /Xam Bushman //Kabbo, who was part of the group of prisoners whom Wilhelm Bleek and Lucy Lloyd interviewed while they were being held at the Breakwater Prison in Cape Town. His crime was apparently cattle theft, an act that had become punishable in an economic and legislative regime in which animals were personal possessions rather than a communal resource.

Cloete points out further in this regard that the key terms 'wilderness' and 'bush' 'have no meaning-system equivalence ... in most of southern and eastern Africa's indigenous Bantu languages. This, should misunderstandings arise, can have significant implications in terms of conservation, social justice, and indigenous knowledge systems' (27).

She then examines some of the origins of notions of 'wilderness'. In Germanic languages, it referred to 'the deep, dark, and dread-full forests of Northern Europe', in which people did not reside, and which were the places of myth and legend. Southern Europe was more densely populated, and the Romance languages do not have the equivalent term. She quotes Roderick Nash on the fact that the closest in Spanish is the term *falta de cultura* (lack of cultivation), whereas Italian uses *scene di disordion o confusion* (place of disorder or confusion) (28). With the rise of industrialization, the Romantic movement especially 'came to see the wilderness not only as forest land but also as those remaining places unspoilt by factories, slums and human degradation' (28).

Within African languages the closest equivalents to the term 'wilderness' are: *indle* (isiZulu: 'the space just outside the hut or kraal where one goes to relieve oneself at night'); *porini lisilolimwa wala kuishi watu* (Kiswahili: 'a grass plain where people do not farm (but could pasture cattle)'); or *muzyonde* (Leya: 'a place that is not used for cultivation but where mostly animals (including livestock) may be found'). 'Wild Africa', Cloete says, translates in Setswana and Sesotho to *Afrika e hlala* ('home for the natives of Africa') (29).

The notion of 'nature' or 'wilderness' 'out there' is not evident in such African languages and cosmologies, and yet it is difficult – using the medium of English, for example – to avoid dualist distinctions between 'society' and 'nature': the language that has always seemed to me so supple and capable of the finest distinction and texture suddenly feels clumsy and inadequate in this respect.

Let me illustrate. The book *Mammals of Southern Africa and their Tracks and Signs* (2013) by Lee Gutteridge and Louis Liebenberg is a fine source for anyone wishing to learn how to read the complex signs and tracks of animals. The detail, nuance and registering of seemingly minute differentiators in the sketches, photographs and descriptors are extraordinary. They identify seven major biomes in southern Africa, defined by their major vegetation types – Forest; Fynbos; Grassland; Nama Karoo; Savanna; Succulent Karoo; and Thicket (28) – and then proceed to differentiate habitats. They identify nineteen for the entire region, some identified by characteristics, such as 'Wetland and Swamp' or 'Bushveld', most by geographical name, such as 'Drakensberg Mountain and Lesotho Highlands', 'Limpopo Valley', and some that seem so generic that one wonders about their usefulness, as in 'Forest', 'Large Rivers' or 'Coastline' (29–47).

In stark contrast, drawing examples from Shangaan society in eastern Zimbabwe, whose geographical area would probably span the equivalent of one of Gutteridge and Liebenberg's more narrowly demarcated 'habitats', Cloete lists examples of words used to differentiate a wide range of features of landscape within the region. They reflect more intimate, 'dwelling' perspectives:

> Kutluma: thicket – favoured as hiding places by hyenas, leopards and lions.
> Mabhiripirini: riverbank gulleys – where pythons are found.
> Mabvungurhi: canopied areas – where owls rest during the day.
> Ndovolo: area of black fertile soil.
> Mathlivi: stone depressions which collect water in the rainy season. Hunters, baboons and birds drink from them.
> Thlaveni: area of red, sandy soil – it is hard to bicycle because of the sand. Good for growing groundnuts and Bambara nuts.
> Magumbitsini: thicket that is hard to penetrate.
> Thangava: portion of the field in which women grow their own crops (such as groundnuts, beans, sweet reds and water melons).
> Tipala: salt pans – where evaporation leaves salt crystals. The salt is often gathered and sold; also: plains favoured by impala during moonlight as it is hard for predators to attack them.
> Marhimakule: outfields – where people dig for tubers (*phomwe*) in drought years.
> Chawunga/mananya: remote, quiet and fearful area where only birds and wild animals are
> found – popular with foreign visitors (30).[5]

Cloete points out that '[p]eople living in the so-called bush have developed a lexicon of terms that is based on experience and a careful reading of the environment. An inexperienced human blundering into a *kutluma* (a thicket where predators hide) could end up fatally misreading that environment!' (31). As suggested earlier, this is a lexicon concerned with use rather than taxonomy – knowing that thickets harbour predators might seem more significant in this context than being able to name each plant species that comprises it. Cloete does, however, note with sadness that many of these terms appear to be little known by people now, as their concept of landscape has been flattened instead by English into a generic concept of 'bush', particularly at schools. Behind this movement away from African languages towards English appears to lie a set of fallacious assumptions that indigenous/non-metropolitan languages occupy 'distinct temporalities': 'Indigenous languages are spoken about either as languages of the pristine past or languages in dire need of intellectualization/modernization in order to become viable for future use. They are seldom seen in their present forms as anything but incomplete, and often disregarded as languages able to voice the contemporary concerns of their speakers' (Stroud, 2018a: 7).

The shift towards English that Cloete describes is not the aggressive, bellicose process articulated by Sir Harry Smith earlier in this chapter, but the effects are no less pernicious or colonial: 'Talk about the natural environment in particular remains westernized and monolingual, with little cognizance of the ranges of knowledges and practices embedded in the various African languages' (2015: 34). At its worst, the abandonment of indigenous languages for English can lead to people inhabiting an environment without an adequate language or knowledge system with which to apprehend it: they become estranged within 'their own' world:

> In rural areas where indigenous languages are mostly 'place-specific', such a 'language shift' to English at school puts at risk traditional ecological knowledge where the prism of a single system of Western knowledge (represented by English) displaces knowledge-systems outside the physical boundaries of the school. Ultimately, this creates the bizarre situation that a person indigenous to a place becomes a kind of 'foreigner' in his or her own country. (35)

Santos (2012: 43) talks of the need in such contexts for 'intercultural translation', involving both a 'deconstructive challenge which consists in identifying the Eurocentric remains inherited from colonialism [...] and a reconstructive challenge which consists in revitalising the historical and cultural possibilities of the African legacy, interrupted by colonialism and neocolonialism'.

Linguistic Citizenship is frequently presented as a political project that, to quote Stroud, 'carries the potential to deconstruct arbitrary divisions between groups in favour of broad coalitions that cut across linguistically based groupings in the interest of a larger, more comprehensive and inclusive strategy' (2018a: 11). But Stroud also connects rethinking the multilingual to notions of economic and environmental crisis, in ways that are suggestive for my project here: 'A major challenge of our time is to build a life of equity in a fragmented world of globalized ethical, economic and ecological meltdown. In this context, language takes on a singular importance as the foremost means whereby we engage with others across difference' (17).

As I hope this chapter has suggested, multilingual citizenship has fundamental implications for how we survive as a species in a world in which climate change and environmental degradation threaten our very existence, and that of the multiple species with whom we share life on this beautiful and degraded planet. It has profound implications for us as academics and students in the seminar room and lecture theatre – and far, far beyond both of those.

Acknowledgement

This chapter was produced as part of the Andrew W. Mellon funded project on 'Rethinking South African Literature(s)' in the Centre for Multilingualism and Diversities Research at the University of the Western Cape. I am extremely grateful to the Mellon Foundation for its financial support of the broader project of which this is a part. The opinions expressed here are my own and are not necessarily attributable to the Mellon Foundation.

Notes

1. I have explored these issues in some detail in the book *Wilder Lives: Humans and Our Environments* (2019), drawing on debates about 'wilding' and 'rewilding'.
2. There are any number of websites listing these terms and their meanings.
3. I am grateful to Jeff Opland for this information (personal communication).
4. I am grateful to Antjie Krog and Stephen Boshoff for checking my translations and making suggestions.
5. Cloete draws this information from Wolmer (2007: 45).

References

Brown, D. (2019), *Wilder Lives: Humans and Our Environments*. Pietermaritzburg: University of KwaZulu-Natal Press.

Cloete, E. (2015), '"There's a Meat down There": An Essay on English and the Environment in Africa', in S. Stephanides and S. Karayanni (eds), *Vernacular Worlds, Cosmopolitan Imagination*, i–xxvii. Leiden and Boston: Brill and Rodopi.

Comaroff, J. (1985), *Body of Power, Spirit of Resistance: The Culture and History of a South African People*. Chicago: University of Chicago Press.

De Kock, L. (1993), 'The Land and its Appropriation by "English"', in N. Bell and M. Cowper-Lewis (eds), *Literature, Nature and the Land: Ethics and Aesthetics of the Environment*, 207–14, Collected AUETSA Papers 1992. Ngoye: University of Zululand.

Gutteridge, L. and L. Liebenberg (2013), *Mammals of Southern Africa and their Tracks and Signs*. Johannesburg: Jacana.

Ingold, T. (2000), *The Perception of the Environment: Essays on Livelihood, Dwelling and Skill*. London: Routledge.

Macfarlane, R. (2015a), *Landmarks*. London: Penguin.

Macfarlane, R. (2015b), 'The Word-Hoard: Robert Macfarlane on Rewilding Our Language of Landscape', www.theguardian.com/books/2015/feb/27/robert-macfarlane-word-hoard-rewilding-landscape (accessed 27 February 2015).

Monbiot, G. ([2013] 2014), *Feral: Rewilding the Land, Sea and Human Life*. London: Penguin.

Poynton, H. (2015), 'The Smell of Rain: How CSIRO Invented a New Word', *The Conversation*, 31 March. Available online: http://theconversation.com/the-smell-of-the-rain-how-csiro-invented-a-new-word-39231 (accessed 23 January 2017).

Robinson, C. and E. Finlayson. (2008), *Scottish Weather*. Edinburgh: Black and White.

Rolston, H.III (1988), *Environmental Ethics: Duties and Values in the Natural World*. Philadelphia: Temple University Press.

Shepherd, R. H. W. (1940), *Lovedale South Africa: The Story of a Century*. Lovedale: Lovedale Press.

Santos, B. de S. (2012), 'Public Sphere and Epistemologies of the South', *African Development*, 37 (1): 43–67.

Stroud, C. (2018a), 'Introduction', in L. Lim, C. Stroud and L. Wee (eds), *The Multilingual Citizen: Towards a Politics of Language for Agency and Change*, 1–14. Bristol: Multilingual Matters.

Stroud, C. (2018b), 'Linguistic Citizenship', in L. Lim, C. Stroud and L. Wee (eds), *The Multilingual Citizen: Towards a Politics of Language for Agency and Change*, 17–39. Bristol: Multilingual Matters.

Wolmer, W. (2007), *From Wilderness Vision to Farm Invasions: Conservation and Development in Zimbabwe's Southeast Lowveld*. Oxford: James Currey.

Index

abyssal line xiv, 21, 34
   'hubris of zero point' 29
   risk of intellectualization and endogenization 26
   strategy of negating/ emancipating/ validating epistemic authority xv–xvi, 30, 32–3
affect (positive affective emotions) 67, 70, 75, 77, 78–9, 80–2. *See also* affinity; care; empathy; love
affinity 10, 81
African newspapers. *See under* isiZulu
Afrikaans
   Afrikaans/English bilingualism 137, 142, 145–6, 147
   and Afrikaaps 34
   language of the oppressor 23, 137, 140, 145–6
   racial and historical privilege 2, 22, 23
   sanitization of /purification 31, 33
   Tswanified Afrikaans 59
Afrikaaps 8, 30–1, 32, 33–6, 38–9, 185
Agar 49–50
agency 10, 33, 69, 99, 105
   citizenship and 196
   collective agency 13, 186
   and custodianship 196
   in decolonial contexts 104–5
   mediation through mutilinguals 85–6
   and participatory spaces 13
   pride and 182
   resemiotization 13
   slow process 12
   and transformation 30, 48
Alcoff, L. M. xvi, 30
Allan, J. 67, 69, 78, 79, 80, 82 n. 6
Andreotti, V. 21, 28, 29
Anglonormativity 135, 137–8, 139, 146, 154, 156 n. 3
anti-Apartheid x, 82 n. 3, 94, 161, 177 n. 9; 181

Apartheid
   affect and cognition 69–70, 71. *See also* witnessing
   Afrikaans as language of oppressor 137, 140, 145–6
   Afrikaaps emergence 32
   bilingualism enforcement 137, 145–6
   decolonization debates 39 n. 1
   forced removals 33, 167
   languages of power and oppression 22, 137, 145–6
   means of subjectification 32–3
   mother-tongue medium 124
   racial classification 15 n. 1, 115, 117, 156 n. 4, 198 n. 2
   sensorial/cognitive 9, 68, 70–2, 74, 75
   separate education 187
   structures of race and class 187
   tiro and *mméréko* 61

Baker, M. 77, 79
Bezemer, J. and G. Kress 165–6, 170
biology teaching 150
black 177 n. 8. *See also* racial labels
Blackledge, A. and M. Creese 139, 142, 154
Bleek, W. 52–3, 54–5, 110
Boler, M. 40 n. 11
Bozalek, V. 38, 71–2
'The Broken String' 52–5

Cabezon E. 3, 5–6, 7
care x, xi, 7, 15, 79, 91–2, 184
   axiology of care 196
   ethics of care 105, 106 n. 5
Casalis, E. 48, 49
Castro-Gomez, S. 29
Cloete, E. 210–13
colonial
   history/conquest 124, 128, 129, 130, 131
   matrix of power 63, 136, 155

coloniality of language 20, 135
  Afrikaaps as site of rebellion 34
  dehumanization 3, 87–8
  endogenization 24, 25–6, 28, 33, 35
  and epistemic (in)justice 21–2
  expansion/retooling of available resources 86
  Fanonian perspective 106 n. 3
  intellectualization and endogenization risks 24–5
  negative effect on education 137–8
'coloured'. See racial labels
Comaroff, Jean 51, 57, 58, 61, 207
Comaroff, John L. 51, 57, 58, 61
'Contraction and Closure of Land' ('Ukufinyezwa nokubiywa komhlaba') 55–6
critical citizenship 113

decolonial 85, 86–7, 89–90, 135
  change 8
  communication 86–7, 88, 91, 92, 94–9, 103–5
decoloniality xiii, 1, 3–5, 6, 8, 19, 183
  centrality of languaging 6
  epistemic diversity 48
  Linguistic Citizenship acts 97, 98
  personal and communal experiences 10, 77–8, 117, 145
  role of embodiment and location 68
  togetherness in difference 10, 62, 81, 89
  and transformation 14
  utopian value 90
decolonization 3, 39 n. 1, 100, 104, 202
De Kock, L 206–7
delinking 3, 11, 138–9, 146, 151–2, 183, 194
Dussel, E. xiii, xiv, xv–xvii, xix, 37

Edwards, E. 118
embodiment 68, 77, 79–80, 98–9
empathy 9, 10, 92
  and conviviality 14, 106 n. 5
  epiphanies 77–8, 80
  ethical 73–4, 76, 91
  and imagination 8
  physical intactness 53
endogenization 24, 25–6, 28, 33, 35

English
  dominance in education 11, 128, 130
  tempering multivocality 35
  value accorded to standard 135, 137
epiphany 71, 74, 82 n. 6
epistemic authority 20, 21, 182, 186, 194, 196, 198
epistemic (in)justice 20
epistemological diversity 48
euphoria 13, 196, 198. See also pride

Fanon xiv, 4, 23, 29, 30, 35, 88, 106 n. 2
Flores, N. 138
Freire, P. xvi–xix, xx, 186
Fricker 20, 21

Garcia, O. xii, 26, 136, 138, 139
Grosfoguel, R. xiii, xiv, xv, 20, 21
Gutiérrez, K. 138, 139, 146

Hengst, J. A. 166, 174
higher education
  increasing access 35, 40 n. 6 (see also #RhodesMustFall/#FeesMustFall /#StellenboschMustFall; language policy(ies)
Hip Hop 10, 86–7, 91–8, 99–101, 103–4
  emancipatory idea of agency and voice 98
  highly stylized performance 86, 94, 101
  voices critical view of colonialism 94
history 6, 11, 32, 51, 52
  colonial 124, 128
  critical citizenship. 113
  decolonial/past as contested terrain 11, 52, 55, 124, 127–9
Hountondji, P. J. 24, 25
human environmental relations 201, 202, 203, 204, 205, 206, 210

Iedema 35, 159–60, 165, 166, 170, 174
immanence of/immanent communicative event 69, 70, 74, 81
Indigenous language(s) 23, 35, 47–8, 62, 124, 127, 130
  abandonment of (for English) 213
  pastness/'in the becoming' 24, 25, 28, 33, 123, 126, 212

isiXhosa
  intercultural translation 47, 49
  language resource (marginalised) 140, 141, 145
  linguistic identity 125
  recognition of embodied knowledge 144, 145
  texts 55, 56–7
  third spaces 138–9
  translanguaging 146–50
  rural (standard) variety 153, 154
  urban variety 152, 153, 154, 155
isiZulu 47, 122, 123, 130–1
  newspapers 112, 124, 125, 126, 127, 131, 132 n. 12
  rich points of poetry 51, 52–61
intellectualization 9, 11, 28, 33, 35, 123–4, 212
  and epistemic (in)justice 24–5, 26

Kress, G. 165–6, 170

landscape 13, 194, 203–5, 206–12
language ideologies
  coloniality 136–7
  critical (awareness) sites 93, 138
  disrupting monolingualism 155, 185 (*see also* translanguaging; *see also* third spaces)
  embodied language ideologies and repertoires 141, 145–6
  monoglossic and normative 26, 135, 140
language of landscape 203, 204–5, 205–12
language policy/ies in higher education 20, 22
  Stellenbosch University 161, 177 n.10
  University of KwaZulu Natal 123–4
  University of the Western Cape 39 n. 3, 161, 195
Leibowitz 38, 40
linguistic and cultural juxtaposition 9. *See also* rich points
Linguistic Citizenship
  critical rethinking of 'linguistic'/ language 89, 90
  decolonial communication 86, 88, 90, 92, 94–105
  and decolonial theory 189
  and decolonization 20–1, 62

disinhabiting 9, 37, 68, 81
engagement across difference 30–2, 62, 69, 81, 88, 112
and epistemic justice 20–1, 33–9
equivocation 34
of language 7
language and subjectification 32–3
language as semiotic resource 185
lens 185
and multilingual practices 38, 48, 85 (*see also* translanguaging)
multimodal articulation(s) 10
multiple modes of articulating knowledge
negotiation of difference 185
participatory spaces 185–6
plurality 32–33
reconfiguring language 29–32
relationality of language 7
relationality of love 8
social/episteme engagement 86, 89, 90
synergies 67, 68, 69
third spaces 155
transformative tool 14
utopian dynamic 185, 186
linguistic identity/ies 123, 124, 125
linguistic repertoire(s) 137, 138, 139, 141–7, 143, 155
linguistics 13, 27, 28, 161–2, 167, 194, 195
Li Wei, 26
Lloyd, L. 52–3, 54–5, 110
locus of enunciation xiv, xv, xix, 99, 100
love x, xi, 3–4, 5–7, 8, 15, 91, 106 n. 5
Love, B. L 91, 92
Lugones, M. xvi, 34, 37, 88

Macfarlane, R. 203, 204, 205
Makalela, N. 26, 40 n. 6, 137, 139
Makoni, S. 24, 136
Maldonado-Torres, N. 136
Marikana massacre 113–14, 130–1, 131 n. 1
Massumi, B. 68, 70, 75
Maturana, H. 3, 6, 7
Menezes de Souza, L. M, xiii, 14
Mignolo, W.
  body politics of knowledge and being xiv
  colonisation xiii
  decolonizing 3, 93, 100, 183
  delinking 3, 63, 77, 135, 138, 183

embodiment and location 68
epistemic disobedience 183
epistemologies of the borders 37
generation of knowledge 82, 138, 183
geopolitics xiii
meaning of graffiti 100
primacy of embodiment and location 68
terms of the conversation 13, 182, 188–9
Western episteme 63
Monbiot, G. 203, 204
multilingual citizenship 111, 202, 206, 209–10, 213
multilingualism(s) xi, 90, 123, 176
   colonial perspectives 11, 104, 123
   enabling ethical engagements 123
   epistemic justice 20, 29, 38
   equivocal translation 37
   in human relations/alities 3, 14
   and landscape 206–12
   Linguistic Citizenship frame/lens 7, 37, 68, 85, 89, 90, 104
   multilingual citizenship
   multimodal pedagogies 136, 159, 164–5, 167–9, 174–5, 176
   pluriversality 29, 32–3, 36, 37
   semiotic conditions 90
   semiotic of relationality 27, 37
   speakers'mediation of agency and voice 85–6
   teaching and learning resource 136, 146, 147–8
   as transformation 36–8
   'ways of knowing' 39
   'zero point', 29
multiliteracies 139, 159–60, 164, 176 n. 2
multimodal pedagogy(ies) 159, 160, 164–5, 167–9, 174–5, 176
   visual history 115–18
multimodality 160, 165, 174, 176
Murphie, A. 67, 67–8, 69, 81

narrative. *See* personal narrative
Ndlovu-Gatsheni, S. 20, 184, 195
New London Group 160, 164, 169, 174, 176, 176 n. 2
Newfield, D. 164
Ngũgĩ wa Thiong'o 20, 55
Nyamnjoh, F. B. 19, 25, 26, 33, 85

Papadopoulos 4, 5, 6, 8, 14, 39
participatory spaces 12–13, 24, 90, 182, 185–6
   in decolonial universities/textbook 13, 98–9, 105
Pennycook, A. 92
performance. *See also* Hip Hop
   aesthetics 67
   comment on 69, 73–4, 75–6, 77, 78, 79–80
   decolonizing/ decolonial act 77–80, 92, 93–4
   engagement across difference 67
   group 146
   photographs 123
   reflexive pedagogy 9
   of ritual 57, 61
   semiotic remediation/semiotics of 79, 166
   Sibande's imagery 118
   of story 140–1
   witnessing 9, 72, 73, 75, 76
personal (reflective) narratives 8, 95–6, 124–5, 168
   comment on performance (*see under* performance)
photography 112, 115–16, 117, 118–22, 123, 126–7, 130
Pink, S. 70, 76
Pinney, C. 118
pluriversality 29, 32–3, 36, 37
post-Apartheid 19, 31, 113
   languages of power 137
   Marikana massacre 113, 130–1, 131 n. 1
   state power 130, 131 n. 1
   university identity 161–2, 166, 182, 187
Prasad, G. 159, 160
pride 25, 182, 185, 194, 196, 197, 198
Prior, P. A. 166, 174

Quijano, A. xiii, 88

racial labels 15 n. 1, 198 n. 2
   black 4 (*See also* racial labels)
   coloured 198 n. 2 (*See also* racial labels)
   white (*see* racial labels)
Recollet, K. 97
re-genre-ing 12, 166–7

relationality 37, 80
   affect in relation to pedagogy 70, 80
   consensual 6
   dialogue and 88
   of language 7
   and love 8
   multilingualism engaging with and across difference 3, 37, 80, 87
   spaces of 4
   teaching with and through Hip Hop, 87, 91
remediation. *See under* resemiotization
resemiotization 12, 35, 38, 159, 165, 166–7
   and remediation 166, 174
#Rhodes Must Fall/#FeesMust Fall/#OpenStellenbosch 19, 23, 135
rich points 9, 49–50
   of indexing 51–2
   listing names 50
   poetry analysis 52, 53, 54, 56, 57–9, 60–1
   whiteness 51

Santos
   abyssal line xiv, 21, 30
   axiology of care 196
   decoloniality 183
   ecology of knowledges 184
   epistemic justice 25, 29, 183
   epistemicide 52, 202
   epistemologies of the South xvi, 21
   ethical translation 37
   exclusionary language policies 20
   intercultural/equivocal translation 28, 184, 213
   sociology of absences 183–4
   sociology of emergences 183, 184, 186, 196, 197–8
Shangaan 13, 15, 211
Stroud (Linguistic Citizenship)
   actors and agents in the process of becoming 7, 196
   acts of language outside status quo. 69, 112, 124
   alternative socialities 90, 100
   Afrikaaps 32, 40 n. 9, 185
   decoloniality of language 88–9, 99
   disengaging coloniality 20
   disinhabiting subjectivity 37, 68, 81
   displaced indigenous/ non-metropolitan languages 22, 123–4, 212

   empathetic connection 69, 81
   epistemic engagement across difference 52
   and epistemic justice 36, 38
   epistemic violence 52
   (more) equitable engagement 48, 112
   ethical engagement across difference 48, 62, 67, 68, 123
   ethics of care 105, 106 n. 5
   lens 23, 86, 89, 90, 195
   monolingual ideology 137, 139, 155
   multilingualism and vulnerability 176
   and performance(s) 67, 69, 85, 92, 98
   pluriversality 29, 32, 33, 36, 37
   sense of re-connect 197
   synergies 67, 69
   together in difference/diversity 10, 81, 89, 185, 212
   transmodal semiotics 99
   transformative agency 30
   transformative approach to language politics 89–90
   utopian dynamic 185
   utopian relations of agency and voice 90
science (pre-service) teaching 53, 135–6, 146–53
'Sempe of the Lešoboro clan' 59–61
sensorial/cognitive knowledge 68, 70–2, 75, 82
SeSotho 48, 122, 195, 210
Setswana 51, 57–61
   texts 57, 59–61
'siswana-sibomvana' 47
situated learning 70, 71
sociology of absence 183–4
sociology of emergences 184, 186, 196, 197–8
Southern theory/epistemologies 183, 201
Stein, P. 164, 165
Steiner, G. 61–2
Stellenbosch University 2, 23, 161, 167–8
   student comments on performances (*see under* performance)
Stille, S. 159, 160

textbook
   axiology of care 196
   decolonial lens 182, 183–6
   euphoria 13, 196, 198
   praxis of fissure 182, 194

recentring local knowledge and voices
    182, 195, 196, 197
third space(s) 9, 11, 12, 135, 136
    delinking from dominant hierarchies
        11–12, 135, 138, 139, 155
    transformative/reconceiving identity
        9–10, 11–12, 138–9, 146
    translingual 146, 138–9
transformation and transduction 165–6,
    170
translanguaging xii, 9, 11, 20, 27–8, 155
    in communication 154
    hushed 38
    intercultural/equivocal translation 28,
        37
    intercultural 28, 184, 213
    modality of social change 26–8, 35
    pedagogy ix, 22, 26–8, 136, 139, 152–3
    retranslation 9
    risks 34

'Ukufinyezwa nokubiywa komhlaba'
    ('Contraction and Enclosure of the
    Land') 56–7
University of Cape Town (UCT) ix–x, 2,
    135
University of Stellenbosch. *See*
    Stellenbosch University
University of the Western Cape (UWC) x,
    26, 39 n. 3, 71, 93, 161, 187
Utopia(n)/utopic 5, 69, 73, 81, 90, 184,
    185, 186–9

Varela, F. 3, 6, 7
Vasquez 21, 24, 34
Veronelli, G.
    agency and voice 106 n. 4
    coloniality of language xvi, 10, 20, 24,
        87–9
    decolonial communication 86, 90, 99,
        104
    disadvantage of metropolitan
        languages 24

engagements with and across
    difference 10
pluriversality 32
visual
    analysis 118, 122, 123
    dialogue 103
    dichotomies 104
    economies 115, 118
    history 115–16
    outcomes 100
    semiotic act 103–4
    texts 116, 122 (*see also* Hip Hop)
Viveiros de Castro, E. 9, 24, 28, 33–34,
    37
voice 48, 77, 86, 90, 104–5, 146, 189
    diversity of 9, 28, 32–3, 62, 185 (*see
        also* pluriversality)
    monovocality and monovocality/
        univocality of 23, 34 (*see also*
        Anglonormativity)
    and participatory spaces 13, 24
    poetic 63
    processes of decoloniality 34, 80
    student 159
(re)voicing 9, 10, 23, 127
vulnerability, 12, 34, 37, 168
    position(s)/ site(s)/ space(s)/site(s)/
        situations 9, 11, 12, 37, 38, 48,
        176
    and rethinking identity 69

Walsh, C. 2, 182, 194, 198
Wetherell, M. 68, 70
white. *See* racial labels
White miners' strike 112
Willoughby-Herard, T. 106 n. 3
witnessing 9, 71, 72, 74, 76

Xam 52–5, 210
    translated texts 52–5

Zembylas, M. 38, 40 n. 11, 71–2, 160, 176

www.ingramcontent.com/pod-product-compliance
Lightning Source LLC
Chambersburg PA
CBHW062144300426